Daily
CREATIVE

A Practical Guide for Staying
Prolific, Brilliant, and Healthy

TODD HENRY

simple **truths**
▶ Small books. BIG IMPACT.

Published by Simple Truths, an imprint of Sourcebooks
P.O. Box 4410, Naperville, Illinois 60567-4410
(630) 961-3900
sourcebooks.com

Library of Congress Cataloging-in-Publication Data is on file with the publisher.

Printed and bound in the United States of America.
VP 10 9 8 7 6 5 4 3 2 1

Contents

Introduction

Creativity is problem-solving. This means that if you solve problems every day, you're creative. It doesn't matter if you are a designer, a writer, an entrepreneur, an engineer, or a lion tamer. And if you work with your mind each day to create value for your clients, customers, or organization, then you are a *creative professional*. This means that you must be creative on demand and likely find that you often need to be brilliant at a moment's notice.

The pressures and pitfalls that affect us as creative pros often go undiagnosed. You know that something isn't *right*, but you can't put your finger on why. One day, you're on top of the world and every word out of our mouth is pure Shakespearean profundity. The next, you find yourself suddenly burned out, lacking insights, and struggling to meet expectations. You're not doing anything differently, but what seemed effortless the day before just isn't clicking in the same way.

In my decades of working with creative pros of all types, I've learned that the best way to prepare yourself to be brilliant when it matters most is to build daily practices that grow you, focus you, and help you stay fresh and engaged with your life and work. As Gretchen Rubin so eloquently put it, "What you do every day matters more than what you do once in a while." Daily practices prepare you for those occasional moments when you need to shine.

This book is designed to help you build a daily practice around your creativity. We'll cover everything from personal passion to idea generation to mindset to collaboration and leadership. If you truly engage with this book, including spending time with the questions at the end of each entry, you will position yourself for creative and professional success for years to come.

How to Use This Book

Daily Creative is designed to be experienced one day at a time. I encourage you to set aside a regular time every day to engage with the daily entry. Each entry is designed to cover one aspect of your life as a creative professional. You'll notice that certain concepts strategically repeat throughout the year because of their centrality to your experience as a creative pro.

Use a journal or notebook to reflect on the day's entry and the daily question. You don't need to write *War and Peace*, but it helps to freewrite a response to the daily prompt. You may be surprised at what you discover about yourself.

Next, plan one action step you will take to help you apply the daily insight.

It can also be helpful to share the daily insight with a peer or friend. In fact, I encourage you to go through *Daily Creative* with someone else as a way to process the material in community. We grow best when we grow together. If you'd like to work through this book with your team, visit DailyCreative.net for a team discussion guide.

I believe that your best work is still ahead of you. We need you to bring yourself fully to what you do every day. I hope you consider *Daily Creative* your training manual for staying prolific, brilliant, and healthy in life and work. I can't wait to see what you create in your remaining time on this earth.

Let's begin!

January

*"If I were to wish for anything, I should not wish for wealth
and power, but for the passionate sense of the potential, for the
eye which, ever young and ardent, sees the possible. Pleasure
disappoints, possibility never. And what wine is so sparkling,
what so fragrant, what so intoxicating as possibility?"*

—SØREN KIERKEGAARD

Every creative project begins from nothing. You simultaneously experience the thrill of a fresh start and the anxiety of the unknown. This month, focus on possibilities, ideas, ideals, dreams, and where the year ahead might take you.

January

1

New Beginnings

There is nothing as thrilling as the moment of inspiration. That fresh creative breath catches you, and you are swept up in a fleeting moment of possibility. Then reality crashes in as you begin to consider what it might take to actually bring your idea into the world. If you're not careful, the gentle, tender seedling that has just sprouted from the ground can be crushed under the harsh boot of pragmatism.

We must learn to cultivate and live in that sense of wonder and possibility, even if for a brief time, every day. We must protect it, because it is what ultimately animates our greatest work.

About fifteen years ago, my friend Lisa Johnson encouraged me to write a list of several things that would blow my mind if they happened and then to review that list regularly. She encouraged me to list career ambitions, relational goals, financial goals, personal accomplishments or experiences, or anything else that excited me. I did the exercise and reviewed the list every morning. And much to my amazement, most of the items on that list have actually happened.

There was nothing magical about writing a list. This is not about wishful thinking. I firmly believe it was my willingness to spend time each morning dreaming about possibility that kept me moving toward my creative ambitions.

Spend a few moments today writing a short list of things that would blow your mind if they happened. Dream big. Dwell in possibility. And keep them in front of you and review them each morning. (Maybe even use them as a bookmark for this book.)

Don't sacrifice what's possible on the altar of what's immediately practical. Your greatest work is still ahead of you if you are willing to stretch toward possibility.

You must learn to root yourself in possibility.

> **QUESTION**
> What is on your "this would blow my mind" list?

January
2

Uncomfortable Questions

You can learn a lot about a person by the nature of the questions they ask. Brilliant, effective creative pros are willing to ask questions that are inconvenient and uncomfortable. Many people avoid these types of questions because they wish to avoid the accountability that comes with any answer they might find. However, those who are willing to ask uncomfortable questions are more likely to get to the heart of an issue faster and are thus more likely to solve the problem more effectively.

There are probably questions lurking in the back of your mind that you've been unwilling to ask because you are—perhaps unknowingly—trying to avoid accountability for the answers you discover.

- Why are we *doing* this?
- What if we tried...?
- What if we're wrong about...?

Cowards only ask safe questions. And their work shows it. Brave, diligent creative pros are willing to tread into uncomfortable places to get to the heart of the matter.

Those who ask the best questions ultimately win.

Is there an uncomfortable question that you've been avoiding? How might you begin to ask it or pursue an answer today?

You must grow comfortable with asking uncomfortable questions.

QUESTION

What uncomfortable question have you been avoiding?

January

3

Unnecessary Complexity

Creative work is *complex* work. You must wade into uncertainty, seek patterns, connect dots, and excavate value that others might not even see. So there is no avoiding the complexity of the work itself. However, there is another kind of complexity that can take root, and it can rob you of the mental bandwidth you need to focus effectively. I call this *unnecessary complexity*.

When your systems, processes, meetings, organizational structure, or any other means by which you do the work become needlessly complex, they generate hurdles you must jump just to engage with the work. Every hurdle is an impediment to creative insight because it's a waste of time and energy.

As you consider your workflow, processes, daily schedule, the tools you use, and other methods for accomplishing your work, is there any place where you see unnecessary complexity?

Today, commit to simplifying your work in one way. It could be in how you structure your schedule. Maybe it's in how you treat your communications with your collaborators. Maybe it's in how you define the problems you are solving.

Save your mental bandwidth for resolving the complexity of the work itself, not the complexity of your process.

QUESTION

Is there any place where you are making things more complex than they need to be?

January
4

Missed Expectations

Think about a few moments in your life when you've experienced conflict. You just *knew* the other person was in the wrong, and you were definitely on the right side of the argument. Or maybe you were frustrated by someone on your team who just didn't seem to pay attention to detail or was perpetually late in delivering their work.

Now, consider this: How much of that conflict was sourced in expectations you had of the other person? And were those expectations ever communicated to the person?

The vast, vast majority of conflict in the workplace is the result of missed expectations. Someone expects something from a team member, customer, or stakeholder, and when it isn't delivered, it almost feels like a personal assault.

Except it *isn't*. Especially if that expectation was never clearly communicated and agreed to by the other party.

We carry so much residue into our relationships and collaborations because we remember slights that were never intended and hold grudges of which the other party is completely oblivious. These unfair grudges corrode our creative process and our ability to collaborate.

Is there an unmet expectation that is causing conflict in your professional life? Your personal life? Have you communicated that expectation in a clear, empathetic way? If not, I challenge you to do so today.

Don't carry the pointless burden of the unmet expectations of others. There's enough on your plate.

QUESTION

Is there any conflict you're experiencing due to missed or unspoken expectations? How can you resolve it?

January
5

Your Principles

How do you define success for yourself, for your work, for your team? Do you have a clear sense of where you are aiming, or are you simply marking your time by projects completed and promotions earned?

Many people end up in a place they never intended because they spend their entire life chasing whatever opportunity crosses their field of view. They just take the next logical step instead of making decisions based on a core set of values that help them determine not just what they *can* do but what they *should* do.

Mature creative pros know what they value and bend their lives toward a clear definition of success.

If you were to define success for yourself this year, how would you do it?

How about in the next five years?

Ten?

Your entire career?

When you look back at the body of work you've built and the people you have impacted, what do you want to see?

Now, try to establish a few guiding principles that might help you make decisions as you navigate toward your ultimate objectives. "I seek to be in the company of brilliant collaborators," or "I aim to do work that stretches me creatively," or "I seek opportunities to grow the skills of others."

Simply establishing a few of these guiding principles will help you filter opportunities that come your way and chart a course toward a body of work you'll be proud of.

You must establish principles to guide your decisions.

QUESTION

What is your definition of success for yourself? Your work? Your team?

January
6

The Back Burner

When was the last time you made something that wasn't going to be judged, poked, prodded, tweaked, and implemented by someone else? Something that you weren't trying to squeeze into a budget or certain time frame? Something that wasn't on demand?

An easy trap to fall into as a talented creative professional is only doing work for other people. Many creative pros get into their line of work because they love the nature of the work and soon realize that they are only doing work that is on demand. When this happens, it can drain much of the joy out of your experience of practicing your craft.

I encourage you to have some kind of "back burner creating" in your life. This is work that you do on your own time, with no pressure from others, and that no one but you will ever see. *This* kind of work allows you to take risks you may not otherwise be comfortable taking, experiment, stretch, and grow in your skills. It allows you to practice being creative without the eyes of the world (or your manager!) on you 24/7.

Build some time in your life this week to make something for yourself.

Why? Because you should also create for yourself, not just for others.

QUESTION
What will you create for yourself this week? When will you do it, or how will you make the time?

January

7

Die Empty

Almost twenty years ago, I was in a meeting in which someone asked an odd, out of the blue question: "What do you think is the most valuable land in the world?"

We all made our guesses. Manhattan. The oil fields of the Middle East. The gold mines of South Africa. But according to the speaker, we were all wrong.

Instead, quoting the late Myles Munroe, he said, "The most valuable land in the world is the graveyard, because in it are buried all of the unwritten novels, unexecuted ideas, unreconciled relationships, dreams not pursued." All that value, all those opportunities were buried in the ground with them, making it the most valuable land in the world.

I resolved that day that I wasn't going to take my best work to the grave. I would do everything I could each day to empty myself of my best work. To put it into the world where it could be useful instead of holding onto it until it is "perfect" or I have more time or whatever other excuse would be easy to cling to.

Is there an idea, a project, a conversation, or anything that you have been sitting on and thinking "tomorrow, I'll start that"? If so, today is the day to get moving. Do something. Start small and build.

Refuse to take your best work to the grave with you. Choose to die empty.

QUESTION

What have you been putting off that you need to get started on now, today?

January
8

Lows and Highs

It's easy to believe that the way things are now is the way they will be forever. If you're going through an especially difficult time, it can be hard to see the end of it. If you're in a season in which everything is going well, it can feel like you're riding an unending wave.

The one certainty in life and work is its uncertainty. No matter how bad things are right now, things are going to change. No matter how great things are, you are certain to face some difficulty at some point.

It's not your circumstances that define you but your responses to them. Resilient people are able to stand in the face of both good and bad circumstances and recognize that the situation doesn't matter nearly as much as what the situation develops inside you. Both success and failure offer the chance to develop character and persistence, which will reap dividends when you are put to the test in the future.

As you consider the present state of your life and work, is there any place where you are slipping into a belief that circumstances are fixed? And what character traits are being developed in you by what you're experiencing?

Everything is temporary. Things will change. How will you?

QUESTION

What character traits are being developed—or do you hope will be developed—in you through what you're experiencing right now?

January
9

Inputs and Outputs

Some professionals pride themselves in the ability to deliver under pressure. They can work for hours nonstop and are always the first to step up and take on any challenge that comes their way. Their output is unparalleled. However, if they don't mind their inputs, they will soon find not only that their output wanes, but they may do significant damage in all areas of their lives and work. If you put the wrong kind of fuel in a car, the engine will stop working.

How are your inputs? Here are a few that you should pause and evaluate:

- *Creative/inspirational:* Are you filling your mind with inspiring stimulus that sparks your curiosity and helps you ask new questions? Are you putting new "dots" in your head to connect?
- *Emotional:* Are you connecting with other people in a deep, meaningful way? Are others filling your well, or are you only filling theirs? Are you ever receiving, or are you always giving?
- *Aspirational:* Are there mentors in your life who challenge you to see new possibilities for yourself? Who push you to expand your thinking and fill you with a fresh vision?

Be mindful of your inputs. If you're not, your creative engine will eventually break down.

Without a steady source of inspiring inputs, you cannot sustain creative output.

> **QUESTION**
>
> When was the last time you were inspired by something you experienced? Which inputs do you need to adjust so that you aren't running on empty?

January
10

Who Else Should Know?

One of the distinct challenges of creative work is that it is highly subjective. What appeals to you may not be what appeals to your stakeholder, client, or manager. A small decision that you make today can set you on a course that leads to a result that you love and they strongly dislike. This means hours or maybe days or weeks of "wasted" work.

Because of this, when making decisions that could significantly affect the outcome of the project, it's smart to routinely ask yourself: "Who else needs to know about this?" While you don't want to annoy your stakeholders with too many check-ins, you want to ensure that you aren't getting too far off course and are able to course-correct if necessary.

Who else needs to know about this design decision? Who else needs to know about this shift in strategy? Who else needs to know about this difficult conversation I had with a team member?

Simply asking yourself this question at crucial moments can not only help you do better work now but save you a lot of pain down the road.

Each day, consider who else needs to be aware of decisions you are making.

QUESTION
Is there a decision that you've recently made that someone else should know about now instead of later?

January
11

Impostor Syndrome

"Who are *you* to say that?"

"Who are *you* to lead this meeting?"

"Who are *you* to start that business?"

Sound familiar? You're not the only one who occasionally has these thoughts. The term *impostor syndrome* refers to a set of beliefs that imply that you don't *really* belong in the room, in your role, in leadership, writing that book, giving that client pitch. If allowed to infest your mindset, these beliefs can cause you to shrink back from opportunities that you are perfectly suited for but have convinced yourself simply aren't for you.

Here's the thing: I've rarely encountered someone who—in their most honest moments—hasn't had these thoughts. I've sat with people at the absolute top of their game, running large companies or influencing huge movements, who confess that they sometimes don't really feel like they belong in the room. It always surprises me. That's how strong impostor syndrome can be. We all have areas of vulnerability, and impostor syndrome tends to know exactly which notes to play to make us dance.

You belong in the room. You belong in the conversation. You have every right to attempt to write that book, give that speech, make that pitch, interview for that job. Sure, you might fall short. But it's far easier to live with a temporary failure than it is to live with never knowing what you might have been capable of accomplishing if you'd only tried.

If you're willing to be in the room, doing the work, then you belong there.

QUESTION

Is there any place where impostor syndrome is preventing you from trying something new?

January
12

Start from Anywhere

There's a famous anecdote of a painter who would always struggle at the beginning of each new project. An empty, white canvas staring back at him was paralyzing. After all, what if he made a mistake and ruined the nice, new canvas? No, it had to be *perfect*, so he had to get off to a perfect start, right?

After a while, he grew tired of his paralysis and developed a new technique. At the beginning of each new project, he would paint a random line or shape on the canvas as a starting point. Then he would begin work on the painting by trying to incorporate the random figure he had made on the canvas. Instead of fretting over where to start, he removed the decision by adding a random starting point. Then the ideas just flowed.

I love this story because it applies to nearly every kind of creative work.

The blank page? Paralyzing.

The blank proposal? Where do you even start?

The empty pitch deck? What if I get it *wrong*?

The best strategy is to simply start *somewhere*. Start typing some words. Create a few slides that you know are terrible but that you can use as a starting point. Put something on the canvas, then shape it into what it needs to be.

Start from anywhere. You can always get where you want to go with it as long as you are moving forward.

QUESTION

Is there a project you're stuck on that simply needs an inciting incident or starting point?

January
13

Stillness

We are learning a fundamentally new way of being human. Our technological development is quickly outpacing our biological adaptation to that technology. The net result is that we spend much of our time glued to our devices, responding to emails and messages the moment they come in and glancing to see if something new is more important than the task at hand.

Creative intuition requires deep thought. This may not seem to be the case, because many ideas apparently come from nowhere in a moment of sudden breakthrough, but those ideas are more often than not being forged for longer than we perceive just beneath the surface of consciousness. If you want to hone your intuition, you must dedicate some time to being still, alone with your thoughts, off the grid, and without distraction. This is so effective because you begin to "hear" things that are often drowned out by the noise.

Creative intuition doesn't shout; it whispers. And if it's not heard, it doesn't press the point. It fades. You must still yourself so that you don't miss these moments.

Dedicate some time each day—in the morning, the evening, at lunch, or whenever works best for you—to simply be still and alone with your thoughts. Be off the grid. Ignore the ping of your technology.

To access deep, creative thought, you must occasionally disconnect and experience stillness.

QUESTION

What keeps you from breaking away and experiencing stillness? When will you be off the grid and hone your intuition today?

January
14

Buffalo, Not Cow

I once heard author and speaker Shola Richards tell a story about the day his father pulled him aside and said, "Son, I need you to be the buffalo, not the cow."

Shola looked at him with a blank expression, clearly confused.

"Son," he repeated, "be the buffalo, not the cow."

Shola said, "Dad, I'm going to need you to explain this to me."

"When a storm is coming," his father explained, "the cow gets frightened and runs away from the storm. By doing so, the cow not only gets wet anyway but actually prolongs the time spent in the storm." He paused. "But, the buffalo, even though it is just as scared, runs directly into the storm. Yes, this means the storm comes more quickly, but it also means that the time in the storm is much shorter."

We spend so much time in life trying to avoid discomfort. When we see it coming, the temptation is to run in the opposite direction. However, by trying to avoid pain, we often prolong it, having the opposite effect of the one we intended.

When we refuse to run from discomfort and instead lean into it, we often find that it's not nearly as bad as we'd feared. Better yet, discomfort leads to growth in ways we couldn't have achieved otherwise.

So choose to be the buffalo, not the cow.

Don't run away from discomfort. Lean into it.

QUESTION

Is there any place where you are running away from discomfort rather than leaning into it?

January
15

Creativity on Demand

One of my favorite quotes is often attributed to William Faulkner, the great American writer: "I write only when inspiration strikes. Fortunately it strikes every morning at nine o' clock sharp."

There is great wisdom in this statement. Many people internalize a romantic notion that creativity is a rapturous, instinctual, spontaneous moment of ecstasy. We want to believe that, like a wild animal, it cannot be controlled and will do what it wants.

Highly productive creative pros, however, have taken a very different approach. Instead of waiting for creativity to spontaneously and mysteriously happen, they plan for it. They schedule time for work, dive deeply into it, and discover the inspiration they need in the midst of their labor. They know that if they work long enough, they will eventually stumble on brilliance.

Immature creative pros wait for inspiration. Mature creative pros chase it down.

Immature creative pros play the victim. Mature creative pros are aggressive.

Immature creative pros want things to happen to them. Mature creative pros make things happen.

Your best ideas and breakthroughs will happen in the midst of your work. If you wait for inspiration to happen to you, it's highly likely you will struggle to produce anywhere near what you're capable of. Pursue creative maturity.

Schedule your breakthroughs even before you know they'll happen.

QUESTION
When does inspiration tend to strike for you? When will you plan time today to dive deeply into your work in search of inspiration?

January
16

Phone a Friend

One pervasive—and damaging—myth is that creativity is a solo sport. We love to envision the lone creative pro, probably alone in a cabin in the middle of upstate New York, working feverishly at their craft, generating breakthrough after breakthrough in total isolation.

Of course, that's not reality. Yes, much of the work you must do has to be done alone, but that doesn't mean that creativity is a solo sport. Rather, we need others in our lives to help us see the full picture of the problem we are solving. Without their perspective and wisdom, we might work much harder and longer than necessary to get to the best result.

Do you invite other people into your work, or do you try to do everything on your own? I challenge you to think strategically about how you might begin to seek the insights of others more consistently. Here are a few questions you might try:

- ► If you were me, what would you do?
- ► Is there anything here that stands out to you?
- ► Have you seen something like this before? What did you do?
- ► If you were me, what would you watch out for?

All these questions leverage the wisdom of your peers and allow them to speak into your work. You will often find deep inspiration in these conversations.

We need others in order to see the full picture.

QUESTION
Who do you need to invite into your work today?

January
17

Simplistic vs. Simple

Everyone wants a quick solution. The temptation when doing creative work is to gravitate toward the very first idea that seems plausible. Mostly, this is because we want to alleviate the discomfort of uncertainty and have something to latch onto, whether because of time pressure or anxiety about not being up to the task. However, that very first solution—while seemingly workable—often doesn't reflect the nuance of the problem. It's not simple and elegant; it's simplistic.

Simple ideas are ones that cannot be reduced any more without hampering effectiveness. Simplistic ideas are those that seem exciting on the surface but that don't fully address the issue you're trying to solve.

As you mature in your career, you begin to notice the subtle differences between simple and simplistic. You may even develop a set of questions to help you see more clearly:

- ► Does this idea solve the problem?
- ► Can it be made simpler?
- ► Does it overlook an important element of the problem?
- ► Is my enthusiasm masking any of this idea's weaknesses?
- ► Could it be improved by adding one layer of complexity?

Questions like these can help you better evaluate an idea and ensure that you aren't falling into the simple/simplistic trap.

Always aim for simplicity but shun simplistic solutions.

QUESTION
Is there an idea you're pursuing that might be simplistic rather than simple and elegant?

January
18

Discernment vs. Judgment

Conflict is a normal and natural part of any organization. Because the work is typically so subjective in nature, there will be a variety of opinions about which direction is best and who should do the work.

As someone working in this kind of environment, it's natural to feel as if you're being ground in the gears. It can seem like certain people are just difficult. To be fair, there are difficult people in the world, no doubt. But we often ascribe ill will to others when they are actually just incompetent.

Managers neglect their teams because they are worried about their own careers.

Peers get testy when you challenge their ideas because they are insecure about their roles.

You fail to follow up with someone by an agreed-on deadline because you were suddenly inundated with urgent emails.

It's tempting to sit and stew on these situations and assume that others are intentionally making your life more difficult, but often it's a series of simple mistakes that are to blame.

Be discerning about the actions of others, and maintain healthy boundaries in how you deal with them, but try hard not to slip into judging their intent.

Don't ascribe ill intent where incompetence is likely to blame.

QUESTION

Is there anyone you struggle to work with whose actions might be explained better by incompetence than by ill intent?

January
19

Art as Protest

We live in a world where it's not only OK to have an opinion about everything, we are almost expected to share that opinion publicly. I often tell creative pros and leaders I work with that it's fine to have an opinion about something, but there is no need to feel as if you must have an opinion about everything happening everywhere at all times. And it's especially OK to keep your opinion to yourself. (What a concept!)

However, if you *do* have an opinion about something and feel the need to share, rather than simply blasting it out over social media, make something. Make a piece of art, write an essay, craft a song, hold an event, or do something that creatively expresses your idea. Opinions are cheap, but art is precious.

As you consider the events in the world that move you right now, what could you create that expresses your thoughts and feelings? How could you use art as a way to help you not only share your ideas but also invite others to consider your point of view?

Don't complain about what's wrong with the world. Make something.

QUESTION

Is there an idea you have or an opinion that is stirring within you that could be expressed through art of some kind?

January
20

How You Do Anything

You cannot control what happens tomorrow. Or in ten minutes. You can't control what your manager or client will say about your latest work. You especially can't control the reception that work might have in the broader marketplace.

What you can control is how you engage the work right now.

Or more importantly, you can control how you do whatever it is you're doing right now.

If you are writing, be writing. If you are designing, be designing. If you are in a meeting with someone, focus solely on being with them at this moment.

Train yourself to be fully and completely immersed in what you are doing at the moment, and it will become a habit. You will—over time—develop the muscle of complete and utter presence. In any given moment, now is all that matters.

We waste far too much time worrying that something "out there" might be more important than what's in front of us. And as a result, we fail to bring our full faculty to the very thing we are doing. We are being robbed not just of our effectiveness but of our very lives.

How you do anything is how you do everything. Whatever you are doing right after reading this entry, focus on doing it with utmost presence and excellence. We will all be the beneficiaries of your diligence.

Focus on what's in front of you, right now.

> **QUESTION**
> What will you devote your complete attention to next?

January
21

Running Away or Moving Toward?

Admit it—at some point, you've probably fantasized about leaving a job. You may have even imagined what it would be like to walk into your manager's office, say a few choice words, quit, and slam the door on your way out.

When things are difficult at work, it is tempting to imagine that there is a perfect situation out there somewhere that will match up to your desires. You may even gravitate toward the first ray of light that appears ever so faintly on the horizon or be willing to follow even vague encouragement from your friends to just quit and move on.

And often, that would be a huge mistake.

Many people spend their careers running *away* from discomfort and frustration. They bounce from job to job in search of the perfect situation. When they find it, they settle in only to learn that it wasn't quite so perfect after all. Then they move on once more.

These people are running away from something. It's far better to run *toward* something. Don't aim to alleviate discomfort and frustration; aim to pursue what you truly value. Move in the direction of what's being called out of you, not away from something that frustrates you.

Move toward your ambitions, not away from your frustrations.

> **QUESTION**
> Are you moving toward something right now, or are you seeking to run away from something?

January
22

Runway and Overhead

There are two things that can instantly suffocate or crush creative work:

1. Not enough runway to get the project in the air
2. Stifling overhead that strangles the life out of the work

Runway consists of the margin necessary to wade through the early, uncertain days of the project. It can be financial runway (so that you have the time to iterate and get the work right), personnel runway (so that you have enough people to make the work manageable), or credibility runway (a project is championed by someone important enough to ensure that it stays on the list of priorities). It's important to determine how much runway you need so that you are certain that you'll give yourself the best chance at success.

Similarly, overhead can stifle a project before it even gains momentum. If there is tremendous pressure to succeed early because of high overhead, whether that's headcount or debt, it can be difficult to shape the work into what it's capable of becoming. Instead, you'll aim for what's most practical, the immediate payout.

As you take on a new project, whether it's launching a new division or starting your own business, consider how much runway you'll truly need to get the project in the air, and always aim to minimize the amount of overhead you carry so that you have the margin to make good decisions.

Successful creative work requires that you have sufficient runway and manageable overhead.

> **QUESTION**
> How can you either increase your runway or minimize your overhead?

January
23

Listen for the Patterns

I grew up in a home situated right next to heavily trafficked railroad tracks. At night, as I would lie in bed trying desperately to go to sleep, I would feel a faint rumble in my mattress. It was almost unnoticeable at first, but then it would send vibrations up and down my legs. As I waited patiently, I began to hear the rumble of an engine, then the wheels on the rails, then finally a loud whistle—*WOOOOOO!*—of a train passing our house.

We tend to think creative breakthroughs are like the *WOOOOOO!* of a loud train whistle. We hear stories of aha moments that suddenly appear out of nowhere. But more often, creative ideas begin like a distant rumble, a faint vibration that signals that something is coming. Those who can hear those faint rumblings are often considered "visionaries" or "ahead of their time," but they are simply listening for the patterns.

How do we hear the patterns? We get quiet, just like I was quiet lying in my bed. We pay attention to fragments of conversation, intuitive hunches, sparks of inspiration. And we attempt to connect them into meaningful patterns. Much of the creative process is simply listening for the patterns that lie just beneath the surface of our conscious thoughts.

Get quiet, and listen for patterns.

You can't force creativity, but you can listen for it.

> **QUESTION**
> Is there a pattern that you're sensing right now but haven't fully recognized?

January
24

Possibility vs. Practicality

"If you had unlimited time and unlimited budget, what would you do with this project?"

I was once asked this question by a client. While they certainly had good intentions, the question is truly irrelevant, because it's based on a fundamental falsehood: We all have limits we must abide by in our work. In fact, much of the *actual* creativity involved in creating for a living isn't about the work itself but about how to do the work in a way that delivers both on time *and* on budget.

It's tempting to resent this tension when the pressure is on or when you don't have the resources to deliver your best idea, but *that's the job.* That's what you do! You are a professional. When someone has a leaky pipe, you don't ask your plumber, "Now, if you had all the time and money in the world, how would you solve this problem?" No, you simply want it fixed well.

Strive not to complain about what you wished you could have done or about the compromises you had to make (that only you see!) in your work. The job of a creative pro is to deliver results, which means dealing with limitations. You may not always be thrilled with every project, but you must always do your job. That's what pros do.

When creating on demand, you must live with the tension between what's possible and what's practical.

QUESTION

Is there a project right now in which you are wrestling between possibility and practicality?

January
25

Complete Your Conversations

Misunderstandings are bound to happen in the course of your work. This is especially true when you are collaborating with or leading multiple people. There are often so many conversations happening in the same day that it can be difficult to keep track of who said what to whom.

One discipline that I believe firmly in is to always complete your conversations. This means never leaving an interaction with someone without having a mutual understanding of what was discussed, a clear sense of next actions based on the discussion, and clear accountability for who will complete those actions and by when. I realize that this sounds incredibly obvious (we're all adults, after all!), but an incredible amount of organizational pain is the direct result of one person making an assumption based on an incomplete conversation.

"Did you think *I* was going to do that? I thought *you* were..."

"Oh, you wanted that by Friday? I thought it was due next week."

Simple misunderstandings like this can trickle down and wreak havoc on the rest of the team. By taking the simple step to complete each conversation, you avoid entirely preventable pain.

As you close each of your interactions today, make certain to complete the conversation.

Don't allow dissonance to emerge simply because you don't close open loops.

QUESTION

Are there any incomplete conversations you've had recently that need to be completed?

January
26

Why Chats

In his book *How the Mighty Fall*, Jim Collins shared some of the key indicators that a company is in decline. One of the early signs is that there is a disconnect between what happens every day inside the organization and *why* it happens. Team members understand what works, but they may not truly understand why it works. This means that when circumstances change, they may not be able to adapt their tactics to meet the new challenge. Instead, they continue to use old tactics to meet new problems.

For this reason, I believe it's important to have regular "why chats" with your team. These are conversations about why certain decisions are being made, why certain systems are in place, and why certain tactics seem to work. Whenever a big decision is made, whether on a project or with regard to the organization, engaging in a short conversation about *why* will help bring alignment and understanding instead of simple compliance.

The same principle applies to those who work with clients. Rather than simply making a recommendation, help them understand why that recommendation is likely to work. Invite them into a conversation about the why behind the what.

Don't allow a gap to emerge between why and what. Keeping them closely aligned will help you avoid inevitable pitfalls and misalignments. **Always ensure that there is a clear understanding of the why behind the what.**

QUESTION
Is there any why/what gap in your work that needs to be closed?

January
27

New Skill

Do you remember when you first learned to ride a bike? I do. It was terrifying. I surrendered my health and well-being to a machine I was barely able to control. Death felt imminent at all times. Well, to a child, a scraped knee *feels* like death, right?

Over time, as I acquired a sense of balance and mastery over the bike, simply riding it wasn't exciting enough anymore. I needed to up the stakes by riding downhill at speeds that would have made my parents cringe or building a ramp and jumping the bike over my sister's Barbie dolls. (She never knew.) My perception of safety had normalized around my developing skills.

This same principle applies to your work. When you first practiced your craft, everything felt new, and each project was a challenge. Now, as you are more mature, the work feels more familiar and less exciting. It doesn't provide you with the same rush as it once did because you are confident in your skill set.

The best path forward? Try something new. Develop a new skill that feels a little uncomfortable. Stretch yourself to find new ways of expressing your ideas. How long has it been since you've learned a new skill or approached your work in a new way? If you feel a bit stagnant, today is a great day to shake things up.

The best way out of a creative rut is to learn a new skill.

QUESTION
What new skill might reinvigorate your work?

January
28

Delusion

I don't want to alarm you, but there is a very dangerous narrative that well-meaning parents and mentors parrot to children, and it's creating an *epidemic* of anxiety. Do you want to know what it is?

"You can be *anything* you want to be."

I know that this advice is intended to give kids the courage to pursue their dreams, but it's simply not true. No matter how hard they practice, the odds of a five-foot-six boy making it to the NBA are very, very slim. (It's happened, but it's extremely rare and accomplished only by athletic outliers.) And the likelihood of becoming a rock/movie/literary star is slim as well.

The problem with this advice is that it focuses on the end result instead of the process. It encourages children to think about where they will end up instead of how they will get there.

Our narratives—the things we choose to believe—in many ways define our experiences of the world. If we are focused on obtaining a rare and glorified position, we will grow disillusioned as we see that dream slipping out of sight. However, if we instead focus on becoming the kind of person who is likely to obtain that rare and glorified position, we win either way.

Instead of focusing on achieving *the thing*, focus on getting better at your craft.

Instead of worrying about whether others notice you, focus on becoming more noteworthy in how you do your work.

Choose to follow a narrative that's about getting better instead of arriving. Focus on process, not outcomes.

QUESTION

How can you shift your narratives to be more about process than outcome?

January
29

End with the Beginning in Mind

You've probably heard Stephen Covey's advice "begin with the end in mind." It's intended to ensure that you don't jump into an initiative without first considering where you'll end up.

With creative work, I like to invert this advice. Always *end* with the *beginning* in mind.

Often, the most challenging part of creative work is getting started. Staring at a blinking cursor or an empty document or a new presentation deck can be paralyzing, so having any kind of initial momentum is valuable. That's why I recommend that each day, as you wind down your work, you consider exactly where you will pick up when you start again.

Let me give you an example from my own work. I tend to write five hundred words per day when I'm working on a book project. When I get to five hundred words, I stop, even if I'm in the middle of a thought. The reason? I know *precisely* where I will begin my work the next day. Just having that as a starting point creates momentum, and once I'm moving, it's much easier to stay moving.

As you wrap each project or each day, make an effort to consider exactly how you will begin again tomorrow. Doing so will go a long way toward preventing paralysis.

Always end your creative work with the beginning in mind.

QUESTION
How will you know when to quit your work for the day?

January
30

Guardedness

Creative work requires vulnerability, because you are putting your thoughts, perspectives, and skills on display for others to critique. It can feel very much like a judgment of your work is a judgment of your worth. Because of this, many creative pros become guarded over time in an attempt to protect their sense of self. They close off to others, only allowing select people into their world.

While you should certainly be careful about those you invite into your personal space, I caution you against taking an initial posture of guardedness. When you greet the world around you with skepticism, you close your mind to possible new connections and insights. When you greet the world with a posture of possibility and hope, you discover brilliance hiding in the most unlikely places.

Don't allow a patina of guardedness and skepticism to cloud your relationships or your experience of the world. Instead, remain open to others, ask a lot of questions, be curious, and choose to seek wonder in the most mundane of happenings. By doing so, you train your mind and your intuition to recognize creative insights in each moment.

Guarded skepticism results in an increasingly closed mind. Hopeful curiosity yields wonder and creative breakthrough. Choose openness.

When you close yourself off to others, you close the door to creativity.

QUESTION
How can you be more open and less guarded today?

January

31

Last Day of Your Life

Some well-meaning advice-givers will tout the phrase "live each day like it's your last!" On the surface, it seems like good advice, right? After all, it emphasizes the importance of cherishing each day, taking risks, and doing things that push you out of your comfort zone. However, I take issue with this advice. If it's my last day on earth, I'm going to eat whatever I want, focus on now regardless of what it means in the future, and generally ignore that little voice in the back of my head that's only job is to keep me viable and healthy.

Instead of living each day like it's your last, I encourage you to live each day like it's your legacy. In *Die Empty*, I proposed a thought experiment: Imagine that a journalist is following you around all day, documenting everything you do. All your activities, conversations, decisions, and relational interactions will be documented for posterity, and how you choose to live that day will define your legacy forever. How would that change the way you approach your life today? What would it say about what's truly important to you?

I think this is a far more valuable way to approach life and work than the "last day" fallacy.

Don't live each day like it's your last. Live each day like it's your legacy.

QUESTION
How would you approach your day today if it were to define your legacy?

February

"Artists cannot be trained. One does not become an artist by acquiring certain skills or techniques, though one can use any number of skills and techniques in artistic activity. The creative is found in anyone who is prepared for surprise. Such a person cannot go to school to be an artist, but can only go to school as an artist."
—JAMES P. CARSE

As a creative pro, perspective is everything. You must shape and hone your ability to see the world in new ways, develop your ability to connect dots, and steel yourself for intuitive leaps. This month, focus on how to push outside your comfort zone and experience the world in new, evocative ways.

February

1

The Artist Date

Life can quickly become a never-ending series of obligations and projects to be completed. The strange irony is that as you strive to become more productive, you often become less so. As you squeeze more and more output from your process, it's easy to neglect the inputs that actually sustain you. So your work increases in quantity but decreases in quality.

Author Julia Cameron suggests scheduling a weekly "artist date" to help you stay inspired, engaged, and outwardly focused. It is a way to fill your well rather than constantly drawing from it. She writes, "In filling the well, think magic. Think delight. Think fun. Do not think duty. Do not do what you should do—spiritual sit-ups like reading a dull but recommended critical text. Do what intrigues you, explore what interests you; think mystery, not mastery."

Visit someplace that intrigues you. Go into the city and explore. Go sit by a stream in the middle of the woods and just listen. Go for a three-hour drive through the countryside. It doesn't matter what it is. If it feels "magical" to you, do it. You cannot draw water from an empty well.

By the way, what fills you might be very different from what fills the person next to you. Don't take your cues from others. Explore your own curiosity.

Schedule a date with your inner artist.

QUESTION

When was the last time you did something that could qualify as an "artist date"? What will you do as an "artist date" this week?

February

2

What Are You Really Trying to Do?

Having grown up in a rural environment, it was common when visiting a friend to park on dirt driveways or wherever there was room. Under normal circumstances, this was fine, but when it started to rain, things became infinitely more complicated. Sometimes the car got stuck in the mud.

When your car is stuck in the mud, the temptation is to press harder on the accelerator, thinking that all the extra force will propel you out. In reality, this method only digs you in deeper. Instead of spinning your wheels, you need traction. Anything—some plywood, a large rock, whatever—can give you the traction you need to move forward and get out of the mire.

We've all experienced the sensation of spinning our wheels and getting nowhere. It seems like the harder you try, the deeper you dig in, just like when you're stuck in the mud. What you need is a little traction.

One method for gaining traction that I often use with clients is redefining the problem by asking, "What are we really trying to do here?" At times, the feeling of "stuck-ness" is really nothing more than a lack of clarity about what meaningful progress truly is. Simply redefining the problem can provide a quick jolt of forward momentum.

When stuck, redefine the problem.

QUESTION

Consider a project you're struggling to make progress on. What are you really trying to do?

February

3

The Daily Mental Checklist

You cannot allow life to just happen to you. You must live it. However, when work and obligations feel overwhelming, you can feel like you're just being carried along by a momentum beyond your ability to influence.

Here is a series of questions that can help you identify your current state and potential order-bringing next steps.

- Is my outer world in order? (Are my projects and surroundings ordered or in chaos?)
- Do I have a clear grasp of what's required of me today?
- Are there any tasks that must be completed today, and how can I ensure that happens?
- Is anyone expecting something of me that I haven't delivered?
- Are my relationships in order? Are there any open loops that need to be closed?
- How do I feel today? Do I know why?
- Are my thoughts in order, or do they feel chaotic? How can I find stillness?
- How can I care for myself emotionally today?
- How does my body feel? How can I care for myself physically today?

I know this is a lot to process, but simply keeping this checklist in front of you and reviewing it consistently can help you find an island of calm in the midst of the storm of life and work.

Don't just move through your life. Manage it.

QUESTION

Plan some time to review the checklist. Are there any responses that require action?

February
4

Blessings into Burdens

"I just have so much work that I don't know how to manage it all!"

"My friends expect me to be at so many commitments, and I don't have the time for all of them."

"All the new clients I'm managing have such high expectations, and I'm worried I'm going to drop the ball."

It's natural to feel stressed and a bit overwhelmed when you are in a season of opportunity. Work is stressful, and expectations rarely go down. However, it's important to protect your mindset from the negative downward spiral that stress can cause and that limits your creative thinking and leadership capacity.

During an especially stressful season a few years ago, our family adopted a new mantra: "Don't let your blessings become burdens." We still say this to one another all the time. It's a reminder that with opportunity comes responsibility and stress but that there are many people in the world (or in your company or industry) who would love just to have those opportunities! Carrying the blessings around like burdens can limit your perspective and cause you to become inwardly focused rather than possibility focused. This limits your creativity.

Yes, work can be stressful, and seasons of abundance can require everything you have to hold things together.

You should always be careful not to allow your blessings to become burdens.

QUESTION

Is there any place where you are allowing your blessings to become burdens?

February
5

Your Portfolio of Passions

If you were to take all your money and invest it in one stock, most responsible financial advisers would tell you that you're taking too much risk. While there's always a chance that your bet will pay off, it's far more likely that you'll end up with middling results or even lose it all. Instead of this "all in" approach, most advisers would encourage you to create a more balanced portfolio, wherein you spread your risk across multiple sectors so that if one goes down, the others can compensate.

In a similar way, some people believe that the key to success as a creative professional is to go "all in" on one thing. We reinforce this story by celebrating people who hedged everything on a single idea and won. But we often fail to recognize the many, many other people who weren't so fortunate.

Focus on building a portfolio of passions. Even if you have a full-time job, consider how you might work on developing opportunities in other areas, like serving a nonprofit, developing a side hustle, or working to build with others in your community. Maintaining a portfolio of passions will not only develop resilience in your career, it will also help you learn new things about your own interests and capabilities, which will pay off in whatever work you do. And doing so will likely awaken passion in your day job as well.

There is no "one thing" you are called to do. Build a portfolio of passions.

QUESTION

Is your portfolio balanced? What should be in your portfolio of passions?

February
6

Your Personal Dashboard

If you wish to be prolific, brilliant, and healthy over the long term in your career, it's important to monitor the gauges on your personal dashboard. If you fail to pay attention to the dashboard of your car, it's very likely that you'll eventually run out of gas, overheat, speed, or end up with a dead battery. If your "check engine" light is ignored for too long, you will probably break down at an inopportune time, maybe on a busy and dangerous highway.

In a similar way, if you fail to pay attention to your personal dashboard, you risk breaking down. You might be unable to perform at a critical moment because you simply don't have the resources.

How is your fuel level? If low, how can you fuel yourself?

And your battery? How is your creative spark? How can you recharge?

Your temperature? Do you need to adjust your mindset toward your peers or team?

Your speed? Moving fast feels efficient in the moment but can cause us to overlook opportunities or make mistakes.

Pay attention to your personal dashboard, and care for your "machine."

To stay healthy and productive, make sure you monitor all the important gauges.

QUESTION
What is (or should be) on your personal dashboard?

February

7

The Very Next Action

It's challenging (and maddening at times!) to attempt to turn a vague notion of an idea into something valuable. It's easy to become paralyzed and incapable of knowing what to do next when it feels like you are making things up as you go. It's like you're driving along a remote road and come across a roadblock. Everything seemed to be going fine, but suddenly your plan is disrupted.

In these moments, it can be helpful to simply ask yourself, "What's the very next thing I need to do to make *any* kind of progress?" Sometimes you'll discover that the reason you feel stuck is that you need some information to make a decision, or you don't have a tool you need to tackle a task, or you need to have a conversation before you feel good about continuing on the path you're on. By simply pausing and considering the very next action that needs to occur, you will often uncover the singular roadblock that is causing you to feel stuck.

If you feel stuck on a particular project, ask yourself, "What is the very next thing that needs to happen to make progress?"

Defining the very next step can get you out of your creative rut.

QUESTION

What is the very next thing that needs to happen on each of your current projects?

February
8

Playing Infinite Games

James P. Carse, a professor of history and literature at New York University, once posited a theory about the nature of life. He said that there are two kinds of games we play, finite and infinite. Finite games are those with clear rules and timelines and defined winners and losers, like most sports or board games. You play a finite game in order to win a title.

Infinite games are those that are played simply for purposes of continuing the play. When more people are included in the game, it gets better for everyone involved. The goal is to keep the game going.

We can get caught up in the stress of finite games—winning a client, closing a deal, getting the next job—while losing sight of the infinite game we are actually playing. It's possible to succeed your way into failure when you lose sight of the bigger picture.

Expand your perspective of what you're actually doing rather than just focusing on the next client, the next paycheck, the next big win. What is the larger, more infinite game that you are actually playing in life and work?

Focus on playing the game that will go on infinitely rather than smaller, finite ones.

QUESTION
What is the infinite game you are playing?

February

9

What Your Work Teaches You

You make your work, then your work makes you. It has taken a long time for me to realize that I am just as shaped by my work—and by the self-awareness that it generates—as my work is by me. As you create, you discover things about yourself that were previously obscured. However, we often fail to notice or document those learnings because we are always on to the "next thing."

How do you respond under pressure? Do you attack or retreat? What does that mean about how you should structure your work and your collaborations? How can you temper your instinctual response?

What happens when your point of view is challenged? Do you see it as a personal attack or a growth opportunity? What does that mean?

Where do your best ideas come from? Is it when you are alone cranking through the work or when you're with a group discussing possibilities?

As George Bernard Shaw said, "You use a glass mirror to see your face; you use works of art to see your soul." By noticing the patterns, we can better structure our lives and work for future success.

Take stock of what you are learning about yourself through your work.

QUESTION

What patterns do you see in your work that might help you be more effective moving forward? What are you learning about yourself through your work?

February
10

The Muse Myth

In Greek mythology, the nine Muses (responsible for inspiration) were the offspring of Zeus, king of the gods, and Mnemosyne, the goddess of memory. So creativity is the result of applying energy/power to memory. Very fitting as this is, in fact, the very definition of creating! When we make things, we apply concerted effort to connect memories (dots) in our minds and forge new patterns that solve problems.

In his book *Daily Rituals,* author Mason Currey described the work pattern of composer George Gershwin. "He was dismissive of inspiration, saying that if he waited for the muse, he would compose at most three songs a year. It was better to work every day. 'Like the pugilist,' Gershwin said, 'the songwriter must always keep in training.'"

Notice that nowhere in that description is the phrase "wait around for the muse to strike." The muse "appears" in the midst of the exertion of effort. In his advice to writers, Jack London once quipped, "Don't loaf and invite inspiration; light out after it with a club, and if you don't get it, you will none the less get something that looks remarkably like it. Set yourself a 'stint,' and see that you do that 'stint' each day; you will have more words to your credit at the end of the year."

Don't wait for the muse. You will discover her in the midst of your work.

QUESTION

What steady, regular stint do you need to dedicate yourself to so that you are making progress on your work?

February

11

Time to Upgrade

After college, in my early twenties, I was a traveling musician. I wrote music and performed for crowds ranging from a handful of people in a smoky bar to seventy thousand people at a giant outdoor music festival. During that time, I wrote a lot of songs and seemed to always be able to "crank one out" on demand.

Then I decided to quit performing and get a "real" job. My guitar sat in the case more often than I'd prefer, and it was rare that I would pick it up to noodle around and write something new. My creativity was finding expression in other ways, like writing essays and books.

A few years ago, I fell in love with an electric guitar that I spotted for sale in a music shop. It was gorgeous and felt incredible in my hands, and I knew I had to have it, so I bought it and brought it home. Then something amazing happened: I started writing songs again. In fact, I wrote a few dozen songs in about six months, more than I'd written in twenty years.

Sometimes the feel of a new tool in your hands is all it takes to create a spark: a new keyboard for your computer, a new pen or notebook. There's no magic in the tool; it's how the new tool makes you feel about working, how it invites you back into your craft.

If you need a quick creative spark, consider upgrading your tools.

QUESTION
What new tool might provide you with a creative spark?

February
12

Doing vs. Leading the Work

If you lead a team of creative pros, I'm sorry to tell you that your entire career has been one giant setup. Early in your career, you are rewarded for getting the work right. For controlling it. For making it whatever it needs to be to please your stakeholders.

Over time, if you do great work, you get promoted. Now, perhaps you are leading others who are responsible for doing the work. However, this is a critical transition point for you. Doing the work and leading the work require entirely different skill sets.

If you continue to attempt to control the work by looking over your team members' shoulders or by telling them exactly what to do, the capacity of the team will never grow beyond your personal purview. You will need to be involved in every decision, or things won't get done.

On the other hand, if you focus on developing your team to be able to accomplish the work and on equipping and unleashing them to tackle it, the capacity of your team is unbounded. You will frequently be surprised by what your team is capable of.

As a leader, your job is to lead the work, not to do it.

QUESTION

Are you spending too much of your time doing the work, or are you focused on developing your team to be able to do it?

February
13

Sound Familiar?

You're stuck and you can't see a path forward. You've tried everything you know to do, but that brilliant breakthrough still eludes you. What do you do now?

One effective method that I've used with teams is to simply ask "Where have we seen something like this before?" It doesn't have to be the exact same problem—it certainly won't be—but it should be something that is similar or parallel. It could be an innovation in a completely different industry, something you experienced at a previous job, or something from a book you read or a magazine article you skimmed. What does this problem remind you of?

The reason this is powerful is because it causes you to examine the problem from a higher perspective. Instead of thinking exclusively about this problem as existing in one place and time, you begin thinking about categories of problems in these kinds of places. You begin looking for patterns and connecting larger networks of ideas. You are thinking systemically rather than functionally.

When you are stuck, consider a similar or sympathetic problem you've solved or encountered in the past and how it might apply to the one you're working on.

To spark ideas, compare your current situation to a past one.

QUESTION

What similar problem compares to the one you're solving now?

February
14

Love of Process

You will become known for the work you produce. That's inevitable, because the work is the tangible representation of your effort. However, the process that produces that end result is far more substantial, consuming, and significant to your life than the end results that others see.

If you fall in love solely with the end results, and especially the recognition of your work, you will do whatever it takes to achieve recognition. You will work as a means to an end, and before long, the results will begin to reflect your priorities.

However, if you strive to fall in love with the process, you will—in the end—produce better results, because you will expend more discretionary energy in the course of your work.

In other words, when you fall in love with the process, your work is self-fueling. Every step of the way will renew you, creatively and otherwise.

By making this simple shift, your reward will be a lifetime of deep engagement and fruitful effort. And you will also likely produce better results.

Strive to fall in love with the process, not just the end results.

QUESTION
What do you love about the process of your work?

February
15

Run Your Own Race

My oldest son was a competitive distance runner in high school. In nearly every race, he would start out near the middle-front of the pack, and it would appear that he was in danger of being left behind by the leaders. Then, slowly, those in front would begin to fade, and some of the stronger runners—who only moments before appeared to be losing—would move to the front of the pack. Often, someone like my son, who seemed destined for a middle-placed finish, would end up winning.

The reason for this is that some less-experienced runners would jolt off the starting line and try to keep up with whoever was in the lead. However, the more experienced runners knew their own best pace and understood how to run a good race. They realized from practical experience that if they just followed the strategy, they would end up just fine.

Every one of us needs to run our own race. You can't compare your productivity or career progress or degree of recognition to the person next to you. That's a never-ending game. The great runner Carl Lewis once said, "I tell myself: 'Get out of the blocks, run your race, stay relaxed. If you run your race, you'll win.'" Be focused on your work, your calling, your career, and the body of work that you are building.

Run your own race.

QUESTION
Where and when do you tend to most compare your race to someone else's?

February
16

Desperate Times and Desperate Measures

You've likely heard the phrase "desperate times call for desperate measures." I believe it's terrible advice. When you are desperate, you will seek any glimmer of hope or even the slimmest thread of an idea to pull on. You will often do things in your desperation that forfeit your future viability. You may build boxes (or cages) that you have to live in long after your moment of desperation has passed. You make deals with devils.

Instead, desperate times call for measured responses. When you feel desperate and need to make an important decision, pause and reflect. Consider all consequences of your decision—not just first-order consequences but second-order consequences. Ground yourself in reality, and refuse to allow yourself to feel hemmed in by your sense of desperation. Don't react; respond. Consider the bigger picture of what you're trying to do, not just the immediate pain you're trying to relieve.

Making big decisions when you feel anxious or boxed in, whether about creative strategy or life in general, can cause mountains of regret later. Always pause, reflect, and respond.

During stressful moments, be extra cautious when making decisions.

QUESTION

Is there a place right now in life or work where you feel desperate and are in danger of making a desperate decision?

February
17

Subtraction vs. Addition

The work that you do is likely very complex. Unfortunately, it's made even more complex by the number of cooks in the kitchen. Everyone wants to add their unique spin to the project, and you probably have to navigate any number of priorities and interests just to do your job.

Work does not get simpler on its own. Left to its own inertia, work will grow increasingly complex and unwieldy. This is why subtraction is a phenomenal strategy for achieving a breakthrough.

Which objective can we remove and still be successful?

How many features can we eliminate for now so that we can focus on the ones that matter?

Who can be removed from this project so that we can achieve more team focus?

When you focus on subtraction, you center your mind on what's essential. You cut through the clutter and noise that is generated by unnecessary complexity.

As you go about your work today, consider how you might be able to achieve more by doing less. How can you achieve addition by subtraction?

Creative breakthrough often occurs when you subtract.

> **QUESTION**
> As you consider your current workload, how can you use sub-traction to gain better focus?

February
18

Work Your Schedule

What would you do if you had all the time in the world?

Your mind may initially run wild with ideas, but the reality is that most of us would simply fill that time with more of the things we are already doing. An object in motion, stays in motion. A schedule filled with busywork, stays filled with busywork.

Have you ever had a wide-open afternoon and thought you were going to accomplish so much only to get to the end of the day and wonder what exactly you did? This is what I'm talking about. It's not that you didn't do things; it's that your time wasn't organized to facilitate doing the *right* things.

I find it incredibly helpful to schedule my time into themed blocks. If I know there are a number of administrative tasks that I need to accomplish, I'll block an hour called "admin." If I need to accomplish some writing, I'll block forty-five minutes called "write." I even have recurring blocks on my calendar for things like planning and interviews. Annie Dillard once said, "A schedule defends from chaos and whim. It is a net for catching days."

Plan your work, then work your plan. It's the surest way to follow through on the important priorities in your life.

Build a schedule, then work it.

QUESTION

What regular time blocks should appear on your calendar? What are the most important activities that might fall to the side if not scheduled?

February
19

Running Out of Time

Loren Long is a friend and neighbor who also happens to be a *New York Times* bestselling author and illustrator of children's books. He once told me that when he was in his twenties, he would see some of his peers doing things like buying nice cars and houses, getting promotions, and checking off all the boxes that many people believe to be the milestones of a happy, productive life. Meanwhile, he felt a bit stuck in his career, and even though he was successful at his work, he struggled with the comparison that inevitably resulted from seeing others on a more traditional career path. In retrospect, he was obviously making the right decisions by pursuing a career he loved, but in the moment it felt a lot like he was falling behind.

It can feel like you are running out of time when your only basis of comparison is what others are doing. You are not running out of time. You might simply be on a different schedule.

Your only job today—and every day—is to pour yourself fully into the work that is being called out of you. You are not responsible for what others do or choose but only for how you engage your work today.

Today, pour yourself into work that you care about. Choose to build a body of work you will be proud of. Let others worry about comparison.

You are not running out of time.

QUESTION

Is there any place where comparison causes you to feel like you're falling behind or running out of time?

February
20

Backward Rationalizing

I love the story about the farmer's cousin who went to visit his family in the country. Upon arrival, the farmer took the city cousin on a tour of the property, and the city cousin was shocked to see an archery target on the side of the barn with an arrow embedded perfectly in the middle.

"Wow!" he exclaimed. "I didn't know you were an archer. How did you manage to hit the bull's-eye?"

"Easy," replied his cousin. "I shot the arrow first, then I painted the target around it."

It works, I guess. Unfortunately, many creative pros and teams apply a similar strategy. When our work fails to live up to our original intent, we invent reasons why the results were actually better than what we meant to do. We backward rationalize. We paint the target after we shoot the arrow.

When we do this, we lose trust with our team, our clients, and perhaps most importantly ourselves. It's difficult to hold yourself accountable when there's no standard to hold yourself accountable to.

Have specific goals and metrics for your work and hold yourself to them. There will always be "happy accidents," but make certain that you don't backward rationalize your results instead of learning from your shortcomings.

Avoid the temptation to backward rationalize poor results. Learn from them.

QUESTION

Is there any way in which you are currently backward rationalizing results?

February
21

Worst-Case Scenarios

Seneca, the Stoic philosopher, believed that the fears that paralyze us are often overblown. He recommended that his followers engage in an exercise of intentional discomfort as a way to better understand real vs. perceived risk. For example, many people allow their fear of failing on a project to escalate into losing their job and ultimately winding up homeless. To that, Seneca wrote, "Set aside a number of days where you will have the most meager of food and clothing. Then ask yourself: Is this what I feared?"

While I don't recommend directly confronting every fear—it's probably not a good idea to run out into traffic just to confront your fear of getting hit by a car—it can be a useful exercise for some of those paralyzing psychological fears that inhibit your creativity and effectiveness. For example, the simple practice of sharing an idea in a meeting or of speaking publicly in front of people you don't know very well can cause some people to break out in a cold sweat. However, by engaging in this kind of activity, you are likely to discover that your fears of these activities are really nothing to fret. Even if things go poorly, you're unlikely to be harmed any real way. Plus you'll have a great story to tell!

By directly confronting your worst fear, you often dismantle it.

QUESTION
Is there a fear that's paralyzing you that you need to confront?

February
22

The Two Kinds of Fear

Since yesterday's entry was about confronting your fears in order to dismantle them, I thought it might be helpful today to discuss the two kinds of fear. The first is fairly familiar and probably obvious: fear of failure. It's what prevents you from taking risks, testing your boundaries, or speaking up in a meeting. It takes root in the unknown and thrives on uncertainty.

But there is a second kind of fear that can also paralyze you: fear of success.

Why would you fear success? Because with success comes increased expectations. With success comes more attention and a higher bar to leap over. With success comes the burden of delivering the same results next time, even if you have less time or fewer resources. As the saying goes, "The tallest blade of grass gets cut." Calling attention to your capabilities only means more responsibility is coming your way, right?

When you fall prey to fear of success, you might purposefully (or subconsciously) underdeliver, because you don't want or need the added pressure. However, allowing fear to control you in any form means you are forfeiting your potential.

Don't allow fear—in any form—to paralyze you.

QUESTION

Is there any place where you might be experiencing a fear of success?

February
23

Interval vs. Snapshot Productivity

Creativity is rhythmic. There are going to be peaks and troughs, highs and lows. You can't treat your creative process (or your team's) like a machine, or you will get machine-like results: highly predictable and no more than asked. You must embrace creativity's rhythmic nature.

It's tempting to measure effectiveness in snapshots. You take a quick glance at how things are going, and you assess what's working and what's not based on that limited view. However, this approach doesn't tell the full story. Instead, you need to measure effectiveness in intervals. What matters isn't how things are; what matters is how things are trending.

Are you gaining more energy for your work over time, or is your energy waning?

Are you consistently having ideas when you need them, or is it becoming more of a challenge?

Do you feel like you are becoming more focused or less so?

Are you delivering on your expectations more consistently or less frequently?

These are trending questions that can help you gain a better sense of what you need to deliver your best work. When you only focus on here and now, you cannot see where you came from and where you are headed, which is what's most important.

Measure effectiveness in seasons, not snapshots.

> **QUESTION**
> Where is your creative process—and your work—trending toward right now?

February
24

How to Fight Fair

Some people believe that any conflict is a sign of a lack of team health. I once had a manager say, "We're the healthiest team you'll ever see. We never fight!" What I wanted to tell him was "You are the most profoundly dysfunctional team I've ever seen!" but I held my tongue. A lack of conflict on a team could mean that you're in a season where everything is just clicking, but it more likely indicates that people don't feel accountable, they don't feel that their opinions matter, or they are terrified of the consequences of speaking their minds.

When you fight, it's important to fight fair. Healthy conflict happens within certain boundaries:

- ► Fight over ideas, not personality. The moment a fight gets personal, everyone loses.
- ► Agree on common ground before attacking the other person's idea. Make sure that you are actually arguing about the same thing. Don't assume.
- ► Articulate the other person's argument before dismantling it. Make certain that the other person feels understood before striving to make your argument.

If you follow these three guidelines, you will have much healthier conflict and more productive conversations.

Healthy conflict is normal in creative work. How you handle it is critical.

QUESTION

Is there any conflict in your work life that would benefit from a good, focused conversation?

February
25

The Long Game

We often become overly ambitious when thinking about the short term but don't think big enough when it comes to the long term. We categorize our ambitions in quarters and years, not decades and generations.

Do you have a vision of what your life will be like in ten years? It won't be crystal clear, of course, but is there any hazy sense of what your life, your work, your portfolio of passions will be in a decade? Here are a few questions to consider:

- How will you have grown and changed?
- What will you have produced, and how will it have impacted people?
- Who will be in your life?
- What value will you be adding to your neighborhood, your organization, your family?
- What will you be most proud of having experienced or accomplished?

This is not a comprehensive list, but if you are able to answer these questions, you can see the rough outlines of a vision forming. And once you have a vision, you can begin bending your life toward it each day over time until you begin to see it taking form.

Effective creative pros bend their lives toward long-range goals.

QUESTION
What is your vision for what your life will be like in a decade?

February
26

Keeping Trophies

I almost died when I was a sophomore in high school. I caught a freak infection in my back that essentially paralyzed me from the waist down. I was in the hospital for a month and lost 53 pounds, leaving me weighing 131 pounds at six foot three. I was told I might not walk the same again and definitely wouldn't play basketball again, my real love at the time. After months of therapy, I did walk, and I did play basketball, and in my senior year, I got to play in the Ohio North/South all-star game after a full recovery to health.

A few years ago, they were tearing down my old high school gym, and my father was able to get a cutout of the floor—the top of the key, which was my favorite place to take shots. It's now in my home office to remind me that however low things get, there's always a path through.

For most of my life, I've been wired to *overcome*, which means that I function best when there is an obstacle in my way or doubters telling me I can't do something. This chunk of wood reminds me every day that I can and will overcome.

When you accomplish something meaningful, keep visual reminders of it around. They will help you keep your mind straight when things are uncertain and difficult.

Keep items around that remind you of who you are and where you come from.

QUESTION

What visual reminder can you create or keep in your environment to remind you of who you are and what you're capable of?

February
27

Morning Pages

There are brilliant insights lurking just beneath the surface of your conscious thought. You may not realize they are there because you are so busy handling your responsibilities that you gloss over them. One excellent method for mining these invaluable gems is called morning pages.

This is a technique introduced by Julia Cameron in her book *The Artist's Way* and involves doing three longhand pages of freewriting every morning before doing any other creative activity. The goal, as Cameron describes it, is to clear your mind of all the things that are cluttering your thoughts. She writes, "Pages clarify our yearnings. They keep an eye on our goals. They may provoke us, coax us, comfort us, even cajole us, as well as prioritize and synchronize the day at hand. If we are drifting, the pages will point that out. They will point the way true north. Each morning, as we face the page, we meet ourselves. The pages give us a place to vent and a place to dream. They are intended for no eyes but our own."

This last point is critical. Morning pages are *only* for you. The only goal is to spill your mind onto the page and let the writing go wherever it leads you.

To keep creative ideas flowing, spill your mind onto the page each morning.

QUESTION

How soon can you try this experiment for yourself? What clutter are you harboring that can be unleashed into morning pages?

February
28

"Not to Do" List

There are more tools for organizing your tasks than at any point in human history. If you're like most people, you likely have a to-do list a mile long, and it may even grow longer every day in spite of everything you've checked off! We are good at getting things done, but what we struggle with is *not* getting things done.

Let me explain. There are any number of priorities that you could focus on each day, but you must become skilled at defining what you should *not* focus on. You have a finite amount of time and energy, so each time you expend any of it, you are choosing not to spend it elsewhere, whether to your benefit or detriment.

One effective way to monitor priorities is to keep a "not to do" list. This is a list of tasks and projects that you are choosing not to focus any of your finite resources on during this particular season so that you might reserve them for what really matters. Items on this list could be projects with plenty of runway, administrative tasks that distract you from the more important creative work you need to do, or even time sinkholes like social media and entertainment.

Craft a "not to do" list, and use it to help you sharpen your focus.

> **QUESTION**
> What should be on your "not to do" list?

February
29

Bonus for Leap Years

Every brilliant act of creativity involves an intuitive leap.

It's always a risk. If it wasn't risky, everyone would do it.

It's always hard. It nearly always feels like you are gambling with your identity. It always involves the potential for failure.

And it's the only path of progress. Without historical intuitive leaps, we would still be scrambling to find food every day and sleeping with one eye open out in the elements.

There is likely an intuitive leap that you know you need to take. Fortunately, today is Leap Day. It's the perfect time for you to move. Follow your intuition.

What idea do you need to pursue, immediately?

What project do you need to make progress on, immediately?

What relationship do you need to move forward (or end), immediately?

How do you need to be aggressive today?

Today is Leap Day. Mark it by making an intuitive leap.

QUESTION
What intuitive leap do you need to take today?

March

The fear of failure can be paralyzing. We don't attempt difficult things because we are concerned about what might happen if we fall short of our objectives. This month, focus on taking small, incremental, challenging steps toward your goals. Small, daily risks build tolerance for the occasional larger ones.

March

1

We Tried That One

A senior manager from a large company once confided in me that he was frustrated that his organization wouldn't allow him to pursue some of his ideas. I replied that perhaps his ideas simply aren't the right ones. "No, it's not that," he clarified. "It's that they are stuck in the past." I asked him to elaborate. It turns out that his manager didn't like one of his ideas because, as he put it, "we tried that back in the 1980s and it didn't work, so I don't think we should try it." Thus I began to better understand my client's frustration.

Have more than a few things changed since the 1980s? Of course. But this company was living with a baked-in assumption based on a thirty-year-old failure that may or may not even be relevant to the current situation.

We are often quick to dismiss past failures and move on, but sometimes it is worth revisiting them. That particular failure may have had less to do with the idea and more to do with the timing. If a brilliant product, message, or system is introduced at the wrong time, it can fail nonetheless. If introduced only a few years later, it's a smashing success.

Consider past failures and any assumptions that might still be affecting your work today.

Past failures may only have been a matter of timing.

QUESTION

What past idea may have failed because of timing, not because of the idea itself? Is there a way you can resurrect it?

March
2

Procrastinate Properly

We tend to think of procrastination as avoiding work so that we can enjoy something more pleasurable. However, there are actually good and bad forms of procrastination.

Obviously, bad procrastination is putting off what you should be doing now in order to avoid discomfort. In his book *Four Thousand Weeks*, Oliver Burkeman argues that we sometimes engage in this kind of procrastination to avoid having to confront our inevitable finitude. It's much more comfortable to live with a perfect idea in your head than to bring it into the world and see its imperfections realized.

But there is also a *good* kind of procrastination. This is when you allow an idea to incubate for a season, even though you could easily act on it now. You intentionally wait to see how the idea develops and if there are any environmental sparks that evolve it into something better. This kind of procrastination allows your creative intuition to develop into something more visible and tangible. Good procrastination is *productive* procrastination. It compromises efficiency for a season for the sake of effectiveness in the end.

Be mindful of how bad procrastination robs your future self of time and energy, but also be mindful of how good procrastination can allow your ideas to fully develop.

Procrastination can be an effective creative strategy, but *only* if done properly.

QUESTION

Is there an idea or project that could benefit from a little productive procrastination?

March
3

Be Your Own Worst Enemy

We all have blind spots. Some of the worst ones involve our favorite ideas. When you are in the "honeymoon phase" with an idea, you only see its positive attributes. That's why it's such a surprise when someone else begins critiquing it. We almost feel personally offended.

"What are you talking about? I have no idea what you mean."

Your blind spots prevent you from seeing the faults in your own idea.

A method that works really well—but must be used with caution—is what I call "be your own worst enemy." It involves spending fifteen minutes attacking your idea from every angle, thinking of every reason why it wouldn't work, and aggressively trying to construct an argument for why it's not worth the time and energy to pursue. As you engage in this exercise, you are likely to uncover some weaknesses that you didn't previously see, but in the process, you are also likely to craft it into a much more resilient idea.

Again, use this technique with caution because it's easy to talk yourself out of pursuing a really good idea.

Be brutally honest about your ideas so that they can become their best versions.

Be your own worst enemy, and once you withstand the attacks, you will be much better positioned for success.

QUESTION

Which current idea that you're working on could use a little scrutiny?

March
4

Spec Work

When you create on demand, it's easy to fall into ruts. You are confined by budget, time, client expectations, past work, collaborative relationships, and more. Thus, you only entertain ideas that you know will be well-received because you simply don't have the time or resources to pursue ideas or projects that might squander your finite resources.

One method to bust out of those ruts is to occasionally engage in spec work for clients, whether real or imaginary. Choose a client, and do a complete reinvention of their product line. Do a total rebrand for them. Imagine what a new organizational structure might look like. Develop a killer product that they might never pursue on their own but that you believe would change their industry.

The incredible aspect of doing this spec work? You don't have to share it with anyone! It's just for you. You can speculate all you want with none of the risk. It's all about imagining a better possible future.

But—and this is key—this spec work will often result in ideas and new paths of innovation that you didn't previously entertain, because you are no longer bound by those limiting constraints.

Creating spec work is a great way to spark fresh, innovative thought.

> **QUESTION**
> What kind of spec work could you engage in this week as a way to spark new, innovative thought?

March
5

Reevaluating the Straw Man

You've likely been in a number of meetings in which—in a moment of desperation—someone exclaims "let me propose a straw man." It's an idea that's known to be compromised and is a soft proposal designed to be shot at and dismantled by everyone else in the room. In theory, the straw-man tactic seems like it should be effective. After all, it provides an opportunity to discuss the problem, and it may feel better in the moment than being stuck. However, you must be careful in setting up a straw man for a few reasons:

- The straw man anchors you. Once you begin to discuss the straw man, you are no longer thinking about what you might be able to do; you begin narrowing your efforts to evaluating that particular idea. So you stop looking for new ideas.
- Some people in the room are relieved by the introduction of the straw man because they are no longer accountable for coming up with an idea. So they might do anything they can to rationalize why the idea works.
- The straw man is knowingly compromised. Starting from a place of intentional compromise is not a way to muster team morale.

I encourage you to replace the straw man method with "What if we...?" Introduce an idea that's designed to be built on, not torn down.

Resist the urge to create a straw man in your creative work. It anchors you and limits your creative thinking.

QUESTION

Are you presently stuck in the straw man trap with a project? How can you navigate through it?

March
6

Trying Hard Things

At some point, you reach a place in your career where work that once felt difficult is now fairly simple and projects that would have kept you up all night several years ago are now quite manageable. You feel in total control of your process and mastery of your domain.

Sounds great, right? However, it's in these moments that you are potentially in danger of slipping into stasis. Similar to muscles that aren't exercised, when you don't sufficiently challenge yourself, your creative process can atrophy.

In the book *The Art of Possibility*, Benjamin and Rosamund Zander relay a story about the great composer Igor Stravinsky. His work was intentionally very challenging to play and required both remarkable technical skill and musical feel. He is once reported to have exclaimed, "I don't want the sound of someone playing this passage, I want the sound of someone trying to play it." Some of the best creative work is crafted not when someone is in complete mastery of their domain but when they are operating just on the edge of it, taking risks, moving just a bit faster and beyond their technical capabilities.

As you consider your work right now, how in control do you feel, and do you believe that is a net positive or a danger to your body of work?

Don't measure creative accomplishment. Measure creative growth.

QUESTION
Are you ever operating on the edge of your abilities? Where might you take a creative risk today?

March
7

Nesting Skills

A few years ago, my family bought me a mandolin for Father's Day. It was a wonderful gift, and it hangs prominently in my home office, where in a moment of pause, I often pick it up and noodle while thinking about the next sentence or a particularly sticky problem. The mandolin is a unique instrument with eight strings tuned in pairs, so four notes total, and is pretty technically complex to play because of its small scale and percussive nature. While experienced mandolin players make it look easy, for novices, it can be much more difficult than other instruments like the guitar. Fortunately, I had a few decades of guitar playing under my belt, so translating my existing skills to the mandolin was a lot easier than starting from scratch. I'm certainly no master, but I can play well enough to make it enjoyable.

All new skills are best learned within the context of skills we have already mastered. Don't feel the pressure to develop a new, completely foreign skill. Instead, consider learning a new skill that's an extension of your existing skill set or nests well within your existing experience. It's like having a secret shortcut to growth.

When learning new skills, consider ones that nest nicely within your existing skill set.

QUESTION

What new skill—that nests well within your existing skill set—should you focus on developing over the coming weeks or months?

March
8

Brilliance Demands Bravery

A reason that many people never step out into the unknown and try something risky is that they are afraid of rejection. There is a narrative playing in their minds that equates who they are with what they do, and the potential of having their self-image violated is simply too much to bear.

They would rather live with perceived invulnerability than take a chance and discover they have limits.

However, the brave souls who are willing to share what they see, make, and think, even if it is incomplete and imperfect, are the ones who move us all forward. The person who speaks up in a meeting, who makes art as a form of protest, or who shows up every single day to do the work (ignoring the gravitational pull of mediocrity) pulls everyone else along with them up the rugged mountain.

I say it's better to appear a fool than to abdicate your contribution and deeply regret your choices later. It's impossible for everything you make to be great, but one thing I do know is this: brilliance demands bravery.

If you make things and share them, your heart will at some point be broken. If you never share, it will harden. Your choice.

Be brave today, friends. Do something that matters to you.

QUESTION

In what way do you need to be brave today? How can being brave today create change for you?

March
9

What's Your Default?

We each have default settings that we tend to revert to when under stress. For example, here's a static default you may have never considered: do you inherently trust someone until given a reason not to or to distrust until given a reason to believe them? When you default to trusting others, you will inevitably be disappointed but might also be surprised by how often they live up to your trust. When you default to mistrust, you create a hurdle for them to jump just to be in relationship with you. While you may anticipate some of some bad behavior, your relationship is covered with an aura of suspicion and oppositional energy. And creativity requires—in fact demands—trust. Without it, your creativity will wither on the vine.

Your default position is a stake in the ground that anchors your future decisions. Thus, you must be mindful of any defaults that you set for yourself or your team. You can easily trap yourself and limit your future options. This applies not only to your inherent position toward others but also your default systems, decisions, schedule, and other personal and team processes. Your defaults anchor you in a set of expectations.

Consider the defaults that you've established in your process, your collaboration, and your leadership. Make certain they aren't limiting your options.

Your default stance anchors your future decisions.

QUESTION

Are there any default positions that you've taken that need to be reconsidered?

March
10

Remove the Earbuds

The next time you go to a grocery store, pay attention to how many people are wearing earbuds, listening to music or the news, oblivious to the sounds around them.

I used to be one of these people. I saw a trip to the market as an opportunity to catch up on my podcasts or to listen to an audiobook. However, one day, I forgot them and found myself immersed in the sounds and stimuli of the shopping experience. I overheard snippets of conversation. I listened to the music the store chose to play over the in-house speaker system and wondered who in the world decided to play *that* song here.

We so rarely allow ourselves to be firmly planted in the place we're standing. We're always "out there" somewhere or filling our senses with other times and other places. However, there's a deep beauty and inspiration to be gained from allowing your environment to happen to you instead of micromanaging it.

I understand that it sounds cliché, but strive to be present today. Take a walk and remove the earbuds. Be in the place you are, and pay attention to the nuance all around you.

Intentionally take in the environment around you. Try not to fall into the trap of perpetual distraction.

QUESTION

How will you attempt to pay better attention to your environment today?

March
11

The Notables

There are moments in your life when you experience something, do something, or are confronted with something that sparks an unexpected response. For example, maybe you experienced some kind of injustice for the first time and felt a strong need to do something about it. Maybe you did work that unexpectedly gratified you and caused you to come alive in ways you didn't expect. We experience these moments, then quickly gloss over them and move on because we're busy or there are any number of other priorities that we need to get to. However, it's by paying close attention to the patterns in these notable moments that we see the tracings of the work that's being called out of us by the world.

What makes you compassionately angry? What makes you think "Ugh! Someone needs to do something about that!" Yes, and that someone is probably you.

What moves you emotionally? Is there any specific kind of situation that brings you to tears every time?

What do you believe that few others around you do? What's the hope that keeps you going?

These are great questions to help you begin to identify your unique response to the world, which will then play out in your work and leadership.

Look for patterns in your world and your work that illuminate your creative calling.

> **QUESTION**
> What patterns do you find in your notable moments?

March
12

The Resistance

Ever notice how just when you are ready to start working on that important creative project that's due in a few weeks, you suddenly have the urge to clean your desk, or you decide it's time to pay the bills, or you realize it's the perfect moment to start episode one of that great show everyone's talking about (which then inevitably turns into a binge-watching marathon)?

It's almost as if there's some great cosmic force working against you, no? In a way, there is. Steven Pressfield dubs this force "the Resistance" and calls it out as the chief opponent of creative productivity. He writes, "As powerful as is our soul's call, so potent are the forces of Resistance arrayed against it. We're not alone if we've been mowed down by Resistance; millions of good men and women have bitten the dust before us." On his first efforts at writing, he said, "I knew I wanted to write novels, but I could not finish what I started. The closer I got, the more ways I'd find to screw it up."

So how do we begin to countermand the Resistance? The first step is to notice it when we experience it. Simply calling it out for what it is helps build a bulwark against it. Notice how you feel as you sit down to write, to design, to think. What is pressing against you?

Then, commit to fighting the Resistance when you feel it. Push back against it, and it usually yields. Make just a little progress, and you will find more progress on its heels.

Be mindful of the forces that want to keep your creativity at bay.

QUESTION
When do you most experience the Resistance?

March
13

Hill Repeats

Two of my children are competitive runners. They typically run in relatively flat environments, and even when running cross-country races, the courses are typically relatively nontreacherous. Regardless, their coach requires them to do what are called "hill repeats" during training. Hill repeats are exactly how they sound—running up and down a hill over and over until you're exhausted.

So why would you do that to yourself—especially when you aren't running on many hills in your races?

Well, hill repeats make normal running feel easy by comparison. When you're used to running straight up an incline and you get to run on flat ground, it suddenly feels like a much more manageable task. It's similar to why baseball players put "doughnuts" around their bats when warming up—once they're removed, the bat feels so much lighter.

Working against an impediment forges strength and resilience. This is why interval training is so effective—you have periods of alternating stress and rest. As you consider your work, how can you structure some interval training into your workload? How can you challenge yourself in manageable, controllable ways today to build capacity for tomorrow?

Mind your intervals, and build capacity for the moments that matter.

> **QUESTION**
> What practices can you engage in today to prepare you for the challenges you'll face tomorrow?

March
14

Little Things Done Well

A friend of mine was once on a trip, trying to secure the business of a large company. The CEO of the company picked him up at the airport and asked if they could stop at the grocery store on the way back to the office. While at the store, the CEO put two small items in the cart, checked out, walked back to the car, and asked my friend if he'd mind taking care of the cart. My friend pushed the cart all the way across the parking lot to the cart corral, and when he walked back to the car, the CEO was standing with his hand extended. "Congrats. You've got the business." Turns out my friend's competitor was in town the day before, and when asked to take care of the cart, he just pushed it between two cars instead of returning it. The CEO said that if my friend did the right but uncomfortable thing in this situation, he was likely to do it when things really matter.

Don't underestimate the power of small, seemingly insignificant acts. They signal to everyone around you that you are a trustworthy collaborator.

Do the little things consistently and well, and you will earn the trust of your team.

> **QUESTION**
> What small act of service can you do today for those you work with?

March
15

Your Intended Audience

Ask a creative pro in the midst of a project who they are making it for, and their answer might begin with "our target audience is…" or "our most coveted segment is…" or "our demographic research shows that…" This is how we've been trained to think about targeting the work; it's all about reaching groups of people who are sympathetic to our products or services.

That said, having a vague target in mind when creating something is often more distracting than helpful. Your aim lacks specificity and nuance. Groups don't use your product or service; individuals do.

Instead, think of a very specific person you are making it for. Don't envision a group, a demographic, or a psychographic but one real person. I've written all my books to individuals, pretending I was sitting across the table from them offering advice. Your intended audience for your work shapes how you make decisions and how you foresee that work finding its place in the world. Don't allow your work to be watered down by a lack of specificity.

Creative work resonates most deeply when crafted for an audience of one.

QUESTION

Consider a project you are working on at the moment. Who—a specific individual—is a good intended audience for the work? How might that change your approach?

March
16

The Challenges of Creative Work

When you solve problems (aka do creative work) for a living, there are three distinct challenges:

1. Your process is largely obscured from many of the people who will be evaluating your work. They don't understand what's required to do the work you do, so they may ask for unrealistic things. You must give them visibility into your process and realistic expectations.
2. The work is largely subjective. The opinions of your stakeholders may be very different from yours, and there is little you can do about it. You must learn to craft the work and be able to argue for why it's strategically correct.
3. There is never-ending fodder for ego and insecurity. Because the job is to confront and resolve uncertainties, less secure people pretend they feel invincible even though they are just as uncertain as anyone. You must be confidently adaptable, arguing for your work but willing to listen to disconfirming information.

Creative work offers some unique challenges. Knowing them helps you navigate through them.

QUESTION

As you consider these three challenges, is there one that you find most common in your work? What can you do to remedy it today?

March
17

Complete Your Projects

Creative work is never really complete because there is always an opportunity to improve it. You might be weeks past the deadline on a project, and even though you turned it in, you can't let it go. Suddenly, you have a brilliant idea that would have completely changed the game. Your mind has continued to work in the background on the project even though you are already on to new ones.

It's natural and normal to experience this. If you had unlimited resources, you could spend as much time as necessary to make the end result amazing. You don't.

Don't allow past projects to obsess you or siphon time, attention, and energy from your current work. (Have you ever met someone who still relives that critical play from an important high school sports game? Don't be that person.)

When you have that "Oh! I should have done X!" moment, log it, learn from it, but don't relive the project. And once the project is complete, close the book and move on. Focus on what's ahead.

Don't second-guess and keep noodling on old work. Close the book and move on.

QUESTION

Is there a past project you're still a little obsessed with? How can you close the book and move on?

March
18

Incubation vs. Stagnation

When you are stuck on a project, it can be helpful to hit the pause button and let things sit for a while. Breaking away from the work for a season can give you a fresh perspective when you return to it. However, there are two types of pauses, and knowing the difference can determine your outcome.

Incubation is when you allow a project to "bake" for a bit while you immerse yourself in new stimulus and experiences. This type of pause is strategic, for a season, and with the express purpose of picking the project back up at a specific time to push it forward.

Stagnation is when you simply drop a project when things grow difficult. It's what Scott Belsky calls the "project plateau." You get tired of the effort, so you jump to a new project that feels more exciting. You allow the project to stall indefinitely because you lack the will to keep pushing forward. It's a purposeless pause.

Discern the difference between a strategic pause and a lazy one.

> **QUESTION**
> Is there a project you're working on right now that could benefit from strategic incubation?

March
19

Cut the Right Corners

In creative work, low overhead is often the key to sustainability, flexibility, and freedom. When you remove the stranglehold of debt and high fixed costs, you increase your ability to spend time and energy where there might be a greater return, even if it's a delayed one.

However, overfrugality can be a significant impediment to the creative process as well. A lack of resources imposes artificial limits on the ideas you pursue. You might begin to unknowingly settle into your overly constrictive boundaries.

When considering how you spend resources, it's best to think in terms of investment and expense. There are things worth spending money on if they are likely to improve or increase the return on the other side. Invest money in experiences, workspace tools, resources, and other things that are likely to give you a creative edge. However, be more frugal about spending money on things that have little ongoing value.

"Is this an investment or an expense?" is a great question to ask when you aren't certain.

Frugality can be good, but don't allow it to lead to creative strangulation. Invest your resources in things that are likely to yield a return tomorrow.

Distinguish between frugality and creative strangulation.

QUESTION

Is there something you should be investing your resources in right now? Or cutting back on?

March
20

5K + 50K

No matter how hard you try, your work is never going to be perfect. You can spend dozens of hours trying to squeeze the final few percent of value out of something, but you're unlikely to ever get there. This sometimes happens when you get too close to a project and begin to see problems that you may not have seen previously. The terrain looks a lot different from five thousand feet in the air than it does from fifty thousand feet. You begin to overthink things. You begin to question prior decisions. You see small areas where you could make it just a little better, even though it means spending 25 percent of your project time to get 1 percent better results.

Take some time to ask yourself if you might be too close to your work. Some signs include the following:

- You are obsessed by new problems that weren't even on your radar a week ago.
- You no longer like the original idea, even though you originally thought it was brilliant.
- You are tempted to blow it all up and start over.

Be cautious not to get too close to the work. Keep a healthy distance. **If you get too close, you will see problems where they don't exist.**

QUESTION
Are you too close to any of your work right now?

March
21

Excess Baggage

We often carry excess baggage—anxiety—driven by worry about things beyond our ability to influence, such as upcoming projects or team dynamics. The anxiety that you feel does not serve you. It hinders you and limits your creative vision. As the old axiom goes, "Worry is like paying interest on a debt that may never come due."

Are dynamics beyond your influence causing anxiety?

If so, I suggest that you consider which conversations you could have to answer your questions, or that might give you a bit of clarity. Or consider if there are any actions, no matter how small, that might assuage your concern. However, whatever you do, don't allow anxiety to rule your life or creative process. Don't pay pointless interest.

Be mindful about carrying excess baggage that weighs you down.

> **QUESTION**
> What excess baggage are you carrying right now?

March
22

Doers and Don'ters

My father-in-law, a consultant, once flew on a client's private jet. His client confessed, "I couldn't have been successful enough to have a jet without you." He replied that the advice he'd given to the successful CEO was no different from similar advice he'd given to numerous executives over time. The difference was that this CEO could actually do something with it. He was in a position to be able to leverage the advice, whereas others would simply hear it, apply it in minor ways, and move on with their lives. Same advice but very different outcomes.

It's not what you know, it's what you do with it that matters. Also, it's important that you associate with people who take action rather than those who just let things happen to them. To summarize singer Frank Turner, spend more time with do's and less time with don'ts. Surround yourself with people who feed you and who challenge you to be better.

Spend time with doers, not don'ters.

Spend time with people who make things happen.

QUESTION

Who are the doers in your life? The don'ters?

March
23

Turning the What If?

"What if they...?"

"What if this doesn't...?"

"What if I discover...?"

"What if....?" questions often sound perfectly reasonable, but they are sometimes driven by a deep fear of something going wrong. In fact, they might keep you squarely in your comfort zone, aiming for the safest route.

And the problem is that we don't think of our comfort zone as a comfort zone. We think we are being rational and cautious and tempered in our approach. But at the root of all these questions is fear.

However, "what if?" can also be asked from a positive slant:

- ▶ What if this is exactly the opportunity I've been looking for?
- ▶ What if I discover I'm actually good at this?
- ▶ What if I enjoy it and it opens up a new world of possibility for my career?

The same question, asked with a different slant, is a courageous question rather than a cowardly one.

Make your what-if questions positive, not negative.

QUESTION

Do you tend to ask courageous or cowardly what-if questions?

March
24

Identity vs. Trait vs. Behavior

The story that plays most loudly inside your head defines your perception of reality. If you are anxious about making a mistake, you will approach every decision with extreme caution, fearful of taking a wrong turn. If you believe you're invincible, you are likely to make careless and potentially dangerous mistakes.

It's important to distinguish between identity, trait, and behavior.

- *Identity (who):* Something that defines your very existence, the source of who you are, the most reliable thing about you.
- *Trait (what):* A tendency that is often exhibited but that isn't a part of your core identity.
- *Behavior (how):* A reaction or response to the world in a moment.

We often promote rare behaviors to traits ("It's just the kind of thing I do") and promote traits to identity ("I cannot perform well under pressure. I cave.").

You are not the sum of your worst behaviors, just as you are not limited to your visible traits. Don't enclose yourself in a false and limiting story. Who you are is not the sum of the things you've done.

Be mindful of the story you tell yourself about who you are and what you're capable of accomplishing. Don't artificially bound your creativity.

QUESTION

Do you ever elevate a behavior or trait into an identity? What is it, and how has it affected you?

March
25

The Next Three Leaps

It's easy to become trapped by the limitations of your current project. You certainly have finite resources, a limited team and time in which to accomplish your work, and probably multiple projects happening at once.

Because of this, many professionals narrow their options to the most practical ones far too early in the process. When you're under pressure, any kind of immediate progress can feel more necessary than making something great. So, you move forward without really giving a problem the right amount of creating thinking.

One technique that works well in these pressure-filled situations for pushing your creative thinking to the next level is an exercise I call "the next three leaps." It works like this:

- ► What would be a huge leap we could take right now if we had the resources?
- ► Then, once we've done that, what would be another huge leap we could take?
- ► Then, what would we do next?

Many people are trapped by a lack of creative vision because they can only see what's directly in front of them or what feels imminently practical.

To accelerate innovation and creative thought, envision the next three leaps.

QUESTION
Which project that you're working on could benefit from the next three leaps?

March
26

What's Obvious

Author and entrepreneur Derek Sivers once made a wonderful observation. He said that many people marvel at the ideas of their peers and exclaim, "I could never come up with something like that. All my ideas are too obvious."

The funny thing is, according to Sivers, those brilliant and amazing ideas often feel just as obvious to the person having them. As he put it, "Everybody's ideas seem obvious to them."

Do you ever feel that way? Like all your ideas are just too easy, too obvious? I'll bet you do. I do too, but I've learned over time that what's obvious to me isn't always obvious to others. I have a different set of life experiences, a different grouping of ambitions, and a different lens I'm looking through to find answers. Because of that, any solutions I've been working on for a while are going to feel vaguely familiar even though they might seem totally revolutionary to others.

As you go about your work today, be mindful not to dismiss an idea simply because it feels too obvious at first. It may be obvious to you but not to others. Brilliance often feels commonplace at first.

Just because it seems obvious to you doesn't mean it's obvious to everyone.

QUESTION

Have you ever discarded an idea because it seemed too obvious?

March
27

The People in Your Life

I once spoke at an event for senior U.S. Air Force officers where one of the other speakers was a former U.S. Army general. In the green room before the event, he caught me by surprise as I was stuffing a blueberry muffin into my mouth and asked, "What's the most important thing to know about creativity?" It was a great question, and to be honest, I can't remember what I replied in the moment.

However, I do remember what happened next. I immediately asked him, "What's the most important thing I should know about leadership?"

Without missing a beat, he replied, "You need people in your life who will speak truth to you well before you realize that you need people in your life to speak truth to you. By the time you realize you need them, it's already too late."

Leadership is only lonely if you're doing it wrong. Who are your trusted truth-tellers? Who do you turn to for honest and frank perspective? Who tells you when you are thinking too small or too big? Who knows you well enough to call out your negative tendencies or encourage your brilliant traits?

Who are your people?

Know who your people are before you need them.

QUESTION

Do you have people in your life who will speak truth to you?

March
28

Leading with Unnecessary Complexity

Most of the difficult people you work with—clients, peers, managers—aren't trying to make your life more difficult. They are just normal people trying their best to do their jobs, and by doing so, they unwittingly make your life more challenging. The truth is, you probably do the same thing to others without even knowing it. This is especially true if you lead a team.

On their own, many of the decisions that you make seem simple and appropriate. However, when you begin to layer those decisions on top of the other decisions you've made, a web of complexity emerges. Very rarely do new systems or processes get removed when a new one is added. Instead, they just layer on top of each other. The same principle applies for every voice added to a project. Each perspective layers on top of the others, adding complexity.

Is there any way in which you are adding unnecessary complexity to your work or that of those you work with? Don't mindlessly add another layer.

Unnecessary complexity often builds one layer at a time in unnoticed ways.

QUESTION

Is there any way in which you might be contributing to unnecessary complexity in your work or with your team?

March
29

Drivers, Drifters, Dreamers

I often like to parse work into three parts:

1. *Mapping* is planning, strategy, developing tasks lists, and deciding on action steps.
2. *Making* is executing on your plan. It's doing the actual work.
3. *Meshing* is the work between the work. It's the small things you do to set yourself up for future effectiveness, like studying, asking inconvenient questions, and developing skills.

When people map and make but fail to mesh, I call them *drivers*. These are people who get a lot done in spurts, but over time, they become decreasingly effective because they aren't developing themselves.

When people make and mesh but fail to map, I call them *drifters*. They are carried along by their ideas but lack the conviction of a strategic plan. They often leave half-finished projects in their wake.

When people map and mesh but fail to make, I call them *dreamers*. They love coming up with the ideas but struggle to put any of them into action.

Which of these profiles do you tend toward when you are under stress?

It's helpful to know how you behave under pressure so that you can build practices to help you stay on course.

> **QUESTION**
> Which productivity profile do you tend toward when under pressure?

March
30

Celebration

When was the last time you truly, meaningfully celebrated an accomplishment? I don't mean that you took a few moments to revel in the joy before diving back into your email or kicking off the next project. I'm talking about truly marking a moment and making it meaningful.

You should celebrate wins. In fact, I'm a firm believer in celebrating often. The key is to find the right balance between "this feels good" and "why are we celebrating that they just cleaned the whiteboards?" Celebration should feel legitimate and substantial. Here are a few questions to ask to help to mark the moment:

- ► What did we overcome to achieve this?
- ► How will the world/our client/our organization be better as a result of this win?
- ► What are we grateful for?
- ► What did we learn about ourselves through this process?
- ► What are we excited about now that we have achieved this?

Marking the moment isn't just an excuse to knock off work a little early. It's a way to prevent work from feeling like a never-ending stream of projects and tasks. Celebrate big and celebrate often.

Take the time to mark the moment and celebrate your wins.

QUESTION
What recent win do you need to celebrate today?

March
31

Ideas Are a Two-Edged Sword

Ideas are weighty and complex things. You crave new ones, but you also don't want them because with every new idea comes accountability.

Accountability to act.

Accountability to share.

Accountability to take a risk.

Accountability to put something in motion that could fail.

Sometimes we don't want a new idea because we don't want the accountability that comes with it. We might *say* that we do, but our actions prove otherwise.

We procrastinate when we know that we need to be thinking. In fact, we avoid thinking because we worry about where all that thinking might lead.

We fail to finish a project that we were previously excited about, not because we aren't capable but because we are afraid to discover whether the project will succeed or flop.

Ideas are two-edged swords, because they come with both opportunity and responsibility.

The opportunity to make something, share something, invent something, collaborate on something, change something that will impact others. That's remarkable.

The responsibility is that you now have to shepherd the idea.

To have an idea is a brave thing.

To have an idea means you are given both an opportunity and a responsibility.

QUESTION

It sounds strange, but is there an idea you are avoiding? Let's face it and look at the opportunity it holds.

April

"All the adversity I've had in my life, all my troubles and obstacles, have strengthened me... You may not realize it when it happens, but a kick in the teeth may be the best thing in the world for you."
—WALT DISNEY

Everyone experiences setbacks from time to time. It's a natural by-product of trying sufficiently difficult things. It's not the setbacks that take us off course; it's our responses to them. This month, consider how you respond to setbacks—minor or major—and focus your efforts on finding a way around or through them rather than allowing them to paralyze you.

April

1

You Can Do Hard Things

I don't know if you need to hear this right now, but here you go:

You can do hard things.

You can handle a challenging manager.

You can tackle that seemingly unsolvable problem.

You can have the difficult conversation.

You can collaborate with that obnoxious person.

You can do more than you've ever done in less time than you've ever done it.

You can be brilliant again when it matters most.

You can endure through this season of hardship.

You can be stronger on the other side.

You can work a job and not lose yourself.

You can both create tremendous value and enjoy yourself while doing it.

You can take that risk.

You can sit for a while and do nothing when needed.

You can study.

You can do difficult physical things.

You can not just survive but thrive under adversity.

You can put yourself out there.

You can start over if you need to.

When things get difficult, remember this: you can do hard things.

QUESTION
What hard thing do you need to do today?

April
2

Thank Your People

You could probably easily list a few people who have made a large impact on your life and work in the past few years. It might be someone in your organization who took a chance on you, a collaborator who recommended you for a job that you wouldn't have otherwise known about, or even a "mentor from afar" whose work you admire and that has inspired you in some way.

The wonderful thing about living in these times is that it's so easy to let those people know how much they've helped you. Carve out some time today to write a short note to a person in your life who has positively influenced you telling them how much you appreciate them. Be specific about how they helped you. If possible, write them a physical note, but if you don't know how to contact them, it's likely you can find them online and send them an email or even contact them via social media. Don't hold any expectation of a response, just send them a note of thanks.

When you put good things into the world—like gratitude and appreciation—everyone benefits. Let someone know how much they've helped you and how. They probably need to hear it.

Express gratitude to those who have helped you. If possible, write a note.

QUESTION
Who could you reach out and express gratitude to today?

April
3

Use Your Voice

So often, creative pros talk about "finding their voice" as if it's some far-off entity that must be hunted down and captured so that it might be put to work. That's not even close to reality. The way in which voice is developed is far less exotic—they try and fail, then they try again, then they adapt and try again, and eventually they make something that feels better and more resonant with their vision.

You develop your voice by using it, a lot. Take small risks with your work each day, and see what resonates. Put work into the world where others can respond to it. Try developing a new skill that gives you unique ways of expressing yourself. Explore a challenging medium. Collaborate with new people. And take in the work of other people broadly and deeply, and see what resonates with you.

Your voice develops over time like film in a darkroom, not all at once like a digital photo. Many people struggle to develop their voice because they don't pay attention to the clues that are found in everyday, resonant moments.

Put work into the world every day. If you want to develop your voice, use it.

> **QUESTION**
> How can you be more purposeful about uncovering and developing your voice through your work?

April
4

Bravery and Boldness

In modern society, we often conflate boldness with bravery. They are not the same thing. Many people who act boldly are simply masking cowardice, anxiety, and insecurity with bold words and actions.

Bold leaders speak in declaratives, while brave leaders are willing to wade through the discomfort of seeing nuance.

Bold leaders identify scapegoats as the source of their problems, while brave leaders take accountability for their own thoughts and actions.

Bold leaders scream against events happening in their circle of concern, while brave leaders focus on what's in their own circle of influence.

Bold leaders listen to what they want to hear, while brave leaders listen to what they need to hear and are willing to change their minds when confronted with new information.

In the face of uncertainty and chaos, it's tempting to act merely with boldness, but now more than ever, our world needs bravery. We need people willing to step into the uncertainty and make brave, nuanced work.

Be brave leaders, friends. Do brave work. Don't settle for mere boldness.

There is a difference between brave work and bold work. Brave work can be bold, but not all bold work is brave.

QUESTION

Is there any place in your life or work where you might be mistaking boldness and bravery? How can you be brave in your work today?

April

5

Challenge - Stability = Anger

Here's a reliable principle of work life: expectations consistently rise. New projects are added on top of existing ones, new systems are put in place, and new meetings are added (which then generate even more work!). Often, you are asked to take on more work than you are capable of managing at a given time. This is normal. However, when this trend continues over time, it can feel suffocating and frustrating. You are challenged without the corresponding level of stability necessary to help you perform. You may lack the resources, clarity, or systems needed to succeed.

When this happens, it's tempting to grow angry and direct that ire at your manager. However, I'd encourage you to seek what you need instead:

- ► Ask for more resources (budget, help, clarity, time).
- ► Explain why the existing process isn't working well, and offer to help fix it.
- ► Ask to reprioritize your existing work so that you can tackle the new, urgent work.
- ► Assess where you feel stretched beyond your capacity, and seek a peer's perspective.

Don't allow your frustration to boil over. Ask for what you need. **Always make certain you have the support structure to facilitate your level of creative challenge.**

QUESTION

Is there any place in your work where you are not getting the clarity or resources you need to meet your expectations? How can you seek what you need?

April
6

Stability - Challenge = Stuck-ness

As an organization adapts to manage the increased challenges of the work by increasing capacity or providing more resources, your expectations may now feel very manageable or even a little repetitive. Another way to put it is that you have high stability but low challenge.

When this dynamic emerges, it's common to feel stuck. You aren't excited about your work because it doesn't challenge you to take risks or develop new skills. You feel like you're in a rut. The only way out of it is to seek a challenge that will help you stay engaged.

Ask your manager if there is new work you can take on. Intentionally develop a new skill—even on your own time—that stretches you. Put yourself in situations where you are a little nervous about your ability to perform. This will ensure that you don't stay in the place of stuck-ness.

While it's great to have stability, without challenge, you will begin to feel stuck.

QUESTION

Do you feel appropriately challenged by your work right now? If not, how can you seek a challenge that would spark deeper engagement?

April

7

Question the Right Assumption

In the 1980s, A&W Restaurants decided to compete head-to-head with McDonald's famed Quarter Pounder hamburger. The idea, promoted by owner A. Alfred Taubman, was to compete on value by introducing an even larger burger, a third of a pound, at the exact same price point as the McDonald's quarter-pound burger. They poured resources into their "Third Is the Word" marketing campaign. As Taubman relayed in his book *Threshold Resistance,* "We were aggressively marketing a one-third-pound hamburger for the same price...but despite our best efforts, including first-rate TV and radio promotional spots, they just weren't selling." Frustrated as to why the burgers weren't selling in spite of being an incredible value, A&W decided to investigate by talking directly to consumers. Was it the messaging? The quality of the food? Something else?

Turns out it was none of that. When asked, customers said that they didn't understand why they would pay the same price for one-third-pound hamburger as they do for a quarter-pound hamburger. They thought one-third was smaller than one-quarter, therefore making A&W's offering a worse value.

Remember that the assumptions you make about your work are founded on your personal experiences but may not reflect the perceptions of your intended audience.

The reason an idea isn't working is often more subtle—or even more obvious—than you think.

QUESTION
What assumption do you need to challenge today?

April

8

The Dailies

In a monastery, there are a certain number of daily actions that take place on a regular schedule. This schedule of dailies is regimented and predictable but is the very reason the monastery is able to function and ultimately perform its purpose. If left to chance or the whims of the monks, it's likely many of these tasks would rarely be accomplished, and the ceremonies would be intermittent.

We can learn much from the regimented life of a monastery. Having a set of dailies in your life can ensure that important activities don't slip through the cracks. For example, here are a few of my dailies that I perform and check off each day:

Study

Meditate

Write

Review goals

Exercise

Have one meaningful conversation with each of my children

Engage in an act of business development

Create one piece of content

I keep a log of my dailies and check them off as I perform them each day. It's not an option for me to skip a day or forget, because the list is right in front of me. Over time, these daily actions become habits that reap big rewards.

Your dailies are most certainly going to be different from mine, but make certain you have some.

Develop a small set of daily rituals to keep you focused and on track.

> **QUESTION**
> What should be on your dailies list?

April
9

Same Old (Stuff)

I recently had the opportunity to see the Piano Man himself, Billy Joel, in concert. He put on a remarkable two-hour show, playing hit after hit and enthralling the audience with banter.

At the very beginning of the show, he paused between songs and proclaimed, "Well, we don't have anything new for you guys. Same old [stuff]! But," he continued, "we're pretty good at playing it by now."

I'd have to imagine there are nights when Joel really doesn't feel like performing some of the songs he's played thousands of times in his lifetime, but it doesn't matter. It's not about him. The work has taken on a life of its own.

Once you put work into the world, it no longer belongs to you. It now belongs to others, which means that their response, interpretation, and celebration of that work matter more than whatever your original intent was. Your work is not about you; it's about others and how they receive it and interact with it. Your work is a gift.

Your work is not for you. It's for others.

QUESTION

Is there any work that you do or have done that you hold onto too tightly, or don't want to allow to take on a life of its own?

April
10

Every Season Ends

Maybe you're in the midst of challenging times right now. Or maybe this is one of the best seasons of your life and career. Either way, know this: it's going to end. There will come a point when you have to move on, and this all will be a memory.

In the moment, it can seem like what's happening now will always be happening. We mentally convert present circumstances into permanent ones. However, everything is seasonal. Everything.

Why is this important?

Because when you fixate on what's happening right now, you begin to lose track of your vision. You funnel resources toward maintaining the status quo or simple survival, and you stop thinking about where you want to go. When this happens, you ignore or overlook opportunity. You get stuck in a moment you can't get out of. (Thanks, U2!)

So I don't know what you're experiencing right now, but no matter how good or bad it feels, know that it's just a moment. It's a season. This is going to end. Keep your eyes fixed ahead.

No matter what you're currently going through, it's going to end.

QUESTION

Is there a present circumstance you are fixated on in some way? How can you shift to the future?

April

11

Craving Boundaries

I'm sure that you've heard, as often as I have, someone exclaim, "I just wish I had total freedom on this project to do whatever I want." They rail against the seemingly constrictive limits their client or manager has put in place and long for complete autonomy. If only they had more freedom, they could do something truly brilliant.

In reality, total freedom is not helpful for the creative process. When everything is a possibility, progress is difficult. After all, how do you even begin to focus when there are no limits?

However, when you have a bounding arc—a place to begin and focus your initial efforts—progress is much easier to achieve. Once you have momentum, you can redirect as needed.

If you're stuck, it's possible that what you really need is some kind of bounding arc. You may be stagnant simply because you lack a place to begin. Having something in place to push against—even if it limits possibilities—can be beneficial to any project in the long run.

Don't decry your lack of freedom. Leverage bounding arcs to your advantage by channeling your energy within them. Innovate within your limits.

Total freedom is not helpful in the creative process. Sometimes all you need to get moving is a bounding arc.

QUESTION

Is there a project right now where you are stuck because there are too many possibilities?

April
12

A Lot of Little Experiments

Innovation rarely results from putting all your eggs in one basket. Typically, the creative breakthroughs you seek will result from conducting several small and diverse experiments, watching the results or responses closely, monitoring progress, then narrowing your options and adapting them until you get closer to something that works.

The experience of progress is key. When you focus all your efforts on one big objective, progress can feel glacial. And that uncertainty and weight can compound and generate negative, self-fulfilling stasis. However, when you center in on small experiments and everyday progress, it has a notable effect on your creative energy. As Dr. Teresa Amabile wrote in her book *The Progress Principle*, "In light of our results, managers who say—or secretly believe—that employees work better under pressure, uncertainty, unhappiness, or fear are just plain wrong. Negative inner work life has a negative effect on the four dimensions of performance: people are less creative, less productive, less deeply committed to their work, and less collegial to each other when their inner work lives darken."

Small experiments represent small pockets of possibility and excitement. And small acts of progress such as learning and iteration can buoy your creative energy and enthusiasm for your work.

Don't put all of your eggs in one basket. Have a series of small, measurable creative experiments going at once.

> **QUESTION**
> What small experiments could you do with your work right now? Make a short list.

April
13

The Unconscious Conspiracy

A favorite pastime that I also share with my oldest son is to visit a local used bookstore and spend hours exploring the multiple floors of books, some of which have been there, unsold, for decades. On a recent trip, the title of one book caught my eye, and upon examination I realized it was written by one of my favorite management theorists, Warren Bennis. Bennis was the president of the University of Cincinnati and a renowned thinker on topics such as leadership and culture. The book, *The Unconscious Conspiracy*, argues that there are certain universal organizational dynamics that inherently inhibit progress. He wrote, "This discovery, or rediscovery, has led me to formulate what might be called Bennis's First Law of Academic Pseudodynamics, to wit: routine work drives out nonroutine work, or: how to smother to death all creative planning, all fundamental change in the university, or *any* institution." He argues that it's not larger marketplace forces that limit creativity as much as the everyday, routine work that must be conducted in order to keep the organization moving forward. These routine tasks crowd out the space required for creative planning and innovation.

Take some time today to consider how maintenance activities and routine tasks might be limiting your ability to explore possibilities.

Don't allow your repetitive, routine tasks to crowd out creative thinking and innovative experimentation.

QUESTION

Are you falling victim to the "unconscious conspiracy"? Which routine tasks get in the way of your creative thinking?

April
14

Good vs. Bad Work

How do you know if your work is good or bad?

To some, it's simply whether their manager or client liked the end product. For some people, it's all about how they feel about the work. For others, it's about the reaction of the end users or audience experiencing their work. But none of these ways are necessarily accurate gauges of what good work actually means.

I wish I could give you a definition of good work, but I can't. That's something you must decide for yourself. And it's something that you *should* decide. If you lack a clear understanding in your own mind of what good vs. bad work is, you will be driven only by emotion and instinct, which can be misleading.

Is good work something you took a creative risk on, whether or not it succeeded?

Is it something that perfectly solves the problem it was intended to solve?

Is it something that was delivered on time and on budget?

Is it something that reflects your personal values in some way?

Is it something that you sacrificed a bit for?

I challenge you to spend some time today considering what good work means to you. Then you have a target to aim for when you go about your day.

To avoid dissonance, develop your own framework for how to decide good vs. bad work.

QUESTION

How do you know good work when you see it? What is the best work you've done recently, and why?

April
15

Superhero Syndrome

I've seen one particular narrative disrupt otherwise effective teams, derail very good managers, and ultimately rob people and teams of the very joy of doing their work. It's this:

"You're all alone. You must not show weakness."

Any indication of hesitation or confusion about a project is perceived as a sign of incompetence. So we forge ahead on our own, projecting confidence but inwardly wrestling with what we should do next. We play the role of superhero, pretending like we have it all figured out.

The problem? Everyone already knows you don't have it all figured out. In fact, no one does. We need one another to see problems clearly and to make meaningful progress.

Invite other people into your problem-solving process. Ask for their input. Ask them to tell you what they see. This is especially important for managers of creative teams, because it builds trust and helps your team members better understand your thought process and how you approach problems. This will strengthen your team's bond and ability to collaborate in the future.

Ask others:

- What do you see here?
- What would you do if you were me?
- What am I overlooking?

Invite others into your creative process. Don't try to be a superhero.

QUESTION
Who should you invite into your creative process today?

April
16

Builders, Fixers, Optimizers

Executive recruiter David Wiser once shared an insight with me that changed the way I coach leaders and creative pros. He said that in his experience, there are three fundamental types of leaders.

1. *Builders:* These are people who love wide-open spaces, a lot of autonomy, and the ability to pursue their vision. If they don't have these elements, they are likely to blow things up just so they can build something again.
2. *Fixers:* These are people who are wired to solve problems. They love to come into situations where others are perplexed and resolve problems. However, once the problem is solved, they are ready to move on. If there isn't a problem to solve, they might go looking for one anyway.
3. *Optimizers:* These are people who love to tweak, perfect, and squeeze the most value out of a system or process. They live for efficiency and maximizing operations. They are perpetually shaping and refining processes to make them better. However, they sometimes lack a sense of "good enough" and can over-tweak to the point of diminishing value.

As you consider these three profiles, which best suits you? Do you like wide-open spaces? Solving problems? Optimizing systems?

What does that mean to your role? Your leadership? Your team?

Knowing which type of work you're best wired for can help you avoid ruts and burnout.

> **QUESTION**
> Which profile best fits you, and how do you see it playing out in your work?

April
17

Fail at Something New

No matter how much you love your job, it's common to grow stale over time. You've seen the same patterns and problems and people over and over, and each day can feel like going around the same traffic circle over and over. "Look, kids, Big Ben! Parliament!" (Bonus points if you get that movie reference.)

One method for pushing out of the rut is to experiment with new creative domains, not in your on-demand work but on the side, in your own time. Identify a new skill or domain you're interested in exploring, and carve out some time for it. If you are a designer, maybe you should try writing or music. If you're a marketer, learn the basics of design. If you lead a team of videographers, try learning a musical instrument. As much as these activities might seem like irrelevant hobbies, they will actually awaken parts of your creative brain that have grown numb due to the repetitive nature of your everyday work. And they just might give you new ways of thinking about that on-demand work as well. You may stumble across a great idea while perusing a book or course that has nothing to do with your job.

To stay energized and alive, experiment with new domains.

QUESTION
Which domain or discipline should you explore as a way to energize your creativity?

April
18

When You Fail, Pause

No one likes to fail. We should always strive to succeed.

However, if you're not failing on occasion, you're probably not trying hard enough. You're simply not doing difficult things.

When you do inevitably fail, don't waste the opportunity. Take the time to pause and reflect on why you failed and to see how you can apply those learnings to your future work. Ask these questions:

- ► Why did I fall short?
- ► What did I learn from this project that I want to remember?
- ► Did I fail because I didn't try hard enough? Because I lacked the skill? Because I didn't have the right insight? What was the source?
- ► Is there anything obvious I could do to prevent this kind of mistake in the future?

You can even craft your own questions to ask each time you feel like you fell short. Taking the time to pause, reflect, and determine how to readjust moving forward can make all the difference between a wasted failure and an invaluable one.

Don't let a good failure go to waste! Pause, reflect, readjust, and move forward.

Every failure or shortcoming is an opportunity to grow.

QUESTION

When was the last time you failed? As you consider that failure, what can you learn from it to help you do better in the future?

April
19

The Adjacent Possible

In his book *Where Good Ideas Come From,* author and researcher Steven Johnson introduced a term he borrowed from evolutionary biology: the *adjacent possible.* According to Johnson, "The adjacent possible is a kind of shadow future, hovering on the edges of the present state of things, a map of all the ways in which the present can reinvent itself... What the adjacent possible tells us is that at any moment the world is capable of extraordinary change, but only *certain* changes can happen."

Good ideas, he argues, arrive when someone commits to playing with ideas that are just at the periphery of lived experience, just beyond the present state. It takes intentional effort to get to these ideas, because you must take the time and expend the energy to toy with combinations of ideas that might not work. However, when you stumble across a combination of dots that click together, it often signals a creative breakthrough.

Do you have time set aside in your life for exploring the adjacent possible? For toying with ideas and experimenting with concepts? While it feels inefficient in the moment, this is often where you will produce tremendous value.

To come up with novel ideas, you must play with ideas, experiment with themes, and explore the adjacent possible.

QUESTION

When can you set aside time this week to choose a project and explore the adjacent possible?

April
20

Occupation and Vocation

It is unrealistic to expect your job to contain the sum total of your creative engagement. It's unlikely to happen. Sometimes your job meshes nicely with your personal tastes and passions, and sometimes you simply need to do your job. That's what it means to be a pro.

Your occupation provides you with resources to live. Your vocation is something much, much more. The word *vocation* comes from the Latin word *vocare*, which means "to call." Your vocation is what's being called out of you in response to the world around you. And it's likely going to be a portfolio of passions that will sometimes overlap with your occupation and sometimes not, but that's perfectly fine and normal. Don't think that something is wrong if you don't always feel fulfilled by your occupation. Ideally, you will navigate to a place where your occupation fulfills you more and more over time, but in the interim, know that you can satisfy your vocation outside your work as well by finding projects to pour yourself into.

Your occupation is how you make a living, but your vocation is what's being called out of you as you engage in life and work.

QUESTION

How would you define your vocation or what's being called out of you? How can you structure your life to pursue it more?

April
21

Your Quirk

Organizations organize. (It's in the name!) An organization can only operate with predictability and stability when there is some degree of conformity throughout its systems. Thus, incentives are often established that encourage people to aim for targets that match established organizational norms and that fit the desired (and expected) culture.

Unfortunately, this tendency toward conformity often rounds off the rough edges of early-career creative pros and managers. Their unique quirks and qualities are pruned so that they can become more of what's expected or "the kind of person who succeeds around here." When this happens, the organization loses some of the qualities that lead to innovative breakthroughs because it is quieting voices of dissension and fresh perspective. The employees lose because they are being asked to conform to a norm that may not be reflective of their true aptitudes and passions.

Remember that many of the most celebrated leaders, artists, writers, marketers, and entrepreneurs in the marketplace today were once questioned or even shunned for their "rough edges" and quirks. Now, those are the very qualities that we celebrate them for.

Don't allow others to round off your rough edges.

The quirk that people criticize you for now might be the very thing they celebrate you for later.

QUESTION

Is there a quality that makes you unique that you often feel the pressure to diminish or get rid of to fit in?

April
22

Ideal vs. Real Days

In his autobiography, Benjamin Franklin outlined his ideal day. It began with a few hours of study and reflection on his upcoming day, followed by work for several hours, a leisurely two-hour lunch, followed by more hours of work, and finally dinner and reflection on his day. This passage has often been quoted by gurus and productivity experts as an example of how everyone should approach daily planning.

Here's a counterargument: How often do you think ol' Ben Franklin actually experienced one of these "ideal days"?

Not often, most likely. They were probably few and far between. If he was able to follow this schedule, it was probably when he was younger and had fewer pressing responsibilities. Predictability is possible where certainty abounds, but in the face of uncertainty, it's nearly impossible to bend your schedule to your will.

However—and this is key—you must have *some* predictability. You may not be able to control all your time, but you must control some of it. Simply knowing when you will have time to do your pressing work will go a long way toward releasing the pressure valve.

Don't strive for ideal days, but ensure that you block some time to do your most important work. Or put another way:

Don't aim for ideal days, but do carve some predictability into your schedule.

QUESTION

How can you protect the time you need today to do your important work?

April
23

Clear Your RAM

When your laptop grinds to a halt or you experience the "spinning wheel of death," it's usually because you have too many programs open. You only have so much random access memory (RAM), and when much of it is utilized by open programs and documents, the computer lacks the resources to spend on new initiatives. There are simply too many dormant programs occupying RAM and not enough of it free to tackle the new tasks.

Similarly, when you have many, many open creative loops occupying your mind—even in a dormant manner—it can stall your progress. It begins to feel a little like you are moving a wall forward an inch at a time rather than making real progress on the work. How do you remedy this? Either close some loops or agree to put them on the back burner until you have the bandwidth to deal with them.

What are your three most important open creative loops right now? Spend the bulk of your effort on these.

The rest? Keep a list and plan when you'll think about them. Simple, but effective.

You only have the bandwidth to process so many open loops at a time. To succeed, clear your creative RAM.

QUESTION

Which are your three most important open loops right now?
Which open loops can be put on hold for now?

April
24

Sit on Your Idea

We've all been there. You have a sudden burst of creative insight, and you think "That's it! This is clearly the most brilliant idea I've ever had!" You share it with someone else, and they stare at you blankly. They don't understand why you're so enthusiastic.

Frustrated, you get even more animated, thinking you haven't explained it clearly enough. And they still stare at you blankly. Then they begin to point out the flaws in your idea. These are things you hadn't considered in your blind enthusiasm.

Enthusiasm masks flaws. Even obvious ones. That's why it can be valuable to take some time to sit on your idea, even for a night or a few days, before sharing it with others. This time will allow you to come down from your creative high and see your insight from a more leveled perspective. If it still feels worth championing, then go for it! However, it's likely that you'll also gain some perspective that will make it even *more* compelling.

All this said, make sure you don't wait so long that you lose energy for the idea. It's also easy to talk yourself out of an idea if given enough time.

In the moment of creative ecstasy, we sometimes lack perspective. Sit on your idea.

QUESTION

Is there an idea you're currently very excited about that might benefit from a few days' perspective?

April
25

Be the Leader

If you've been in the workplace for long enough, it's likely you've had at least one really bad manager. Maybe they were obviously only in it for themselves, phoning it in, or completely unable to empathize with your needs. It becomes nearly impossible to do your work when you report to someone who feels more like an impediment than a benefactor.

However, your tenure on their team was not a complete loss, because you can learn from the experience. Ask these questions:

- What did you need from them that they couldn't provide?
- What frustrated you the most about how they made decisions?
- What qualities did they exhibit that made your life more difficult?
- Why didn't you trust them?
- What skills did they lack that you needed them to have?

Now, as you consider your own life, work, and career development, what do your answers to the questions above mean about where you should be focusing your own growth? How can you leverage what you learned from your bad experiences into something that will benefit those you lead, collaborate with, or work for?

Choose to be the leader, the collaborator, the peer you wish you'd had.

QUESTION

What qualities do you need to develop to be the leader or collaborator that others need?

April
26

Fads vs. Trends

Are you old enough to have owned a pet rock? I'm not either, but I've read about it. Apparently, the inventor came up with the idea when he grew tired of hearing his friends complain about their own pets. After chewing on the conversation, he realized that the perfect pet was a rock because it didn't need anything from its owner! He pulled together the resources and launched the pet rock in 1975, selling over a million rocks and earning the equivalent of $27 million in today's dollars.

By early 1976, the pet rock fad had faded. Imagine if someone paying attention to the market thought "Wow! Apparently there's a huge market for inanimate pets! We need to launch one of our own!" They would have obviously missed the point entirely. The pet rock was a fad because it arrived at the perfect time, meeting a cultural moment. However, there's a difference between a cultural moment and a trend. A trend is a series of cultural moments that point in a specific direction. Often, they begin in smaller pockets before going mainstream.

Pay attention to fads, but don't chase them. Instead, scan the horizon for patterns of cultural moments that could signal a trend.

As a creative pro, ignore the fads but pay close attention to the trends.

QUESTION

Do you see any patterns in cultural moments that could signal creative opportunity?

April
27

Avoiding Collective Delusion

No idea is perfect. However, at times a team's (or client's) energy for an idea can cause everyone to overlook its potential weaknesses. As discussed in an earlier entry, everyone has individual blind spots. However, there are also collective blind spots that result from a kind of collective group delusion generated by excitement for a particular idea.

A little delusion is necessary in order to do difficult things. However, too much delusion will cause you to take irresponsible risks. To avoid this, play the role of the idea's biggest critic. Look at it from every angle with the sole purpose of proving why it will fail. Ask these questions as a team, or with your client:

- ► Why is this too obvious?
- ► Why is this impossible to accomplish?
- ► Who else has tried this and failed?
- ► Who won't give us the buy-in we need to get started?
- ► Why is this a logistical nightmare?

Pay attention to your answers, because they give you clues about how to strengthen your idea. If you identify some weaknesses, consider how you can circumvent them. If you discover that selling the idea will be challenging, consider how you can alter your messaging.

Arguing against your own idea is a powerful way to make it more resilient and to avoid collective delusion.

To strengthen and refine your idea, argue the opposite.

QUESTION

Which of your current ideas would benefit from a little self-critique?

April
28

Luck vs. Skill

When an endeavor is successful, people almost always claim that it was due to strategy. When something fails, they will often talk about how circumstances conspired against them. To some extent, they may be right in both cases. Success or failure is always a mix of skill and luck. However, when you fail to notice the difference between these two forces, you will struggle to see the connection between your efforts and the results you experience.

By focusing on developing your skills and intuition—the things you can control—you are positioning yourself to take advantage of opportunities when they arise. You can't control whether the breaks fall your way, but you can ensure that you're ready to pounce on them when they do.

Focus on controlling those things you can control:

- ► Your skill set
- ► Your attitude
- ► Your collaboration skills
- ► Your communication, especially when writing
- ► Your clarity of thought
- ► Your leadership conversations

If you really hone these aptitudes, you increase your chances of success. By controlling what you can control, you place yourself where "creative accidents" are more likely to occur. Isn't that lucky?

Don't confuse luck with skill. Control what you can so you are positioned to take advantage of opportunities.

QUESTION
Which skills can you focus on developing so that you're better positioned to take advantage of opportunity?

April
29

Incentives and Outcomes

Imagine that you hire a contractor to work to renovate your kitchen. After seeing how quickly the contractor is working, you decide that instead of paying him a lump sum for the job, you might be able to save a little money by paying him by the hour. After all, your research showed that this job would typically take about three-quarters of the time you have allotted to it. So you and your contractor agree to an hourly wage and work resumes. Then, suddenly, the pace of work slows. The contractor is making frequent trips to the hardware store. It seems to take forever to do small tasks.

What happened?

Your incentives are now misaligned! Before, when the contractor was paid for the value created, he had an incentive to do the work quickly so that he could move on to the next project. However, once paid by the hour, his incentives shifted because he is being rewarded for taking longer to complete the work.

Are there any misaligned incentives in your organization? In your life?

Ensure that your incentives are aligned with your desired outcomes.

QUESTION

Is there any place where your incentives and desired outcomes might be misaligned?

April
30

The First Dumb Idea

No one wants to appear incompetent or naive. It's one of the worst fears that many people have. So they keep their mouths shut even when they have a hunch that could be helpful to others. Often, this dynamic can paralyze a team to the point that no one is willing to share an idea. Everyone seems stuck, but the reality is that no one wants to speak first.

In these situations, someone has to be brave enough to toss out the first dumb idea. I realize it's uncomfortable to do so, but the willingness to appear foolish is sometimes an act of creative bravery that opens the floodgates for more and better ideas to follow. Once people think "Well, at least my idea isn't *that* bad!" they will be willing to share their own.

A few caveats:

- This only works in an environment of trust. If you don't trust your teammates, this technique may lead to bad things. You've been warned.
- This works best if you have a track record of good ideas. People know that you're not incompetent but are just trying to kick-start the conversation.

When stuck, be brave enough to toss out the first bad idea. It won't be the last.

QUESTION

Have you ever felt too paralyzed to share an idea in a meeting? Why?

May

*"Unless you feel good about what you do every day,
you won't do it with much conviction or passion."*

—MIA HAMM

What do you *love* about the work you do? Don't just reflect on the tasks you do each day but also consider the outcome that you get to experience, the process you get to participate in, or the people you get to collaborate with. This month, spend time reflecting with gratitude on the things you love about your work, your craft, and your community.

May
1

Part-Time Passion

Gustav Mahler wrote much of his brilliant music in between his responsibilities as a conductor. In fact, he wasn't even known as much of a composer during his lifetime, only having his work broadly celebrated after his death.

Albert Einstein developed much of his theory of special relativity while operating as a patent clerk, a job that afforded him the time and space to work out his theories in his spare moments.

As discussed earlier, we tend to want our jobs to contain the sum total of our creative output, but that is impossible. While your job will hopefully accommodate more and more of your creative ideas over time, you simply cannot—as a professional—expect a job to completely fulfill you creatively. You should have a side outlet that allows you to express yourself in ways your on-demand work cannot.

Have you ever wanted to write a novel? Record an album? Develop a mathematical theorem? (OK, maybe that last one was a stretch...) Do it! Develop a plan, and start working on it in the spare moments of your life. You don't need permission or a paycheck to start. And the best part is that these side projects will often bring additional clarity and energy for your on-demand work as well.

Your body of work will be much larger and more nuanced than what your job can contain.

QUESTION
What part-time passion should you pursue?

May
2

Challenge a Convention

What's something that you believe that few people around you do? It's likely that—if you've ever had a conversation about whatever that thing is—it's ruffled some feathers. When conventional thinking is challenged it sometimes feels to others like a personal indictment. Survival is often achieved through consensus, and when you challenge the sentiments of your community, you risk being cast out to the fringes.

But—and this is a big but—those who advance our understanding of the world, build products that transform society, and create art that resonates deeply are typically those who challenge deeply entrenched conventions.

"Films are best in black and white. Who needs color?"

"No one wants to buy British rock and roll!"

"It's impossible to put a computer on every desk. Who would even want one?"

In retrospect, every breakthrough seems inevitable. However, in the moment, it was only possible because someone challenged conventional thinking. They believed something that few others did and were brave enough to share their point of view, sometimes at great personal cost.

What convention are you convicted to challenge? What entrenched belief is worth fighting? What is the thing you believe that you can't shake and that others think you're crazy for believing?

That could be the start of your most important work. Brave people who challenge conventional thinking sometimes change the world.

Big creative breakthroughs often happen when you challenge an entrenched belief.

QUESTION

What convention do you need to challenge?

May
3

First Things First

Many creative pros have discovered the value of tackling their most important creative projects at the very beginning of the day. Simply making measurable progress on an important creative project before you do anything else does a few things for you:

- ► You feel productive, regardless of whatever else happens that day, because you've moved the important thing forward.
- ► You relieve the uncertainty of knowing when you're going to get around to that important work.
- ► You are giving your best, freshest thinking to an important project.
- ► You eliminate the possibility that an unexpected priority arises that keeps you from doing that important work, which is almost certain to happen if you push it back to the afternoon.

Now, to be clear, different people do their best work at different times. Understood. However, instilling the discipline of making some kind of progress on your important work at the very beginning of the day can generate momentum that carries through the remainder of your day. **Make a little progress on your most stressful creative problem first, before anything else.**

> **QUESTION**
> Right now, which project should you be tackling at the very beginning of the day?

May

4

Quit While You're Ahead

Writer Ernest Hemingway's work life was decidedly ordered and very serious. One of his practical habits was to never quit his work having exhausted himself on its subject. Or in his own words, "Always stop while you are going good and don't think about it or worry about it until you start to write the next day. That way your subconscious will work on it all the time. But if you think about it consciously or worry about it you will kill it and your brain will be tired before you start."

Completely spending yourself on a project every day may feel like a badge of honor, but then you have to gear yourself up during the next work session and do it all over again. You're tired, spent, and empty of energy after spending everything you have only the day before. (Who wants to run a marathon on two consecutive days?)

It's best to consider ending each work session knowing exactly where you're going to pick up the next day, while you still have energy for the idea you're pursuing. If you work until you're stuck or completely spent, you may struggle to reengage during your next work session.

Don't work until you're exhausted. Stop while you still have energy for the work.

> **QUESTION**
> How will you know when it's time to quit work for the day?

May
5

The Everyday Work of Art

I used to be a drip coffee guy. Just give me a large mug of whatever generic brand of coffee grounds you just poured hot water through, and I'm good to go. Then few years ago, a friend introduced me to the art of using a French press to brew my coffee. First, you heat the water to a specific temperature. Then, you grind a precise amount of beans and add them to the press. Finally, you very slowly add perfectly heated water and stir, letting it brew for just the right amount of time. Press the grounds, pour, and enjoy. I've come to enjoy this morning coffee ritual because I get to slow down just a little before diving into my work. I do a lot of thinking while I'm crafting my morning coffee. It's meditative.

It can be helpful to build these small, seemingly insignificant crafted moments into your day. Maybe for you it's preparing your lunch, lighting a few candles, organizing your drawer, or preparing your desk for the next day. Choose an activity or two to approach with craft and care, and it will force you to slow down and be present, both of which will benefit your creative process.

Take time to craft moments in your day. Be purposeful and artistic about the small things.

QUESTION

What small moment can you craft into your day?

May
6

Efficiency and Effectiveness

Oliver Burkeman spent years researching every productivity tool available. He tried them all. Some of them even helped, for a while. However, many of these methods just made him more efficient at doing largely meaningless things. Burkeman told me that he calls this the "efficiency trap." You tweak, improve, and expend a ton of energy to get more done, but more priorities just get piled on top of the things you're already doing. There's never an end to it. So you strive to become more efficient at doing those things too, but you only clear room for even more things...and the cycle continues.

Burkeman's point really strikes home. I've found myself in that very predicament before. I'm getting a lot done, but does any of it really matter? I mean, *really* matter?

The only key that I've discovered to overcoming this efficiency trap is to focus on effectiveness. Effective use of your time and resources might mean investing thirty minutes now to do something that won't pay off for days or weeks but is valuable nonetheless. When you begin to think about your time more like a financial portfolio, in which you make both safe and risky investments, you begin to think differently about how to spend it.

Don't fall into the efficiency trap. Focus on effectiveness.

QUESTION

What can you invest time in today that may not pay off for weeks or months?

May
7

Pay, Prestige, Process

When I was in what I now jokingly call my "misguided twenties," I was a full-time musician. As the opening act, I got to meet a variety of big-name performers and observe their behavior up close, along with some new up and comers.

As I watched the behavior of some of the newer acts, I noticed that while some were quite accommodating and kind, others were very cruel and dismissive. They almost seemed angry to have to do a show. It was *strange*. I came to a conclusion as to why they behaved this way: they were chasing the benefits that came with being a successful musician—fame, attention, money—more than they were chasing the ability to perform their music on stage for people who loved it. When they realized that the side benefits didn't satisfy them in the way they anticipated, they grew disillusioned. On the other hand, those who were kind and engaging—some of whom were very big, household names—seemed to be in it for the music, not for the side benefits of being on stage.

There seem to be three things that typically drive people, in some combination.

1. *Pay:* The money or benefits you get.
2. *Prestige:* The recognition that comes with it.
3. *Process:* The love of your craft.

Something to consider: most of the healthy, happy creative pros I know are primarily driven by process.

Understand what drives you, and strive to center your motivation around process.

> **QUESTION**
> How can you fall deeper in love with the process of your work?

May
8

Tilting at Windmills

In Miguel de Cervantes's *Don Quixote,* the namesake character sees several windmills off in the distance and—confusing them for giants—believes that fortune has given him an opportunity to rid the world of several hulking beasts. He tries to fight them but falls off his horse. This is the source of the phrase *tilting at windmills,* which means inventing enemies to fight where they don't exist.

Some people are driven to fight battles even where there are none to fight. They are perpetually championing a cause or complaining that someone is wronging them. They are tilting at windmills. It's a waste of energy.

It's not only these extreme cases that we must be cautious of. It's easy to slip into the same trap on an everyday basis. For example, stewing about the person you don't get along with and who you just know is working against you behind your back. Or obsessing about the client who never likes your idea and you just know is trying to get you taken off the account. You may be tilting at windmills. You are imagining giants where there are none. Save your valuable spark for the true battles that you must fight to deliver your work and serve your stakeholders.

Don't invent enemies to fight. It's a waste of valuable energy.

QUESTION

Are there any illusory battles you get pulled into? Are you tilting at windmills?

May
9

FRESH

Effective creative pros who remain at the top of their game for a long time have practices in their life to sustain them. These practices help them stay creatively energized and focused. In my decades of working with top performers, five key categories of practices have appeared over and over:

1. *Focus:* They have discipline around how and where they spend their finite attention.
2. *Relationships:* They have deep and regular connections with people who inspire them, challenge them, and help them do their best work.
3. *Energy:* They are good at managing their ability to bring emotional labor to their work and are willing to say no when necessary.
4. *Stimuli:* They seek valuable inspiration for their work and challenge themselves with the thoughts and work of others.
5. *Hours:* They are really effective at investing their time in efforts that will pay off later, not just activities that pay off in the near term.

Fittingly, these five areas form the acronym FRESH. I encourage you to spend some time thinking about a few practices you might implement to help you stay creatively engaged and energized. You make your rituals, then your rituals make you.

To stay creatively viable, focus on building FRESH practices.

QUESTION

As you consider these five areas (FRESH), what regular practices or rituals might you implement?

May

10

In the Arena

Do you know where the phrase *peanut gallery* came from? It was a term from the days of vaudeville, when traveling shows would go from town to town selling tickets to the locals. The cheapest seats were—of course—in the very back of the stands. To increase the revenue per customer in these cheap seats, the show would sell peanuts as snacks. Often, these cheap seat holders would express their dislike of the show by hurling peanuts at the performers. So as you were onstage pouring your heart into the performance, you might be pelted with peanuts by people who barely paid anything to be there. Talk about demeaning.

Often the loudest people in today's metaphorical peanut gallery are the critics. They love to pelt you with their virtual peanuts—snide comments, mockery, uneducated critique—the moment you put your work in the world.

Don't listen to them. Listen to the people in the arena with you. Listen to those who also vulnerably share their work with the world. As Brené Brown wrote, "If you're not in the arena with the rest of us, fighting and getting your ass kicked on occasion, I'm not interested in your feedback."

Trust feedback from someone who understands vulnerability. Ignore feedback from those who critique from their safe, cheap seats.

Listen to people who are in the arena with you. Ignore the others.

QUESTION

Do you ever let the critiques of the peanut gallery get to you? Whom should you be listening to instead?

11

The Noise Floor

In audio production, there's something known as the "noise floor." It's the amount of unwanted signal coming from any source other than the one that you're actually trying to record. Listening to someone speak in an environment with a high noise floor is like trying to have a conversation at the beach with a crashing ocean ten feet away. You can make out what they're saying, but it's not easy to do.

Many of us not only allow but invite a high noise floor into our lives. We have signals coming at us from every direction, inputs, requests, demands, and marketing, then we fill our lives even more with noise via the apps we interact with or the stimuli we allow into our lives. Our noise floor is so high that we can't discern the signal pattern. It's too buried.

Here are a few signs:

- You feel overwhelmed but don't know why.
- You have difficulty with short-term memory and often confuse simple concepts.
- You are perpetually distracted and struggle to maintain attention on one project.

As creative pros, it's important that we monitor the noise floor in our lives and ensure that we are able to discern the signals we're trying to pay attention to. Be still. Stop. Think. Clear the signal chain so that you can focus deeply.

Be aware of the amount of latent noise in your environment. Lower the noise floor.

QUESTION
Do you have a high noise floor? How can you lower it?

May
12

No Choice

If I placed you in a room, put a piece of broccoli and a cookie in front of you, and said "You can eat whichever you want and no one will know," which would you choose? Right now, you might reply "The broccoli, of course! I care about my health." That's easy to say when this is a pure thought experiment. However, in the moment, your body may scream for that infusion of chocolate and sugar, and you might be unable to resist the temptation.

We make good, objective decisions when we have time and space to think. However, it's under pressure that our principles are tested.

Given the choice between doing your uncomfortable creative work and doing something that might give you an immediate surge of productive energy, it's tempting to choose the latter. (Let's see, work on that marketing plan or achieve inbox zero? Inbox it is!)

The key in these moments is to not give yourself the choice. While you are thinking rationally, commit time to doing the things that need doing. Then, in the moment, treat it like a commitment to your manager or client. Don't allow yourself out of the commitment.

Plan your work, then work your plan. Don't make important decisions in a moment of weakness.

Don't give yourself a choice about doing the hard work.

QUESTION
What is the "cookie" that often distracts you from your most well-rounded meal?

May
13

Now and Later

OK, just a quick confession from your author. I'm tired.

There. I said it.

I'm in the midst of a long, steady, uphill run, and I'm definitely feeling its effects. Have you been there? I'm sure you have.

But in our culture, it's not always appropriate to admit that you're tired. You're supposed to be made of steel and nuclear powered. No weaknesses allowed!

Whoever is responsible for the maxim "find work you love and you'll never work a day in your life" was irresponsibly wrong. You'll work a lot. And hard. And it will be worth it, later.

And that's a key point, right? We work hard now so that we experience results later. But life is lived *now*, which also means we must make choices to protect what's most important and preserve our energy for the things that can't wait until later. Some things can never be recovered once lost. You must take care of them in the moment.

I've been saying no to a lot of discretionary things because I have to protect my energy. There are commitments I have in my life that can't wait until later, like family, friendships, and personal growth. You cannot sacrifice these now and recover them later.

Also, like every hard, uphill run I've ever done—literally or figuratively—this one will end. Yours will too. Take care of yourself.

Know your limits, and care for the things in your life that can't wait.

QUESTION

What are the commitments in your life that cannot wait until later? How will you care for them?

May
14

First Drafts

I recently did an exercise that both depressed me and encouraged me at the same time. I decided to take a look at my first drafts of each of my books and compare them with the final, published manuscript. My key takeaways:

- My first drafts are pretty awful.
- The way in which I conveyed the most resonant ideas in each of my books appeared through revision, *not* in the first draft.
- I can clearly see moments when I was struggling vs. when things were flowing clearly. I struggled more than I flowed.

It was a pretty depressing exercise because I—probably like you—look back with pride on my finished work and sometimes forget the struggle involved in getting it to that place. I was also encouraged because I realized that I don't need to fret when a draft doesn't "sing" to me initially. It will *eventually*, after a lot of work and revision.

Your goal with any project is to simply get to a first draft that can be revised, augmented, and adapted into its final form. The struggle is getting to that draft. As prolific writer Joyce Carol Oates once quipped, "Getting the first draft finished is like pushing a peanut with your nose across a very dirty floor." It's not glamorous, but it's the most important milestone in your work.

Your goal with any project is to simply get to the first draft, which can then be revised.

QUESTION

Is there a project right now that just needs you to buckle down and get to a first draft, whatever it takes?

May
15

Decisions

Most people like to keep their options open. We wait until the last minute to commit to social engagements in case something better pops up. In the workplace, we wait until we absolutely must make a decision before doing so just in case a better idea comes along. However, that indecisiveness typically trickles down to our teams, our collaborators, and our clients. There are others who are waiting for you to make a decision in order to make their own.

The root of the word *decision* is *cis*, which means "to cut." (Think scissors, incisor, etc.) When you make a decision, you are literally cutting off other options to focus on the one in front of you. You are making a commitment by saying no to good options so that you can say yes to a potentially great one.

When you fail to make decisions, your work becomes obscured and foggy. Your world becomes needlessly complex. When you make a decision, you part that fog. As Danish philosopher Søren Kierkegaard wrote, "The thing that cowardice fears most is decision; for decision always scatters the mists, at least for a moment." If you want greater clarity in your work, make a decision and follow it. You can always redirect.

Remember: you must say no to a lot of good things to say yes to one great thing.

QUESTION

Is there an area of your life or work where you simply need to make a decision right now?

May
16

When to Build

The tendency in many organizations is to ride the momentum when the market is good, squeezing every ounce of opportunity, then when things slow down, to rest until the opportunity returns. However, I believe this is a waste of opportunity. Those slower moments, which cycle through predictably every so often, are ideal seasons in which to focus on building. They are the perfect moments in which to do spec work, prototype, experiment, and invest in whatever might be your next thing.

Innovation happens in the "white space," the gaps between your frantic work. These are the moments when you can reflect, iterate, and take small strategic risks because the pressure is (generally) off. You can't always do this when you're busy, because every moment away from your work is a wasted opportunity to generate revenue.

Take some time today to consider projects you might want to experiment with the next time you have some "white space." What do you envision? What would you love to build but simply don't have the time or space to at the moment? What spec work might you want to experiment with that could eventually become something you pitch to an actual client?

Take advantage of the spaces in between. Build when things slow down so that you can take advantage of that momentum when things pick back up.

When things slow down, build.

QUESTION

What project should you begin the next time you experience a bit of white space?

May
17

Find Your EST

I know it's not polite to brag about yourself, but I want you to take a few minutes right now to do just that. What are you great at? What do others come to you for because they know that you're the only one who can deliver the results they need? What do people praise you for all the time?

Author Mike Michalowicz challenges people to identify their "EST," as in the superlative of whatever quality they have. Are you the happiest, the absurdest, the coolest, the quirkiest, or some other "EST" that describes what makes you truly unique? You can even make up a word like "inventive-est" if you'd like. But what is it that truly separates you from the pack?

Define and seek to cultivate those qualities that separate you from your peers. What could you be the best in the world at, given the effort? It can't be everything, but it must be something. Spend some time considering the qualities that set you apart from everyone else, then commit yourself to identifying ways you can develop them and leverage them more consistently in your life and work.

To thrive, you must cultivate the quality that sets you apart from everyone else.

QUESTION

What are the unique qualities that make you different from everyone around you?

May
18

Where Nobody Has Gone

One of my favorite books is *Orbiting the Giant Hairball*, written by Gordon MacKenzie, who was a long-time creative leader at Hallmark. The shortest chapter in the book—and probably the shortest chapter I've ever read—simply says this:

"Orville Wright did not have a pilot's license."

That's it. That's the whole chapter. But I remember it to this day because it's so punchy and relevant. How often do we wait for others to certify, ordain, or otherwise bless our ideas before we're willing to take a first step toward putting them into the world? Had the Wright brothers waited for official permission to attempt powered flight, who knows when we would have escaped the confines of gravity and taken to the sky.

How about you? Is there any place where you are waiting for someone else to tap you on the shoulder and give you their blessing? Are you seeking official approval that your idea is worthy of your attention?

Yes, there are moments when it's wise to go through the proper channels. (I'm grateful my doctor isn't just winging it but has a medical degree!) However, we often excuse inaction by blaming it on the lack of official consent. Don't wait for your pilot's license, unless of course you are *actually* trying to become a pilot, in which case...please do.

Don't wait for permission to act on your idea. No one is going to give you a license to be creative.

> **QUESTION**
> Where are you waiting for someone else to ordain your idea or give you a license to act?

May
19

Your Idea + Someone Else

One of the most valuable moments of growth in my professional life occurred in my early thirties when I was leading the restructuring of a creative team. I had the right idea, and the timing was perfect, but for a number of reasons, the initiative just wasn't working. After a few months, my manager called me into his office to discuss what was going wrong. He agreed that it was the right idea at the right moment, but then he said something that I didn't expect: "Just because it was your idea doesn't mean that you're the one who should execute it." I'd never considered it. I assumed that because it was my idea, I would be the one leading the charge. It was an eye-opening moment.

Recognize that you will have many ideas in your life, and some of them will fall right into that sweet spot of personal passion and competence. However, you may also have some ideas that would have a much better chance of success if they were executed by someone else. It's difficult to acknowledge this reality in the moment, but with a little distance and perspective, it's often obvious to others.

Just because it's a brilliant idea doesn't necessarily mean it's a brilliant idea for you. Maybe you need to find someone else to help you execute it.

Just because it's your idea doesn't mean you should execute it.

QUESTION

Are there any ideas in your life right now that you might need to find someone else to help you execute?

May
20

The Mind Sweep

Much of the stress we experience as creative pros has less to do with the work itself, and more to do with the weight of all that's left undone. This weight is always with us, even when we're not working. We're stressed about letting things slip through the cracks. We're stressed about all the ideas we need but don't yet have.

One effective technique for mitigating this stress (that I learned from author David Allen) is called a "mind sweep". You simply freewrite all the commitments, tasks, topics, and ideas that are weighing on you. It might take some time—twenty to thirty minutes—to really capture most of what's on your mind, but once you're finished, you'll have much of what's actually stressing you out right there on paper.

"But wait," you say. "Won't seeing all that just make me more stressed?" Actually, no. Much of the stress has less to do with the tasks you need to accomplish than your fear of not having the time to accomplish them. Having it all on paper in front of us can somehow—mysteriously—make the workload feel much more manageable. And once you have it all on paper, you can organize it, plan for it, and make meaningful progress.

A mind sweep can clear your mind and open new pathways of creative thought.

QUESTION

Could you benefit from a mind sweep right now? Take twenty minutes in the next week to do one.

May
21

Shabbat

In the Judeo-Christian tradition, one day per week is to be set aside as a day of rest. The guiding principle is to take a complete break from labor one day out of seven. The Shabbat (or Sabbath) is not to be violated.

While many will nod their head to the principle of Shabbat, a complete day of rest feels impractical in today's busy world. After all, a day without email, or without progress on that big project, or without prep for the week ahead and everything will fall apart, right?

No, I don't believe so. In fact, throughout the centuries, many scholars have agreed that a core meaning behind Shabbat is to prove that you are not the center of the universe. The world goes on just fine without you. A regular rhythm of rest provides you not only with replenished energy but a fresh reminder that the world is not dependent on your existence. As Abraham Heschel wrote, "The Sabbath is the day on which we learn the art of surpassing civilization."

I understand that it's difficult in today's frantic world, but strive to plan one day a week in which you rest and do no work. You will discover wonder and replenishment in the midst of your pause.

One day of complete rest per week can refuel your creative energy.

QUESTION
When should you plan your Shabbat? How will you unwind?

May
22

Encouragement

Think back to a time when someone gave you a word of encouragement that lit your fire. What did they say? Why did it matter to you? How did it change your perspective or energy?

Isn't it strange how one comment at the right time can stick with you for years? One person speaking directly about who you are or praising something you've accomplished can be a vector changer for your day, your week, or even your career. The funny thing is, that person may not even know how their words affected you. To them, it may have been an offhand comment at an opportune moment, but to you, it meant everything.

To encourage means to "put courage into," which is precisely what you're doing. You are putting another log on their fire. You will likely move on, but their world might be changed.

Who have you seen do something extraordinary in the past week? Maybe others didn't even notice, but you know what it took for them to do it.

Who is acting bravely right now but may think no one sees them?

Who does the little things that hold everything together, even when no one is looking?

Who has had a series of losses and just needs someone to remind them of who they are and what they're capable of?

When you encourage, you put courage into the world. And it will likely come right back to you.

Take a moment to encourage someone else. It may change their life and yours.

QUESTION
Who can you encourage today?

May
23

Patient vs. Passive

There are times when the best strategy is to wait. Maybe you need to see how dynamics develop before investing time or resources into work. Maybe a key decision-maker has yet to weigh in, and it would be unwise to take any step forward until you know your efforts won't be in vain. You need to be patient.

However, sometimes we conflate patience with passivity. We excuse inaction by claiming that we're being "wise." However, often we're only abdicating responsibility.

Patience has a plan and knows when to take a step. Passivity is waiting for things to work out.

Patience is forward leaning. Passivity is backward leaning.

Patience is strategic and as needed. Passivity is a mindset and lifestyle.

Patience is poised to make things happen when the time is right. Passivity will let things happen.

Do you see the difference between these two? Patience has a bias toward action, whereas passivity embraces the pause as a relief from the necessity of action.

As a creative pro, you must occasionally exercise patience as ideas develop and team dynamics play out, but your bias must be toward action the moment you see an opportunity. Don't excuse passivity under the guise of patience.

Know the difference between being patient and being passive.

QUESTION

As you consider your work, is there an area where you are being passive rather than patient? What will be the signal to you that it's time to move forward? How will you know when the time is right to make an aggressive move?

May
24

Center of Attention

Some people are driven by a desire to be close to the center of the action. They want to be "in the room where it happens," so to speak. Their energy comes from being in the spotlight, delivering the key presentation, or speaking on behalf of the team.

When they aren't recognized for their contribution or they aren't able to be at the center, they experience frustration or even embarrassment. In fact, they may even wish that they weren't driven in this way, because it feels selfish or arrogant to want to be at the forefront or to be the person in the spotlight.

However, all motivations are a gift! We need people who are driven to be central. We need them to share our ideas, champion our causes, entertain and educate us. So, if this is how you are motivated, take heart! Your motivation is a gift. Don't bury it. And if you are sometimes frustrated by someone who seems to be motivated in this way, it's fine to have a conversation with them about how to appropriately leverage it and how to temper it when necessary.

It's OK to want to be at the center of attention, assuming your intentions are right.

QUESTION

Have you ever felt embarrassed by your drive to be at the center of the action? Why?

May
25

The Squiggly Line

Ask any mid- to late-career professional, "Did you see yourself doing what you're doing now when you were twenty-two?" and more often than not, they will laugh. Very few people follow a linear career path throughout their career. Instead, most people follow opportunities as they emerge through their life experiences. They learn things about themselves and their field of interest, and over time, they begin to spot trends or see opportunities that they couldn't have imagined when they were younger. (I didn't even dream of being a writer until I was in my midthirties, and now I've published six books in twelve years.)

My friend Mitch Joel calls this the "squiggly line." When you look back on a career, you can clearly see how you got from point A to point B, but it's something you couldn't have imagined from the beginning. That's because it's not typically the job or industry that's the through line; it's the unique skills being called out of the individual.

As you consider your next few career steps, ask these questions:

- ► What patterns do I see right now that I'm uniquely positioned to take advantage of?
- ► What aptitudes have I developed that I couldn't have foreseen two or ten years ago?
- ► What opportunities excite me right now that I may not have even known about before?

Pay attention to the patterns, and follow the squiggly line.

Most careers are squiggly lines. They only make sense in reverse.

QUESTION

As you consider your future career moves, what excites you the most?

May
26

How to Give Feedback

Think back to a moment when you were presenting your work to someone who simply didn't get it. Maybe they poked at your work and started making suggestions about how to improve it. Maybe they started deconstructing it before you even had a chance to explain your rationale.

It's frustrating, right? After all, you've just spent days or weeks on something only to have someone who's thought about it for two minutes tell you what's wrong with it.

Because creative work is often so subjective, offering feedback requires an empathetic approach. Rather than critiquing the end product, aim to understand the mindset that led to that result so that you can understand the rationale for decisions and offer corrective ideas with context.

Instead of immediately poking holes in the work, identify something about the work that doesn't seem to work well. Then offer something like, "This is an interesting choice. Help me understand why you took this approach." As they share, listen for any comments that indicate that they possibly misunderstood the objective or made an error of judgment. Then ask, "Instead of doing X, what if you chose to do Y? How might that change your approach to this project?" Allow them to work through the problem. By doing this, you not only ensure that this project will be successful, but you also help them better understand how to think about future ones as well.

When giving feedback about creative work, don't prescribe. Ask questions about process.

> **QUESTION**
> Do you need to rethink the way that you—or your team members—offer feedback?

May
27

Framing

It's easy to slip into mental ruts and assumptive behavior when working on a project. If you don't have a model or method for challenging those assumptions, it can be easy to spin your wheels for days or weeks before realizing that you're off course.

One simple model that I've taught organizations of all sizes is what I call the four As. It's a series of frames to help you think about the problem differently.

1. *Assumptions:* Which assumptions do I need to challenge right now? What am I assuming to be true, and what am I assuming to be false? What if they weren't?
2. *Aspirations:* What would complete success look like with this project? How will we know that we've done what we set out to do? What would the world look like if I was wildly successful?
3. *Affinities:* Are there any parallel problems or projects that are similar to this? What can I learn from other industries or other work that I'm familiar with that might help me here?
4. *Attributes:* What are the core attributes of the problem I'm solving? What are three words that perfectly capture the issue? How can I use those words to help me solve it?

By framing your problem in these four ways, you are likely to discover a different perspective than the one you were previously using.

When you're stuck on a problem, try to reframe it.

QUESTION
Is there a problem you're stuck on that could benefit from the four As method?

May
28

The Three Ps

What happens in your private world will eventually become public. If your inner world is in disorder, then your team will eventually experience the fruit of that chaos.

There are three primary areas that comprise the inner life of a leader, each of which needs to be ordered:

1. *Philosophy:* These are the outer-facing expectations you have of others about how they interact with you and what you expect of them. In some ways, it's like the user manual for you as a leader.
2. *Principles:* These are the internal guidelines that you use to make decisions and lead your team. For you to maintain the trust of the people you work with, they must see you make decisions consistently and by principle, not reactively.
3. *Practices:* These are the regular activities you engage in that help you stay aligned and energized for your work. Things like study, meditation, reviewing your goals and values, and analyzing your areas of responsibility fall under this category.

When all three areas are consistent with one another, they provide a strong foundation for both creativity and leadership. When one is lacking, there will be at some point be public consequences.

The inner life of the leader consists of philosophy, principles, and practices. They must be aligned. Inner chaos will ultimately affect your team and your work.

QUESTION
How are your three Ps? Which do you need to work on?

May
29

Room for Spontaneity

It's tempting to squeeze as much efficiency out of your days as possible, but in doing this, you risk forfeiting your best insights. Ideas rarely arrive just on time. It's best to accommodate the unpredictability of the creative process by allowing yourself some margin. If you think something will take an hour, give yourself ninety minutes. If you think it will take a week, plan for a week and a half. Yes, I'm aware that these inefficiencies make many managers squirm. However, this is anything but wasteful. It's necessary.

Creativity is not efficient, but it utilizes everything. If you are purposeful and mindful, nothing goes to waste. By leaving a little bit of room in your process, you allow yourself the freedom to follow mental trails that arise or to play a bit with an idea before feeling the need to refine it. You grant yourself creative latitude. When the time pressure is off, your mind is free to roam without its executive function staring at the clock.

As a pro, you don't have the luxury of unlimited time, but that doesn't mean that you should artificially limit yourself either. Carve out margin for creativity, and you will experience insights you would otherwise miss.

Leave some room in your process for spontaneous insight and action.

> **QUESTION**
> How can you give yourself more space in your creative process?

May
30

Rejection Proof

Jia Jiang knew he had a problem. He was terrified of being turned down, of failing, of embarrassing himself. However, he recognized that this fear was potentially keeping him from meaningful life experiences. So he hatched a plan: he would become rejection proof. The goal was to engage in a rejection exercise each day with the sole purpose of actually being rejected so that he would become inoculated to its effects. He showed up at a neighbor's house dressed to play soccer and asked to play in their backyard. He asked for a "burger refill" at a fast-food restaurant. Dozens of times, he was rejected, but nearly as often, people actually accommodated his requests.

No one likes rejection, because no one likes to be judged. If you choose to make things for a living and share them with others, rejection in some form is inevitable. It's not rejection that we should fear but rather the fear of rejection. That is what prevents us from taking creative risks that lead to valuable breakthroughs.

I believe that far too many brilliant projects, great ideas, or remarkable relationships never begin because of the fear of rejection. It's unfathomable what the compounding loss of those never-seen efforts actually is. Do not allow the fear of rejection to prevent you from acting on your ideas and ambitions. It is a sure pathway to regret.

Creative pros must overcome the fear of rejection.

QUESTION
Is the fear of rejection leading you to inaction?

May
31

Input and Output Metrics

How do you measure great work? Which metrics really matter?

Right now, I'm (obviously) in the midst of writing this book. As part of the process, I measure how many words I write in a given day, but that metric isn't all that useful. Rather than just focusing on word count, I focus on the number of high-quality ideas I generate each day for entries and the number of entries I actually write. The former is a measurement of my "idea factory" and the latter a measurement of my creative output. Both are valuable and useful. Without measuring the number of ideas, I could quickly get to a place where my needed output outstrips the quantity of ideas in the pipeline. Without measuring output, I will fall woefully behind in my work and may miss my deadline. One metric is an input metric and the other is an output metric.

Do you know both the input and output metrics for your work? How are they measured? Measure what matters not only in terms of output but also upstream in your creative pipeline so that you always have the inputs and ideas necessary to do your work.

Make certain you are measuring both your creative inputs and your creative output.

> **QUESTION**
> What are the input and output metrics for your work?

June

"Whether you succeed or not is irrelevant—there is no such thing. Making your unknown known is the important thing."
—GEORGIA O'KEEFFE

How do you define success? So often, we chase a vague, distant idea of what success might look like, but we haven't fully considered what the word even means. This month, center your efforts on producing work that you can point to with pride and that represents your best.

June
1

From Here

Some of the career decisions you make may turn out to be happy accidents, but some may later feel like mistakes. It's understandable in those moments when things feel desperate or you feel trapped to begin to think you may have made a mess of things.

And maybe you have. We all do at times. But wherever you are and whatever your circumstances, you can navigate to where you want to be from here. It might take more time than it would take someone else who didn't make your same choices, but it can be done. It will take sacrifice—maybe a lot of it. It will require you to make some difficult decisions. But you can get there. You can.

The worst thing to do is allow yourself to become overwhelmed to the point of inaction. To accept your status as "trapped" and fail to develop a plan for moving forward. In a crisis, those who freeze from fear are often the ones who end up being harmed, hence the phrase you often hear in emergency situations: "Keep moving!" When you're moving, you can redirect. When you're standing still, you have no momentum.

Keep moving and keep your destination in mind. You *can* get there from here.

QUESTION

Do you ever feel overwhelmed or trapped by your circumstances? Where are you moving toward?

June
2

Your Heroes

Did you ever play superhero as a kid? (My favorite was Aquaman, which in retrospect truly baffles me, because he was only useful for solving nautical crimes.) We would run around our neighborhood pretending to be our favorite hero, blasting one another with invisible rays and "flying" across fences to confront the supervillains (played by our coerced younger siblings). Of course, we heroes always won the day.

In some cases, childhood play can be a good model for adult creative play as well. Emulating your heroes is a valuable method for sparking new pathways of thought or breaking out of process ruts and mental traps.

How would Abraham Lincoln resolve the argument you're having over the direction of your current project? How might Mary Barra approach leading your team through this season of change? How would Steve Jobs lead the design of your new app? What advice might MLK give you about your team's dynamics?

Thinking about the work of your heroes can help you bust out of ruts and take a fresh look at your projects. Read deeply and broadly about great contributors of the past, then reflect on them when you need a fresh perspective. Consider the problems they encountered and how they approached them. Consider their mistakes (everyone makes them!) and how you can avoid them.

Spark fresh creative insight by emulating your superheroes.

When you're stuck, ask what your heroes might do.

QUESTION
Who is someone you deeply admire? Is there a method they used that you can borrow?

June

3

Ego vs. Confidence

The creative workplace is often a parade of ego and insecurity. Because of the subjective nature of creative work, people sometimes feel the need to posture themselves to appear "strong" and confident, but they are really only masking their uncertainty and lack of confidence. Worse, entire teams sometimes bend to the will of those who are the loudest, most aggressive, and most seemingly certain, even when they are abusive. Because their egos have made them inflexible to the point that they cannot be persuaded, everyone just accommodates them. But ego is not the same as confidence. Confident people are adaptable to new circumstances, whereas ego-driven people are inflexible and only interested in protecting their own interests. Confident people look outward, while ego-driven people only look inward to their own needs and ambitions.

Confidence says, "I believe I can get this right," whereas ego says, "I can do no wrong."

Confidence says, "I'm valuable," whereas ego says, "I'm invaluable."

Confidence says, "Get out of my way," whereas ego says, "Here's my strong, considered perspective."

These are fundamentally different mindsets. Unfortunately, some people defer to ego because it always comes across boldly and loudly. However, volume is not truth and aggression is not true insight.

You must cultivate the trait of creative confidence, but be wary of leading with ego. One path leads to strong, trustworthy collaboration and the other to isolated, lonely creative dysfunction.

Don't confuse ego (self-protection) with confidence (self-projection).

QUESTION

Do you need to increase your level of creative confidence? Have you ever encountered someone who led with their ego? What happened?

June
4

Outside

If you are a designer, do you only read design-related magazines or visit websites that show others' work in your field? As an entrepreneur, do you only read business books and magazines? If you write, do you seek inspiration from other writers in your genre? Or if you're a photographer, do you only follow photography social media accounts?

It's easy to slip into the rut of only seeking inspiration from tried and true, trusted wells. It makes sense to attempt to see what others in your fields are doing. In fact, it is smart to stay abreast of trends. However, you're also likely to slip into comparison mode rather easily when you're only looking at others who do what you do, and you risk the danger of copying someone else's idea and mistaking it for your own.

Instead, strive to seek creative inspiration from those who are outside your field. One studio creative director told me that he never sought inspiration through video and film but instead sought all his inspiration through reading fiction. He was able to make intuitive leaps and connections between what he was reading and the work he was doing, and many of his ideas felt really novel because they were sourced outside where his peers were looking.

Identify a handful of resources outside your field to peruse for inspiration.

Seek inspiration outside your core domain.

QUESTION

Where do you regularly find inspiration for your work? What are some sources outside your field that might spark new ways of seeing the work?

June
5

Creative Day

There were several key moments in my career when I needed a clear next direction. In fact, this has happened in the wake of the release of every one of my books, when I'm very busy talking about my past work but uncertain about what my next thing should be. In those moments, I declare a "creative day."

I get up in the morning, have my coffee and breakfast, then drive downtown in my city and walk along the river. Then I walk through the city, visit bookstores, pay attention to the stimuli around me, cross the river and walk through the neighborhoods on the other side, and sometimes even see a movie if the mood strikes me. All along the way, I take notes, listen for patterns, and see what the world offers in the way of inspiration.

Here's the thing: every single time I do this, I come away with a strong sense of what to do next. Simply breaking away from the email, the daily grind, and the pressure to produce and allowing myself to meander, think freely, and wander the world gives me fresh perspective and enthusiasm for my work. I come home from those creative days tired but refreshed at the same time.

When it's time for a bold move, declare a creative day.

> ### QUESTION
> When might you schedule a creative day in your life?

June
6

Like What You Like

Once, a youth worker friend of mine told me that one of his high school students came to him distraught. Thinking there was something wrong at home or maybe that he'd experienced a nasty breakup with his girlfriend, he inquired about what was wrong.

"It's terrible," he said. "You see, I really like this band [name redacted]."

My friend nodded and asked, "What happened? Did the band break up? Did something happen?"

"No, it's not that," the high schooler continued. "It's that a bunch of people in my school just discovered them, so now they're ruined. I can't listen to them anymore because they're not cool now that everyone *else* likes them."

True story. It's tempting to modulate our own likes and dislikes based on popular opinion. It's not "cool" to like cheesy pop music or pop art. It's considered artistically immature to laugh at a silly comedy. You're supposed to only like dark, dense films that force you to confront the dysfunction of contemporary society, right?

Here's my advice: like what you like, unapologetically. Everything is useful in your creative process. If it makes you feel the way you want to feel, like it without remorse and don't worry about what other people think.

Worry less about how others perceive your taste and seek to let the world inspire you in whatever way it does.

Just like what you like, unapologetically.

QUESTION
Is there something you enjoy that you find a little embarrassing? Why?

June
7

Gatekeepers

My friend Lionel is a brilliant musician. He wrote and recorded several hits, including a smash number one record. A few decades ago, when he was active on the performing side of the music business, the pathway to success was: get the attention of a record label executive, secure a recording or publishing deal, let the label shape and refine you and make you marketable, spend tens or hundreds of thousands of dollars making a record, and follow their lead and hope that you "catch on." But no matter what, that first step was to get the gatekeepers to let you in.

Since recording technology has been democratized and studio-level equipment is available to almost everyone, Lionel has been joking with me for years that it was only a matter of time before some kid wins a Grammy for something they recorded in their bedroom.

He was wrong. She won five with her debut album.

Billie Eilish has officially driven a stake through the heart of what we used to think was the sole path to creative success. It's official—you can make music from anywhere.

Now, there's a big difference between *making* something and *gaining attention* for it. Attention for your work is not a birthright. However, the old excuses of needing someone to give you permission to make your art are officially dead.

You don't need a gatekeeper's permission. You just need to do your work.

There are no creative gatekeepers, especially in this day and age. Do your work.

QUESTION

Is there any place where you are waiting for the permission of a gatekeeper before you do your work?

June

8

Now vs. Later

Every creative pro reaches a juncture in which they must ask, "Do I want quick success or lasting success?" These moments don't scream at you. They're often subtle. But if you pay attention, they come along often.

Do you follow the fad or follow your intuition?

Do you do what's expedient now or what will deliver results for a long time to come?

Do you do what gets you the most attention in the moment or what will grow a body of work you'll be proud of later?

These are subtle decisions that require you to understand your values. They require you to subvert your ego for the sake of your body of work. As Thomas Merton wrote, "There can be an intense egoism in following everybody else. People are in a hurry to magnify themselves by imitating what is popular—and too lazy to think of anything better. Hurry ruins saints as well as artists. They want quick success, and they are in such haste to get it that they cannot take time to be true to themselves. And when the madness is upon them, they argue that their very haste is a species of integrity."

Stay focused on the body of work you are building, and resist the urge to follow the pack for a quick moment of recognition.

QUESTION

Where are you tempted to go for quick results at the expense of your long-term body of work?

June
9

Stretch for Capacity

A few years ago, I tore my ACL while playing in a basketball league. (It was inevitable—I was playing with people twenty years younger!) Sidelined for months awaiting surgery, I realized that my basketball days were likely over and that once I recovered, I would need to find a new way to exercise. Against my better judgment, I decided to take up running. I'd tried before and always hated it, but with two of my kids now running competitively, I decided to give it another shot.

In my first attempt, I made it about two blocks before slowing to a walk. The next time, I went about half a mile. It was then I made a decision: I was going to run a mile, no matter how slow and no matter how I felt.

I did, and I felt awful. But you know what? The next time I ran, I made it a half mile before I even felt tired. I'd proven I could do it. Now I run for miles nonstop because I've stretched my capacity.

There are moments in your creating when you simply need to push through the discomfort. You need to stretch your capacity to create so that when you need endurance, it's there. Today, focus on pushing through the moments of discomfort when you want to give up. You'll be glad you did.

Press yourself to go beyond the moment when you feel like quitting. You will increase your creative endurance.

QUESTION

When are you most tempted to give up in the midst of your work? How can you push through those moments today?

June
10

Own Your Mistakes

Deflect, rationalize, and blame. These tactics have become more common in the workplace, and they're destroying team culture. "It's not my fault!" is something a child says when caught breaking a lamp, not something an adult should say when they fail at work.

Often, people deflect and blame because they are afraid of losing the trust of their peers. They fear being seen as incompetent and will do anything to protect their reputations. However, this tactic often has the opposite effect. Everyone likely already suspects who's really at fault. The denial only breaches trust even further.

Own your mistakes. Assume responsibility for making them right. In fact, don't wait until it's too late. Speak up early and often, and you might be able to prevent the worst from even occurring. It might sting a little in the moment, but in the long term, people will trust you to do what's right, not just what's comfortable. When you make a mistake:

- ► Acknowledge and own it.
- ► Determine how you can fix it or prevent it from happening again.
- ► Communicate your plan to your manager, your stakeholders, or your peers.

If you are running fast enough and trying difficult things (which you should be!), you are going to make mistakes.

To build trust in your peers (and yourself), own your mistakes.

QUESTION

Have you ever known someone who refused to own their mistakes? How did it feel to collaborate with them?

June
11

Shooting for the Three

Back in the 1990s (the ancient days!), a friend in the music business told me how record labels chose which songs to release as singles to radio. (Keep in mind that I've never been able to verify this story, but the source was credible.) They would record a number of songs for an album, then would begin to market test them by playing snippets over the phone to survey participants. The participants were asked to rate the song on a scale of one to five, with one meaning "I would definitely change the radio station" and five meaning "I love this song!" Then they would compile the data to determine which songs should be radio singles.

You would think they would release the songs with the most fives, right? Me too. But that's not the case. What they discovered is that many songs that had a lot of fives also tended to be somewhat polarizing. There were a lot of ones. You either loved these songs or hated them, so they were risky. The songs that tended to perform best overall were the ones with the most threes, because they were just good enough to keep your attention but not nearly as polarizing. Over time, much of the music started sounding the same—predictable, sonically one-dimensional, safe. The goal wasn't to release great music; it was to keep radio listeners glued to the station so that it could sell more ads. Keep more listeners, and your song plays more.

Are you aiming for the right objectives today? Are your metrics aligned with your creative ambitions, or are you in danger of "shooting for the three" instead of producing your best work?

Invisible, subversive objectives can lead to subpar work.

QUESTION

Is there a project in which your assumed outcome is not aligned with the actual desired outcome?

June

12

Working Hard vs. Striving

Urgency and diligence are the foundation of hustle. If you want to succeed in your life and work, you will need to work very, very hard and in a focused way. However, there's a difference between hard work and desperate work. Hard work is sourced in intent and is focused and resourced. Desperate work expends a lot of energy but is unfocused and often unproductive.

How can you know the difference?

- Hard work is targeted, whereas desperate work flails.
- Hard work has a clear end point, whereas desperate work feels never-ending.
- Hard work is from a position of strength, whereas desperate work feels like you're always behind.
- Hard work feels good, whereas desperate work feels empty.
- Hard work has a plan, whereas desperate work is reactive to urgency.
- Hard work is measured in intervals of progress, whereas desperate work is measured by how much it temporarily relieves your anxiety.
- Hard work pursues the right idea, whereas desperate work latches on to the first available idea.

Of course, you must work hard. But be mindful of the subtle differences between working hard and working out of desperation. When you feel desperate, you don't think clearly, and you feel too anxious to take the necessary time to play with your thoughts and experiment with ideas. **Work with diligence and urgency, but don't work desperately.**

QUESTION

Can you think of a time when you worked desperately rather than hard? What was it like?

June
13

Awe

Think of a card, any card in the deck.

When I was a child, I fell in love with magic. I remember watching a Doug Henning special on TV and actually believing that there were people in the world who could bend the laws of physics by making things levitate, disappear, and switch places. As I grew into my late childhood, I knew that these were only illusions, but I was still in love with the feeling of awe that a well-performed magic trick could inspire. Although my sleight of hand skill has waned from a lack of practice, I still have a suitcase of magic gear ready to pull out whenever the occasion calls for it. (Hey, look under your chair right now. Just kidding.)

What is it about magic that excites us? My friend Harris, who is a professional illusionist, calls it "wonder" and believes that it's an essential element of creativity. To make things that the world has never seen, we must first be able to imagine their existence. This requires us to traffic in a kind of shadow world, just beyond our senses. It almost feels like wishful thinking or willing something into existence. It's very similar to childlike play. We must believe in impossible things.

Do you have a sense of wonder in your life, or has it faded a bit? Take a few moments today to remember what it felt like to be a child and to see possibility in the world around you. That sense of wonder is the antidote to cynicism and snark, which are the enemies of creativity.

Embrace wonder in your life. Don't allow the magic to die.

QUESTION

What inspires awe and wonder in you? How can you experience it today?

June
14

Self-Editing

When I was younger, I was easily embarrassed when I had an idea that I didn't consider "cool." It was as if there was an inner critic poking holes at my internal dialogue and shaming me for not being as good as I thought I should be. This resulted in a lot of unnecessary self-editing. While we may decry the overreach of the *actual* editors in our lives or workplaces, our internal, self-editors can be even more brutal.

We don't share an idea in a meeting because our editor nixes it before we have the chance.

We don't explore a slightly fringe idea because we're afraid we don't have time to bring it back into the realm of possibility before the deadline.

We keep a concept to ourselves because we're afraid it will look "too obvious" to everyone else, and we'll be laughed at.

This kind of self-editing early in the creative process can stifle your energy for the work and cause you to underperform. Instead, allow yourself the freedom to think, write, speak, and develop any idea that gives you energy, knowing that there will always be time for editing later.

Be free now, and edit later.

Don't self-edit too soon in your process. Allow ideas that make you uncomfortable.

QUESTION
Do you tend to self-edit? How does it affect you?

June
15

Change Your World

The phrase "change the world" is often in the mission statements of organizations I work with. There's nothing wrong with the desire to bring positive change to the world, but it's important to note that very few people have created large, systemic, lasting change in the world. Even some of the more famous and influential people in the history of any particular country—while certainly impactful—came nowhere near changing the world in the grand sense. However, they each made a significant dent in their own corner of the world.

That's all we can do. Very, very few people are truly capable of changing the world. However, every single person is capable of changing the world around them. All macro change begins with micro effort. Be the leader that other people need you to be. Bring enthusiasm and courage to your work. Make life easier for the people you collaborate with. Dwell in possibility and challenge others to be the best version of themselves each day. Refuse to settle for mediocrity, and run alongside others who are struggling.

Many people become paralyzed by the size of the macro problem and simply give up. Instead, focus on the micro problems around you and pursue them with full vigor. Don't try to change the world; just focus on changing the world around you.

Very few people are called to change the world. Everyone is called to change the world around them.

QUESTION

What change do you want to see in the world around you? How can you contribute to that effort today?

June
16

Master the Rules

As we've already covered, complete freedom is not helpful to the creative process. Without a clear bounding arc, any creative effort can feel paralyzing. That's why a clear, precise, specific directive from a client or manager can be helpful, at least in getting you moving in the right direction.

Sometimes these bounding arcs are the generally accepted rules of your craft. Whether you're a marketer, entrepreneur, designer, writer, musician, etc., it's important to have a deep and firm understanding of the basic tenets of your profession. How have others succeeded at your craft over time? What are the various schools of thought? The tools of the trade? The tried-and-true methods?

Some people want to tag themselves as "contrarian" and toss the rulebook out the window, but it's important to understand that there is a specific reason why those rules exist to begin with: they generally work! You must earn the right to break the rules, and the way you do that is by proving first that you know them and understand why they work. Strategically breaking a rule of the craft is a great way to achieve a creative breakthrough, but not until you first understand why that rule is there to begin with. As Pablo Picasso is claimed to have said, "Learn the rules like a pro, so you can break them like an artist."

Before you try to break the rules of your craft, master them.

QUESTION
Are there generally accepted rules of your craft or discipline?
Have you ever broken one? What happened?

June
17

Obnoxious People

You've likely heard the phrase "you can't change other people!" Coach and author Peter Bregman disagrees. In fact, he's made a career of changing other people, or more accurately, helping people change themselves. He believes that our approach to trying to change others is often the biggest impediment to the other person actually changing. We tend to confront them and explain why their behavior isn't working. However, that method often generates even more conflict, with the other person digging their heels in and refusing to budge. Instead, Bregman says that we should strive to become an ally of the other person. Rather than telling them what they should do, we must help them discover why that change would be beneficial for them. By taking this approach, we prove that we aren't their sworn mortal enemy but are actually striving to help them succeed.

There are certainly times when confrontation is necessary in the workplace, but those moments should be saved for when behavior is so egregious that it rises to the level of insubordination. In most cases, it's far better to come alongside the other person and help them grow. You will build stronger organizational relationships, and you will also be more likely to get the results you want.

No one changes their behavior until they want to, and you can help them want to.

QUESTION

Is there anyone in your organization (or whom you have to work or live with) who is exhibiting an undesirable behavior? How might you—by becoming an ally—help them change their behavior—for their own good?

June
18

Empty Your Mind

A leader I admire once explained the most important ritual in his day. He said that he gets out of bed, grabs a cup of coffee, then makes his way to the chair in his living room. Then he sits down and zones out. (When he was telling this story, he exhibited an almost confused, dazed look.) He simply sits there for twenty minutes or so with no agenda. He allows his mind to wander. Sometimes he'll think of a person on his team, and he'll make a quick note to reach out to them. Sometimes he'll have a flash of insight about a project, and he'll jot it down and go back to spacing out. The point of the entire exercise is to simply sit, allow his mind to wander, and pay attention to whatever happens in those quiet moments.

I've adopted this method over the years, and some of my best ideas have emerged from it. In the hustle of the day, there is so much noise in my mind that I often can't hear the quiet whisper of insight trying to break through. When I take a strategic pause to empty my mind, those whispers become crystal clear. You discover what's really on your mind, which is often nothing like what occupies your executive brain throughout the day.

To see things more clearly, take a strategic pause and clear your mind.

QUESTION

When might you schedule a strategic pause in your day to allow your mind to wander?

June
19

Failure

When was the last time you failed? I don't mean you struggled at making a new dish for dinner or couldn't complete a crossword puzzle. When was the last time you took a risk, you really tried, you gave it your all, and you came up short? (Bonus points if it was in public.)

For many, failure is their biggest fear. They've spent much of their life shielding themselves from the potential of falling short to the point that they can't even remember the last time they did. They take on projects that are well within their abilities, and when they don't quite hit the mark, they rationalize why what they did was actually a success if you think about it the right way.

If you don't occasionally fail, you aren't trying sufficiently difficult, ambitious things. You aren't stretching yourself and testing your abilities. Most people can easily lift a ten-pound dumbbell, but you don't build muscle that way. Instead, you lift a challenging weight over and over again until your muscle begins to fail. When you reach your absolute limit, you push harder, then you quit. The next time, your capacity is greater.

When you don't fail, your capacity never changes. You simply live and work within safe, predictable limits. And you never know what you're capable of.

If you aren't failing from time to time, you are playing it too safe.

> **QUESTION**
> When was the last time you failed? Do you think you are stretching yourself enough?

June

20

Prune Relationships

You only have so much energy to exert. Any energy that you spend necessarily comes at the expense of other things in your life. It's easy to prune redundant tasks, old projects, and recurring calendar commitments from your life, but sometimes what needs pruning feels a little more personal and awkward. There are some relational commitments that simply outlive their benefit to each person, and the time comes when you simply need to prune the relationship and move on.

This can be a difficult conversation because the decision is not always mutual. For example, an old colleague may want to continue to meet up for coffee every two weeks to chat about how bad his work situation is, or your college roommate wants to grab a few beers after work to relive the past. Neither of these situations is bad on its face and may have even brought you energy at one point but has now outlived its merits. It may be time to prune so that you have the energy you need to bring to the fulfilling relationships in your life.

A quick caveat: I am *not* endorsing walking away from your commitments to others. Those must be honored. However, pay attention to when relationships seem to have withered, and be courageous enough to prune when necessary so that you have the energy you need to pursue your productive passion.

Sometimes we need to cut ties with people who drain us.

QUESTION

Are there any relationships in your life that need to be pruned?

June
21

Small Diversions

If you are old enough, you recall the days when researching a topic meant walking over to a shelf, pulling out an encyclopedia volume, shuffling through the pages until you found the topic, and hoping that the article was written at some point in the past ten years. (Or you may have visited the library to search through microfilm of hundreds of newspapers until you found the exact article you were looking for. Fun times.) Now, you can find the answer to nearly any question with just a few clicks. If you are curious about something or get the urge to follow a hunch, you can do it in an instant, which will likely lead to another click, and another, and soon you are down the rabbit hole of distraction. These distractions driven by curiosity are easy and cheap to follow but actually very costly to your process because they fracture your focus.

To curb the instinct to bounce from click to click, it can be helpful to keep a small notepad handy to write down interesting thoughts that cross your mind while doing your work. Experiencing a desire to follow a clickbait article? Write it down and follow it later, when you aren't in the middle of something. Want to read an article about your favorite band? Great! Write it down so that you can do it later, when you have time.

Keep a log of potential diversions, then schedule some "diversion time" to pursue them all.

Be mindful of small diversions that sidetrack your work.

QUESTION

What small diversions tempt you the most when in the midst of your work?

June
22

Big Vision

In 1966, Walt Disney announced his vision for EPCOT through a series of videos. For those who have visited Disney World, you know EPCOT as just another in a series of Disney parks containing exhibits for countries around the world and its own rides. However, this wasn't his original intent.

In his promotional videos, Disney exclaimed a vision of a futuristic city (EPCOT stands for Experimental Prototype Community of Tomorrow), with people living, working, and creating in an enormous planned community. Transportation would be accomplished via the "people mover," which is still in use at the park today. It was an ambitious vision and one that would fall short. After his death, the company decided that Disney's plans for a "city of tomorrow" were simply not practical and would distract from other business interests. They were shelved until the early 1980s, when a less ambitious EPCOT was opened to the public.

I am deeply inspired by Walt Disney's vision of possibility. At a time when he could have focused solely on growing his successful entertainment interests, he was dreaming about how to change the conversation around city planning. He was tackling the problem of urban sprawl. He was thinking bigger.

It's easy to become obsessed with the work in front of you, but I challenge you today to think bigger about your role in the world. How can you expand your view of what's possible?

Dream big. You won't get everything, but you'll come closer than if you aim for "reasonable."

QUESTION
Is there a big vision you have that scares you?

June
23

Creative Discontent

What propels you forward? For many creative pros, it's the sense of discontent they experience when their in-process work doesn't match their vision for the work. They desire to close the gap between the aspirational and the practical, and they feel ill at ease until they do. Whether it's a design that isn't quite right or a phrase that doesn't capture the essence of what they're trying to say or a system that isn't humming in just the right way, they can't seem to rest until they solve it.

That's the nature of creative work. It goes with you everywhere, because your mind is always at work. There's often an ever-present feeling of discontent because of the gap between your vision and your results.

Being unsettled in this way is necessarily unhealthy, nor is it always anxiety. Anxiety consumes you and is counterproductive. However, healthy discontent can propel you toward better work and more mastery over your craft. You may never achieve a perfect match, and that's also OK. It's the effort to close the gap that leads to growth and fulfillment.

It's fine to feel discontent. When you are unsettled, you may just produce your best work.

QUESTION

Is there an area of your work where you feel unsettled, like your vision doesn't match your results? What would it take to close the gap?

June
24

Five Snapshots

A few years ago, I was asked by an organization to help them rethink their brand and how they communicate their story to others. As part of the engagement, I sent the team out into the surrounding neighborhood with a few instructions:

- ► You are allowed to snap five photos that—in sequence—tell the story of your brand.
- ► You may not use anything (symbols, language, signs) that is currently a part of how you talk about yourself and the brand.
- ► You must all agree on the five photos you choose.

I sent them out, and after ninety minutes, they returned to share what they'd discovered on their trek. One by one, the group shared their photos and the story they told. Each presentation was completely unique, and at the end, we had a trove of words, images, phrases, and sentiments that were previously absent from the conversation. The simple act of venturing out into the neighborhood to spark new insights had pushed everyone outside their mental ruts.

You can do this same exercise for product development, marketing, writing, designing, or any other kind of creative project where you need some fresh thinking. When you're stuck, it can be helpful to explore ideas through different media. If you're a writer, draw or photograph it. If you're a designer, write it out. It will force you to think about the problem in new ways.

It's often beneficial to force yourself to explore ideas through different media.

QUESTION

Is there a project you're working on that could benefit from exploration through a different medium?

June
25

Never Too Late

In my book *Die Empty*, I shared an old anecdote that has resonated with me since I was young. A man wanted to learn to play guitar his entire life, and now at almost age fifty, he was afraid that it might be too late. His friend encouraged him to take lessons.

"Nah," he replies. "It'll take five years to really learn. By the time I'm any good, I'll be almost fifty-five years old!"

His friend paused, then softly asked, "Tell me, how old will you be in five years if you don't learn how to play guitar?"

So many people give up on their passions, their curiosities, their hunches because they believe they're too late to the game, they're too old, or that they missed their window of opportunity. I was hesitant to start a podcast in 2005 because I thought I was too late to the podcasting space. Can you imagine? Seventeen years, tens of millions of downloads, and six books later, I'm glad I didn't listen to that naysaying voice.

It's not too late for you. Wherever you are, whatever your situation, you can begin now. Learn the craft. Have the conversation. Start the thing. Take the risk. Plant your flag. The time is now.

As the old saying goes, the best time to plant a tree was twenty years ago. The next best time is right now.

It's never too late to begin. Start today.

QUESTION

What have you wanted to start or do but felt like it was too late? What do you need to start?

June

26

Action

Some creative pros are so afraid of making a mistake that they'd rather freeze in place until they can figure out the right path forward. The one thing they are absolutely certain about is that everyone around them has it all figured out—that they are surely the only ones who are treading water. After all, look at all the confidence everyone else conveys!

The irony is that when you freeze in place, you only dig yourself deeper into your rut. Inaction is the enemy of discovery. The path to self-discovery is not through thought but through action. As Ellen Langer wrote in *On Becoming an Artist*, "Action is the way we get to experience ourselves. And so, we act not to bring about an outcome but to bring about ourselves." We discover our unique contribution—our giftedness—not by contemplating what we might do but by actually doing things, feeling the resistance of the world when we act, learning about our response to that resistance, then adapting, trying again, and continuing the cycle.

Action is the only way to self-discovery. It's the only path to fulfillment. It's not what you know, it's what you do about it that matters.

Be a person of action.

QUESTION

Is there an action that you know you need to take but have been hesitant to do so? Why are you hesitant to act?

June
27

Shadow Artists

Some people flirt with the idea of pursuing their dream of making art or launching a business but settle for doing something close enough to the edges to still associate with their dream without the requisite risk. Author Julia Cameron calls them "shadow artists." They are close to where the art is being made but aren't willing to take the necessary risks to actually make it themselves. For example, people who want to write books but instead choose to edit or people who want to be musicians who become road managers. She writes, "Artists love other artists. Shadow artists are gravitating to their rightful tribe but cannot yet claim their birthright. Very often audacity, not talent, makes one person an artist and another a shadow artist—hiding in the shadows, afraid to step out and expose the dream to the light, fearful that it will disintegrate to the touch."

I would argue that this term applies not only to artists in the classical sense but also to anyone who chooses a safer version of their dream rather than risk failure. It might be the person with the entrepreneurial idea who instead chooses to work for someone else's venture because it's easier and less risky.

Don't settle for something less than what you're capable of. Be audacious enough to try.

Make your art. Don't settle for being a shadow artist.

QUESTION

Is there an area where you are settling for the shadow version of your craft rather than the real thing?

June
28

Fear and Wisdom

"Are you sure you want to..."

"Wouldn't it be better to..."

"Maybe you should wait until..."

"What if they say..."

"What if they don't say..."

"It would be safer to..."

These narratives play inside our heads each time we confront uncertainty and choose to take a creative risk. On the surface, they sound like the voice of wisdom, but their motivation is often rooted in fear, driven by self-protection.

The problem is that you cannot take a creative risk and self-protect simultaneously. They are antithetical to one another.

How can you tell the difference between wisdom and fear?

Fear only cares about preservation, whereas wisdom seeks the best possible result. Fear exaggerates the perceived consequences of failure, whereas wisdom is realistic about both the upside and the downside of action. Fear tends to grow once it's entertained and become more consuming, whereas wisdom maintains perspective. Fear dissipates when exposed to facts and reality, whereas wisdom thrives on accurate information.

When you operate in wisdom, you recognize the potential consequences of failure but also consider the benefits of success. Wisdom calculates the cost and chooses to act anyway when action is warranted. Fear only desires inaction and self-protection.

Pay attention to the narratives inside your head, and strive to parse the voice of fear from the voice of wisdom.

Fear often comes disguised as wisdom. Learn to differentiate them.

QUESTION

Do you think you ever confuse the voice of fear with the voice of wisdom? How so?

June
29

Contingency and Ownership

I often ask managers, "If you could snap your fingers and change one thing about your work situation right now, what would it be?" There are two distinct types of responses I get.

The first response is what I call the "contingency" response. This contains statements like "If only (insert name) would listen to me, then..." or "If we would take on better clients, then..." or other types of contingency-based responses. These responses nearly always target someone else for the problems they are experiencing.

Then, there are what I call "ownership" responses: "I would like to assume more responsibility for..." or "I would pursue bigger clients so that we can make more of a name for ourselves in the industry," or "I would give our team more time for personal development so they can expand their capacity." These are responses that are positive and vision focused. Those who respond in this way focus more on what's possible than on what's being withheld from them.

To succeed in life, you must assume full ownership of both the problems and opportunities in your world. When you focus on possibilities, you begin to marshal your resources toward bringing them into being. When you focus on limitations, you train yourself to wait for someone else to fix the problem.

Own both your problems and opportunities.

QUESTION

If you could snap your fingers and change one thing in your work world, what would it be?

June
30

What You're Missing

Regardless of how experienced you may be, you cannot see all things at all times. You need the perspective of others in order to gain a full sense of reality. I share what I see, you share what you see, then we try to figure out the reality in the midst of our mutual perceptions.

One technique that is incredibly effective at bringing visibility to potential blind spots is to simply ask someone you trust "What is something obvious that you think I'm missing?" It's very likely that others have spotted potential oversights or mistakes in waiting but haven't felt permission from you to talk about them. Simply opening the door to the insights of others can help you better understand how others see the world and help you avoid potentially damaging mistakes that others could see coming well before you could. Try these questions:

- ► Am I missing something?
- ► What do you see that you think I don't?
- ► What would you do if you were me?
- ► What should my next action be?

These are all good variations of the same question. Any one of them can help you gain better clarity and ensure that you're not overlooking potential value. There is no shame in seeking help from others. And you should be ready and willing to do the same for them.

Seek the perspective of many people to ensure that you're seeing reality correctly.

Ask others to help cover your creative and leadership blind spots.

> **QUESTION**
> Who should you seek perspective from today and about what?

July

"Some writers confuse authenticity, which they ought always to aim at, with originality, which they should never bother about."

—W. H. AUDEN

In order to grow, we need models to emulate. However, the inevitable temptation is to compare your in-process work and growth with those who are much further down the path and thus much more skilled or advanced. This month, focus on incremental, meaningful growth rather than unfair comparison with the work of your heroes.

July
1

Best, But Unpopular

I still remember the day I reached out to a very well-known and respected author for some advice. At launch, my new book was inexplicably not selling as well as my previous ones, and I was terrified that this was a signal of some imminent career doom.

I'll never forget what he told me. He said, "Don't beat yourself up about market reception at launch. The market is just about always stupid." He was right. But not just about the market. He was right about the "don't beat yourself up" part.

There are two parts to the work of any creative pro: making and marketing. The first part is completely under your control, but the second part—how the market receives your work—is not, which is what drives a lot of creative pros to prematurely shape their work to make marketing a lighter lift. But this is backward thinking. Your job is to do work that is so compelling that it will eventually find its footing, regardless of the initial reception.

As the opening act for the Monkees, Jimi Hendrix was once booed offstage several nights in a row. Monkees fans had no grid for what Hendrix was doing, so they rejected him. It didn't make his work any less brilliant.

Since that launch, I've received emails from around the world—from celebrities, business titans, and everyday creative pros—that said the book referenced above had made a huge impact on them. It still hasn't sold as well as my others, but it is doing its job with the people who discover it. And to this day, I still believe it's my best writing. As difficult as it may be to understand, your best work may not be your most popular. And that's fine. Don't beat yourself up.

Your best work may not be your most popular work.

QUESTION

Is there work you've done that was not received the way you wish it was? Are you still holding on to regret or beating yourself up about it?

July
2

Humility

Have you ever met someone who can't take a compliment? You try to tell them how wonderful their work is and they reply with, "No, not really," or "I was just lucky," or "Other people are so much better," or something similar. They apologize all over themselves whenever they feel like they are intruding on your space or taking up too much of the conversation. They seem to be apologizing for their very existence.

Often, this mindset is reinforced at a young age by well-meaning authority figures who repeat axioms like "Be humble!" or "No one likes cocky people!" We learn early that to be humble means to downplay your own achievements and elevate those of others, even when it means being self-deprecating.

However, that's not at all what humility means. Humility simply means having an accurate assessment of yourself. The root of the word is *humus* meaning "ground." It simply means not elevating yourself above your place. In fact, false humility is often a form of ego. People downplay themselves publicly but secretly think they are better than everyone around them.

Embrace your giftedness! When someone pays you a compliment, simply reply "thank you." Be confident in your abilities, and learn how others see your unique gifts and abilities from the way they pay you a compliment. We know ourselves best through the eyes of others.

True humility means embracing your giftedness but recognizing your limitations.

QUESTION

Are you ever tempted to shrug off compliments or downplay your own giftedness? How does that affect your mindset and work?

July
3

Peace

When people use the word *peace*, what they often mean is "I want to get what I want, and I don't want you to complain about it or cause trouble." That's not peace; in a way, it's a form of selfishness. For peace to exist, there must be harmony or order. This requires all parties to strive for the well-being of the other parties involved. When one party refuses to seek the well-being of another, there can't be true peace.

There will always be conflict when groups of talented, creative people bump into one another. If people on your team are striving to do great work and take accountability for delivering results, they are naturally going to disagree from time to time. However, healthy conflict always has a common objective and the well-being of the other parties in mind. Teams who fight in a healthy manner do so within clear boundaries and with the intent of making each other better at the end of the day. There is order, not chaos. This is the essence of peace. It doesn't mean a lack of conflict; it means we are all on the same side, and disagreements are with the intent of achieving our mutual objectives.

Commit to being a person of peace. Bring order, and strive for the well-being of your peers.

To achieve peace in your process and collaboration, strive for increased order in your world.

QUESTION

Have you ever experienced unhealthy conflict in your organization? What was the source of it, and what made it unhealthy?

July
4

Inner Freedom

As a creative pro, it can sometimes feel as if there are too many constraints placed on you. You must navigate the expectations of your client, your manager, your peers, the marketplace, and any other stakeholder who wants to ensure that their particular needs are met through your work. It can feel as if each of those constraints is a limitation of your creative freedom. However, true freedom is not sourced in permission from others; it is internal. Others can only limit your creative freedom if you surrender it to them. Your job as a pro is to leverage your intuition and skills to deliver something great within those constraints, even when they feel artificial. At times, the constraints may be so numerous that your options are truly limited, but that doesn't mean you've been robbed of your creative freedom. It simply means that you must self-limit in order to deliver on your expectations.

When you see others as the arbiters of your personal creative freedom, it's easy to adopt a victim mindset, which can lead to a downward spiral both mentally and emotionally. Instead, embrace the default position of creative freedom. Do the best work you can within the constraints you're given, and you will experience fulfillment. Rail against your constraints, and you will struggle. Remember: no one can rob you of your freedom—you can only surrender it.

Your creative freedom is sourced internally, not externally.

> ### QUESTION
> Do you ever feel as if your creative freedom is being taken from you? How can you embrace the ethic of inner creative freedom?

July
5

You Are Not the Hero

Because creative work is subjective and often very personal, it's easy to forget that your work is not for you but for others. The point is, in some way, to help others achieve their ambitions and find fulfillment. Your perspective is valuable only in as much as it helps others along their own journey. You are *not* the hero of the story; they are.

What does your intended audience desire? What are their hopes? What do they dream about? What are the obstacles in the way? What do you know that they don't yet see but that could help them surmount those obstacles and achieve their goals?

You should spend as much time thinking about the ambitions of your intended audience as you do actually creating for them. Place them at the center of the story where they belong. Enter into that story with them and they will feel an intimate connection to your work. You will be their ally. Their guide.

The essence of empathy is the ability to enter into the lived experience of another person. Spend time today placing your intended audience at the very center of your thoughts. Dream like they dream. Make them the hero.

Your best work results from making others the hero.

QUESTION

How can you make your intended audience the hero of the story today? Spend some time entering into their story.

July
6

Success and Failure

Two things that will quickly stall the creative process:

1. A lack of definition of success.
2. A lack of definition of failure.

If you haven't defined (and agreed upon) what a successful project looks like, it is entirely possible that you're aiming at a much different target than everyone around you. Or the target might shift in the midst of the work, and those micro drifts of scope could steer you far off the intended course.

If you haven't defined failure, it will be difficult to know the difference between a bump in the road and a catastrophic sinkhole. How do you know when it's time to give up? To try a new approach? To adjust your strategy?

To define success, ask these questions:

- ► What will it look like when we've succeeded?
- ► How will we know?
- ► What problem will we have solved?

To define failure, ask these questions:

- ► How will we know we are off course?
- ► What are the limits of the resources we can spend?
- ► What are we trying *not* to do?

Have clear definitions of both success and failure, and you are much more likely to steer your work successfully.

QUESTION

Do you have a clear definition of both success and failure for your current work?

July
7

On the Perception of Safety

I once printed a series of bumper stickers for my team that read "Safety Is Not an Option." (In retrospect, it's possible that a bumper sticker wasn't the best forum for that message.) The principle that I was trying to instill is that safety and brilliant work rarely coincide. Our best work occurs when we do things that might very well fail but where the payoff for success is great.

Consider this: when was the last time you gathered everyone around and told the story about a time when you chose the easiest and most comfortable option?

How many projects have you completed that you point to with pride, knowing that you did the most convenient and safe thing?

Of course not. All our stories and moments of deep satisfaction are sourced in times when we did the right thing, even when it was the difficult one.

Playing it safe is dangerous because it prevents us from exploring options that only become visible when we get out on the edge, where things might fall apart. As Neil Simon said, "Don't listen to those who say, 'You're taking too big a chance.' Michelangelo would have painted the Sistine floor, and it would surely be rubbed out by today."

Now, I'm not advising you to throw caution to the wind. Risk mitigation is an important part of any work that we do. But mitigation is not avoidance. Risk is a necessary element of doing effective creative work.

When you always choose the safest route, you take the greatest risk of all: never knowing what you might be truly capable of accomplishing.

Safety is not an option.

QUESTION

Is there a place in your life and work where you are taking the safe route, even though you know that something more might be possible?

July
8

The Work Is Never Complete

Could it be better? What if we got it wrong? Maybe I should tweak it just a little.

One unique challenge of doing creative work is that you are never certain when a project is truly complete. There is always something you could do (or could have done) to make it better. It's difficult to let go of work once a project is complete, and sometimes—maybe even weeks or months down the road—you have a sudden flash of brilliance and the perfect solution comes to mind, long after it would have been useful.

If you read my books in sequence, you will notice that ideas introduced in one book are often fully fleshed out in the next one, because I just couldn't let go of a concept until I knew I had it just right. Or I had a sudden insight that led to a new breakthrough in how I approach a topic. This is very typical of long-arc creative work. It becomes what it's supposed to be over time, in layers.

It is unlikely that you will ever be fully satisfied with your completed work. Or if you are, you will look back later and wish you'd done something differently. That's the nature of the creative process.

So what do you do with this? Learn. As you consider the work that you've completed or are struggling to complete, what doesn't quite sit right with you? Where do you now realize that you could have done something differently? What can you learn and apply to future projects to cut short the process and get it right quicker?

We don't have the luxury of tweaking until we are satisfied. So we need to learn from the observation of our own work and apply those learnings to future work.

Become comfortable living with open loops.

> **QUESTION**
> As you reflect on your past work, is there an insight you can gain and apply to something you're working on right now?

July
9

Reclaiming the Meaning of Passion

We have a very misguided sense of what the word *passion* means. We often toss out phrases like "follow your passion" to young professionals, and what we mean is "do things you like" or "enjoy the tasks you do every day." However, this is a very, very deceiving use of the word.

The word *passion* is derived from the Latin word *passiō*, which means "suffering or enduring." So when we tell someone to follow their passion, we are really telling them to "follow your suffering!" Doesn't quite have the same ring to it, huh?

But that's exactly the advice we should be giving them.

When you discover productive passion, you are willing to stay with a project longer than you otherwise would. You will endure hardships, late nights, difficult problems longer than others around you. That doesn't mean that you chase after suffering; it means that you are willing to suffer when necessary for the sake of something that matters much more to you than your temporary discomfort.

Your productive passion is not a set of tasks; it's an outcome that you are driven to achieve. Maybe it's bringing order to things. Maybe it's surprising and delighting others who experience your work. Maybe it's bringing compelling clarity to a message.

Once you connect deeply with your productive passion, you can bring it to the work you do each day rather than waiting for your work to inspire you. Don't follow your passion. Bring it to your work!

You must discover and unleash productive passion.

> **QUESTION**
>
> As you consider your work, what outcomes seem to bring you to life? Do you notice any patterns? Are there certain kinds of projects or situations that cause you to stick with things a little longer than you otherwise would? Now, consider what that might say about your productive passion.

July
10

Channeling Your Finite Attention

You have a finite amount of attention to spend on behalf of your daily work. How you allocate that finite attention is critical to your success. However, there are any number of distractions that can arise and pull you out of focus.

There is a dynamic that I like to call "the ping." It's a perpetual pinprick in my gut that says, "You should go check your email!" or "You should go check your voice mail!" Or "You should go check your phone, because maybe the president of the United States is calling you with a national security crisis!" That's the level of urgency the ping delivers, and it has us living in a state that researcher Linda Stone calls "continuous partial attention." I'm always kind of here, but I'm also kind of somewhere else at the same time. Do you think you do your best work that way?

Of course not.

Focus is an act of bravery, because to say yes to one thing, you must say no to many, many others. Yes, you may always fear what you are missing out on, but that is the price that you must pay for the clarity that comes with sharp, honed focus.

Be brave today and protect your attention. Dedicate some time off the grid to delve deeply into your most important, focused creative work. You will be rewarded.

Focus is an act of bravery.

QUESTION

Do you ever have time off the grid when no one can reach you? Carve out time today to focus on your most important work.

July
11

What Gets Pruned Grows Stronger

As creative pros, we don't struggle with new ideas, new projects, new meetings, new initiatives, new businesses, etc. What we often struggle with is saying no. We add thing after thing to our lives until we are suffocating. There is simply no room left for another commitment. Then, of course, we add another.

This dynamic often plays out in organizations as well, where we love to add new systems and initiatives and expectations but rarely remove any of the old ones.

In a vineyard, a good vine keeper knows the value of pruning. If not regularly pruned, a vine will not produce up to its potential. Over time, it can bear a lot of mediocre fruit or a select amount of very good fruit.

The same principle applies in your life. Without routine pruning, you will settle into mediocrity because you simply won't have enough resources to support your ambitions.

What very good thing in your life might need to go away so that something better can be born in its place? It might be a meeting, a project that once showed promise but now has become an energy drain, or even a relationship that is hanging on by a thread but neither of you wants to stop meeting for coffee. You must grow comfortable with pruning if you want to have sufficient energy and mental space to pour yourself into what matters most.

You must create space in life for the things that matter.

QUESTION

What needs to be pruned so that you have the focus, energy, and time to pour into what matters most?

July
12

Understand Why

Imagine that I took you into a field and told you that somewhere in the field is a target, and your job is to hit it with a bow and arrow. No other rules—just hit the target. However, there is one small caveat: you'll be blindfolded. You'll have no idea where the target is.

Now, imagine that after a lot of trial and error, you somehow manage to hit the target by sheer luck. You'll be glad that the exercise is over, but how gratified do you think you'll be?

I'd argue that you wouldn't be very gratified, because there's little gratification that comes from work that's not sourced in intent and purpose. As humans, we are wired to derive a sense of satisfaction and even a sense of self from the work that we put into the world. When the results of our work are not connected to a deeper sense of why we are doing the work, even success can feel hollow.

It's important that you are able to understand the meaning behind the projects you are working on. What is the deeper theme, or through line, that explains why the work you do is important to begin with? Otherwise, it's possible to work for days, weeks, or months on end and accomplish a lot that means little or nothing to you.

There is little gratification in work that's not sourced in intent and purpose.

QUESTION

Do you understand why you are doing the projects and tasks you're accountable for? If not, do whatever it takes to learn the why before diving into the what.

July
13

Difficult Conversations

Whether as leaders, teammates, clients, or friends, no one (except a masochist) enjoys difficult conversations. Yet they are inevitable any time we are doing difficult, complex work in a community of others. There will be differences of opinion and perspective that are necessary to sharpen and refine ideas. There will be personalities that grate against one another and cause friction.

Here's the good news: friction is what creates progress. Without it, we have nothing to push off against. If handled well, difficult conversations leave us in a better place than before. We reach an understanding. We clear the air. We are free to collaborate without the residue of suspicion and mistrust. Douglas Stone wrote, "Difficult conversations are almost never about getting the facts right. They are about conflicting perceptions, interpretations, and values."

It's often the case that neither party wants to be the first one to engage in a conversation that might become difficult. You should be that person. Clear the air, remove the dissonance, and build trust.

Have the difficult conversation.

QUESTION

Is there a difficult conversation that you've been avoiding because you simply dread the idea of having it? Make a plan for having that conversation.

July
14

Diving into Stimulus

When was the last time you intentionally did something that forced you out of your comfort zone? For many of us, it's a difficult question to answer. We fall into habits, routines, certain ways of doing things that feel comfortable and familiar but that do little to help us spark new ideas and do our best work.

If we want to get outside our heads and connect new and interesting dots, we must seek out those dots. I call this a "stimulus dive." It involves engaging in activities that cause your mind to fire in different ways than it typically would during your normal routine. I've led teams on dumpster dives in New York City to see what new stimuli we could discover (I wouldn't recommend it), and I've sent teams on photography expeditions into a neighborhood to snap just a few pictures that tell the story of their brand. The core principle is that new ideas are unlikely to result from sitting and staring at the problem. You need to get out into the world and allow patterns to emerge and dots to connect.

Brilliant ideas emerge in a place of bounded unfamiliarity. Today, put yourself in a situation where "creative accidents" are more likely to occur.

To spark new insights, put yourself in unusual or even uncomfortable situations.

> **QUESTION**
> When will you do a stimulus dive in the next week? Put a time on the calendar!

July
15

The Trust Balloon

You've probably heard people talk about trust like a bank account. You can put a little trust in and occasionally make a little withdrawal, and as long as you maintain a positive trust balance, you're fine. However, in creative work that's not how trust works. Because doing risky work—projects where your efforts might not pan out in the end—requires you to spend time, energy, and focus now for a potential later payoff, it's important that you are able to trust the character, competence, and intentions of the person who is leading the charge and of those you are collaborating with.

Because of this, I often say that trust is more like a water balloon. You can fill it as full as it can go, but if you puncture it once, even in a tiny way, you are likely to lose it in other areas as well.

The problem is many of us are unaware of places where we might breach the trust of our team or our peers. It's small things we do that cause us to forfeit our relationships with them, like showing up late to a meeting consistently or forgetting to get them something by the deadline we committed to. Over time, these small acts of trust breaking can make it difficult to depend on one another when it matters most.

Most people don't breach trust in the big ways. It's the small things that trip us up. Commit to getting the small things right, and you'll have the trust you need to take creative risks together.

You must earn trust every day.

QUESTION

Is there a small place where you might be breaching trust with your team, your peers, or your friends? How can you remedy it?

July
16

The Second Wall

Beginning a new project can feel daunting. The blank page, endless possibilities, and a concern that a wrong move early in the process can take you off course might leave you struggling to take those first few steps. An object at rest wants to remain at rest. You hit the wall before you even begin.

Then, in the midst of your work, an insight emerges. You make some progress, and you are feeling good about your direction. You finally feel some momentum building. Then you suddenly stall again. You are tired, or you encounter a thorny new problem that needs to be solved, or you somehow lose your passion for the project. You've hit what I call the "second wall." It's the moment when you're tempted to just push the project to completion and get it over with or give up and move on to something else.

It's important to recognize these moments, because they are crucial. When you've arrived at the second wall, you must push through it. Don't stall out at the moment when you're stuck, or you will struggle to reengage with the project the next time you begin your work. When you feel like giving up and moving on, push on for a short while until you feel some momentum building again. Then that momentum will carry you into your next work session.

There are two walls you must surmount in your creative process. The second one is the most challenging.

> **QUESTION:**
> When are you most tempted to give up on your work? Do you ever experience the "second wall"?

July
17

Idea Time

If you really, really wanted to ensure that something happened on a particular day, what would you do? Would you simply try really hard to remember to do it? Would you write it on a Post-it and hope that you'd see it at some point that day?

No, of course not. You would put it on your calendar.

The things that are important to us get coveted space in our schedules. We block time for them, because it's the best way to ensure that they are accomplished.

Yet when it comes to idea generation, we somehow believe that it will simply happen at some point when we least expect it. We hold these mythical ideals of "eureka moments" as uncontrollable, spontaneous strokes of luck. This is untrue. We can increase the likelihood of experiencing them more often.

How? By scheduling time for them. By dedicating blocks on the calendar for thinking about problems and sparking ideas for them. I will often schedule an hour on the calendar with the title "XYZ Training Idea," or "Chapter 21," or something similar. These are placeholders for time to think about and generate ideas for important work I'm accountable for accomplishing.

If it's critical, it goes on your calendar. Block a bit of time today (or this week) to work on ideas for a project that's still unresolved. You'll be surprised at how often creativity shows up right on time when you plan for it.

Don't expect ideas to happen in the cracks and crevices of life.

QUESTION

Which project has open loops that you need to plan time to close? Do it today.

July
18

For the Love

My friend Ben is a brilliant creative director. He has led teams that have produced work that you are almost certainly familiar with and that has been experienced by hundreds of millions of people around the world. He once gave a talk about the nature of creative work, and he asked a provocative question:

"Are you loving people or using people through your work?"

At first, you might be taken aback or even offended by the question, right? I mean, you're a good person. You're doing good work. You're trying to serve your clients. But there's a much more subtle aspect to Ben's question. You see, it's really about generosity vs. manipulation.

If I lead a team and I do things that really serve my best interests rather than those of the team, I'm using my team.

If I'm creating a product and I don't really believe in the claims I make about the product, I'm using my potential customers.

If I'm collaborating with a peer and I win an argument at the expense of our relationship, I'm using them to get my way.

Love doesn't mean that we all get along or that the work is liked by everyone. What it means is that you are aiming to be generous in how you create. You are giving a gift to those who experience what you do. You might get something in return, but it all begins with an act of generosity.

In his excellent book *The Gift*, Lewis Hyde writes, "The more we allow such commodity art to define and control our gifts, the less gifted we will become, as individuals and as a society."

Our job as creative pros is to be generous, to make work that serves those who experience it, and to unleash possibility for others. Let's aim for that as pros and leaders today.

The best creative work unleashes possibility for others.

QUESTION

How can you be generous today through your work?

July
19

Bad Ideas

There's an old cliché about creative work that states, "There's no such thing as a bad idea." It's wrong. So, what do you do when a bad idea is tossed into the ring? Here are a few best-practice suggestions:

- Immediately address the potential merits of the idea. Use phrases such as, "What I like about that is...," and "What's different about that is...," and show how the idea could possibly be used in a productive manner. Don't make the first comment a critique, especially in a group setting.
- Use the merits you suggested as fuel for a new and more productive direction: "What if we used the core of that idea, and instead we..." This way, the person feels like they've made a valuable contribution, but the idea has been reshaped in a way that makes it more valuable to the team.
- Have a rule that no one can shoot down an idea without offering an alternative or building on the existing idea. If the climate in the room is negative, it will squelch the conversation.
- Refocus on objectives. When an idea can't be salvaged or restructured, simply address the fact that it might be valuable in some context but that it doesn't really match the current objectives.

How you handle bad ideas can set the tone for the entire group and subsequently for the effectiveness of your efforts on the project. Set clear objectives, and be brutally honest with one another, but make sure to do it in a way that moves the conversation forward rather than stifling it.

Deal with bad ideas immediately and directly.

> **QUESTION**
> Have you ever had to deal with a bad idea? How did you handle it?

July
20

Drop Your Guard

In *Herding Tigers*, I wrote, "Do you feel the need to power up every time someone disagrees with you or offers disconfirming information? These power plays aren't typically obvious but include subtle hints of your position or importance within the organization. You might rationalize your actions to others by pointing out that they don't have the same information that you do or that you have more experience. You might patronize them and pretend to be listening while sending them subtle signals that you don't respect their opinion."

How receptive are you when someone challenges your perspective?

If you lead or work with bright, talented, capable people, you want them to push you and challenge your ideas. In fact, if they're not doing that, it might speak to a bigger issue of accountability within your organization. (They might not feel it's expected that they bring their perspective!)

However, when you get defensive when someone (respectfully) challenges your idea, you are communicating to them that you don't really want to hear their thoughts, and you aren't willing to rethink your opinion. While you might think defending yourself will bolster your stance, it often has the opposite effect.

Is there a situation in which you tend to get defensive? Do you find yourself pushing back against even the remotest criticism of your ideas?

This week, I challenge you to drop your guard. Recognize that you need a marketplace of ideas to succeed as a team, and the fastest way to squelch those ideas is to dig in your heels and defend your own perspective. Your team and your collaborators will stop trying.

Defensiveness closes your mind to growth.

QUESTION

Is there a particular area of your life or work where you tend to get overly defensive? How can you drop your guard today?

July
21

Embrace the Tension

The one constant you experience as a creative pro is also the one thing that you probably despise the most: tension.

There will rarely be a moment when you aren't weighing the pros and cons of a decision, dealing with a conflict on your team, or trying to figure out how to do what's right for the organization, your client, and your team simultaneously. This is tension.

Now, some people attempt to deal with the tension by ignoring it or by prematurely resolving it. In their insecurity, they are willing to settle for a suboptimal solution and "kick the can down the road" rather than dealing with the discomfort of walking through the season of tension.

Mature creative pros recognize that responsibility means tension. There is no reprieve except to recognize it and walk through it.

Here's my question for you: Is there a place in your work (or leadership) where you are attempting to prematurely resolve tension rather than dealing with it directly?

If so, recognize that the temporary reprieve you feel from pushing off the discomfort will only come back later and probably amplified.

Create means to resolve tension. That is the work of a creative professional. However, you must not try to resolve it prematurely. Resolve it properly and be willing to deal with the discomfort it brings. That's how you get to the value on the other side.

Tension is a necessary part of healthy creating.

QUESTION

Do you ever try to prematurely resolve tension? Why do you think that's the case?

July
22

Reject Perpetual Hustle

I was recently reading *Titan,* the biography of John D. Rockefeller, and came across this quote from the iconic oil tycoon: "It is remarkable how much we all could do if we avoid hustling, and go along at an even pace and keep from attempting too much."

Now, to be clear, Rockefeller certainly did not heed his own advice early in his career. That said, there is much truth in what he said. When you are in a state of perpetual hustle, you often find yourself becoming increasingly efficient at doing decreasingly effective things. You think you're making progress, but in reality, you're only running in place.

Hustle drives you, but rhythm sustains you.

You are not a machine. If you don't care for your mind and your body, sooner or later, something is going to give. You have to build infrastructure into your life to support your ambition, which means taking time to think, cultivating relationships that help you see the world in new ways, and managing your energy so that you are able to perform at critical moments throughout your day. However, when you are in a state of perpetual hustle, you may miss opportunities to shine because you are simply stretched too thin.

Hustle yields incremental results, while rhythm facilitates intuitive leaps.

Yes, work hard. Of course you need to put your full effort into whatever you're doing at any given time. However, be careful not to fall into the hustle trap.

You might find you're only sprinting on a treadmill rather than making true progress.

Reject the cult of perpetual hustle. Build rhythm instead.

QUESTION

Is there any place where you are striving for results, but no matter how much you hustle, you can't achieve a breakthrough? Could it help to step back and approach the work differently?

July
23

When You're Stuck

It's bound to happen sooner or later. No matter how skilled you are and no matter how well you've prepared, you're inevitably going to find yourself stuck on a tough problem without a clear path forward.

Choose a project you're stuck on, and ask these questions:

- ▸ Is an assumption in the way?
- ▸ What is the worst-case scenario?
- ▸ Could I do the opposite?
- ▸ How can I thrill the end user?
- ▸ What am I afraid of?
- ▸ Do I understand why?
- ▸ Where else has something similar been done?
- ▸ What is expected and why?
- ▸ Who is the enemy, and how do we foil them?
- ▸ Who could solve this problem with ease and how?
- ▸ How would my favorite movie character do it?
- ▸ Could I change the medium?
- ▸ Could I ask the question differently?
- ▸ How would a third grader approach this problem?
- ▸ Is there a resource I'm lacking?
- ▸ Who can I call for help?
- ▸ Can I create a metaphor for the problem?
- ▸ How would I start over?
- ▸ What's the primary block and why?

Refuse to remain stuck. Ask new questions to spark new insights.

QUESTION

Is there an assumption you're making that needs to be challenged? How can you unblock yourself?

July
24

Failure Is Not a Name

Imagine you're walking across a rope bridge that you've walked across a hundred times. Suddenly, the planks shift and fall. What you do next is incredibly important: Will you panic and fall? Will you freeze and perish? Or can you find a path forward?

How do you get moving again? You have to tell yourself a story about all the times you've successfully crossed the bridge

If you work long-arc projects, you probably know the frustration and pain of having a project fail to live up to expectations. After expending so much time, energy, and focus on something you care about, it can be devastating when it just doesn't click. What you do next is very important. The story you tell yourself in those moments may define the next few years of your life and work.

Psychologist Martin Seligman explained that there are three ways in which our internal beliefs or narratives become damaging: we make them personal ("I've failed, so I must be a failure."), pervasive ("I failed in this instance, so I'll probably fail in every instance."), and permanent ("I failed once, so I'll probably fail always.")

Of course, each of these three narratives is a lie, but in the moment, they feel very true. The narrative fills the vacuum previously filled by our unmet expectations. It's collateral damage we experience when walking through the refining fires in the depth of the valley of the creative process.

Don't answer to the name "Failure." For better or worse, the story you choose to live out establishes your boundaries.

Failure is not a name to answer to or a badge of shame to wear.

> **QUESTION**
> Is there a false narrative about failure that is preventing you from doing good work?

July
25

The Tyranny of the Adequate

What's the greatest barrier to brilliant work? Adequacy.

Since most of us are being tasked with making more and more with fewer and fewer resources, the first or most reasonable answer is the one that lets us move on to the next project as quickly as we can. We equate moving simply through our work with actual progress.

Frankly, this isn't always the wrong strategy. Sometimes adequate is appropriate. However, not as often as we likely employ it.

Why do we settle so easily?

- *Mind-numbing repetition:* When your work is highly repetitive, it's easy to succumb to a sense that you're being carried along by your work rather than driving it. The counterstrategy is to make sure that you have clearly defined edges for your work (objective and defined success criteria) so that you don't drift with the tide.
- *Fuzzy boundaries and definition:* When accountability is lacking, it's easy to let someone else make the bold decisions. If you want to have a culture in which everyone reaches for brilliance, each person must feel accountable for the end result.
- *Lack of a through line:* Finally, if your tasks lack "connective tissue" to tie them all together into a greater sense of purpose, it's easy to lose your passion. Try to understand the context of your work in the overall why of your role and your organization.

Sure, there are times when it's wise to settle for the most reasonable answer, but don't allow the daily grind to lull you into mediocrity.

Don't fall prey to the tyranny of the adequate.

> **QUESTION**
> Is there a place in your work where you are just settling? What should you do about it?

July
26

Encouragement

Self-centered people are creatively stuck people. They are so focused on what they do and don't have, what others do and don't get, and how credit gets doled out that they have a difficult time celebrating the success of others. Or if they do, it's in a backhanded, "I really wish I didn't have to say this," kind of way.

The best thing you can do for your personal creative energy is to add some to another person. You do this by encouraging them, which literally means to put courage into them. And the word for courage is derived from the word for heart, so you are giving them heart. You are fueling their fire.

Why does fueling someone else's fire give you creative energy? Because it shifts your mind from scarcity to generosity. You begin to think generatively instead of conservatively. There is a multiplier effect, both psychologically and emotionally.

Be free and generous with your encouragement. Write a handwritten note to someone today telling them about a way they've impacted you. Pick up the phone and have a conversation with a peer about work that impressed you. Put courage into someone today.

The best way to build your own creative fire is to stoke someone else's flames.

QUESTION
Who will you encourage today?

July
27

Your Sweet Spot

A theme that I often discover when I meet young creative pros is a fear that they will never discover their "thing." They are worried that they'll somehow fail to deliver the contribution that they are uniquely wired to make and will miss their window of success. They have what I call "purpose paralysis," which is an inability to move forward because they don't know for sure which direction is the right one. So they feel stuck and anxious.

I do believe that everyone has a sweet spot of contribution, where they can have more impact for the same amount of effort than anyone around them. However, I also know that you don't suddenly discover it or figure it out by accident. It comes into focus over time, in layers. Your sweet spot is not like a digital photo; it's more like film that must be developed in a dark room. It takes time, process, and patience. Then, over time, you'll begin to see a pattern forming.

It's important to pay attention to little clues that point you in the direction of your unique genius. What are you able to do that others marvel at but seems commonplace to you? Where do you seem to get more return for your effort than others do? What work brings you to life?

As you begin to note these moments in your life and work, you'll begin to recognize where you should spend more time and energy each day.

Remember, friends: you'll discover your unique genius over time, not all at once.

QUESTION

Is there any place in your work where you are experiencing purpose paralysis? How can you take a step forward, even in the midst of your uncertainty?

July
28

Hunting Trails

Our neighbors have an outdoor cat named Leo. Several times a day, Leo will stop by my home office window to say hello.

Well, at least that's what I like to think she's doing. In reality, Leo is on the hunt. She loves to explore the bushes in front of our home for small game. In fact, Leo has a defined hunting trail that she follows each day that runs in front of our house, around the side, through the neighbor's landscaping and around their house, past the bushes in our side yard, back to the firewood pile, then finally into the woods where I assume her trail continues.

Leo follows this path because it's been a successful one for her. She routinely finds what she's looking for. She doesn't invent a new path every day, hoping that somehow she will discover a chipmunk.

As creative pros, we can learn a lot from Leo's habits. We need to establish well-defined hunting trails that help us spark new ideas. This means having sources that we routinely check for insights, habits, and rituals that help us review our notes and make new connections, or places we go that introduce new and valuable stimuli.

As you consider your life and work patterns, where are your hunting trails? Which of them can you build into your life to help you have ideas more consistently? Be like Leo—hunt where there is likely to be game.

Plant yourself in the places where great ideas are likely to occur.

QUESTION

What sources of inspiration, habits, or places tend to spark new ideas for you? How can you build them into your routine each day?

July
29

Waiting for Permission

It is easier to blame others than it is to assume responsibility for results. Now, most of us don't overtly blame others for our own shortcomings. We are far too subtle and clever for that. Instead, we develop narratives that grant us permission to avoid anything that might fail.

We would rather live with the delusion of invulnerability than test our limits and discover that we actually have some.

One narrative that we adopt is "as soon as...":

"As soon as my manager seems to be in a good mood, I'll..."

"As soon as I get all my things in order, I'll..."

"As soon as I have a perfect strategy, I'll..."

We are waiting. But what are we really waiting for? If we're honest, we're waiting for someone to give us permission to take the risk. Many people spend their entire lives and careers waiting, and that permission never comes.

Stop waiting for permission as a means to avoid taking risks.

QUESTION

Are you waiting for permission before doing something you know you should do? Take a step today.

July
30

A Little More Definition

One reason we get stuck looking for a creative breakthrough is that our minds need more clarity about what—precisely—we are trying to do. When something is too familiar, we tend to make assumptions or develop shortcuts to get us where we know we are headed. However, those shortcuts and assumptions can limit where we look for new and fresh ideas.

When you feel stuck, step back and ask yourself, "What am I *really* trying to do here?"

Answer in as few words as possible. Be precise. Speak in concrete terms and specifics. Get to the real heart of the problem. (It's possible that it's changed since you began the project!)

The better you get at identifying the core problem, the more effective you will be at generating ideas.

When you're stuck, give the problem a better definition.

QUESTION

Is there a problem you're stuck on right now? How might you redefine it?

July
31

Optimism vs. Wishful Thinking

Wouldn't it be great if you didn't have to do anything at all, yet all your work showed up completed each day, in a neat, organized pile, ready for your manager or client to review?

Actually, no. That would be terrible. It seems like it would be wonderful, but the reality is that you need to experience struggle and tension to feel alive. There is no growth without tension. There is no gratification without challenge.

Optimism is a belief in a better possible future, knowing that it might require some work to achieve. Wishful thinking is lazy optimism that wants everything to just happen. Optimism is willing to put in the work, while wishful thinking wants to live with the delusion that things will just work out.

We need optimism to do creative work. Without it, we cannot take intuitive leaps. But we are still responsible for the work necessary to bring our vision into being.

Believe in a better possible future, then develop a plan to bring it about.

Optimism is creative fuel. Wishful thinking is lazy optimism.

QUESTION

Are you falling into the trap of wishful thinking? Where do you need a plan vs. a dream?

August

"Be regular and orderly in your life...so that you may be violent and original in your work."
—GUSTAVE FLAUBERT

If everything in your world is chaos, you cannot focus your finite time, attention, and energy on the work that truly matters. Instead, you will waste valuable resources trying to put things in order just so you can begin. This month, focus effort on bringing order to areas of your life or work that are misaligned, disordered, or chaotic.

August

1

Clear the Decks

Have you ever seen that famous photograph of Albert Einstein's office, taken the day after he died? It's made the rounds in creative circles as an example of what genius looks like at work. Piles of books and papers, disorganized files lying about, and no space to set anything on the desk.

Yes, that's fine. It's true that the creative process can be messy and disorganized. Right up until his death, Einstein was working on a grand unification theory to unite all the underlying laws of physics. It was heady stuff, and he must have known that he was running short on time.

But I think many people use examples like this as a justification for being disorganized and messy. It's not that the mess leads to the creativity; it's that the creativity generates the mess, which then must be reorganized.

One trick that I've found tremendously helpful is fairly simple: when I don't know what to do next, I clean. I find something to organize, file, put away, tuck into a drawer. I organize my desk or my computer desktop. I do something to bring a little more order to my world.

The funny thing is, in the process of doing that, I often experience a creative spark. Order often yields chaos, but it's rare that chaos leads to order.

When you have a few minutes today while thinking about a project or how to reply to an email, spend that time organizing or cleaning your workspace. You might find that the additional order makes even your thoughts clearer.

When you don't know what to do, organize.

QUESTION

Is there anything in your life that needs to be ordered right now?

August
2

This Might Not Work

In an interview with author Seth Godin for my podcast, he introduced a phrase that has since become a personal mantra: *this might not work.* It's something that I say whenever I'm working on a new project or a new idea, giving a new speech, or trying a new medium. This phrase embraces the reality that all creative efforts confront the possibility of failure, but only because they are difficult.

All the easy things have been done. What's left—and what's valuable—are the hard things. And there is no guarantee of success when doing difficult, uncertain work.

So "this might not work" becomes a kind of permission slip to try hard things without worrying about the consequences. You can always recover from a short-term failure, but if you choose to shun risk over the long term, you will most certainly fail in much, much more important ways.

Today, embrace the ethic of "this might not work."

Failure is rarely fatal. Never failing almost certainly is.

QUESTION

Where are you paralyzed by a fear of short-term failure? What step can you take toward progress today, with the mindset of "this might not work"?

August

3

Slow, Steady, Deliberate

How many times have you heard the phrase "slow and steady wins the race" trumpeted as a recipe for success?

The problem? While in essence, it's a solid principle, the way it's applied is often more harmful than helpful. Slow and steady definitely do not win the race alone. Slow, steady, and deliberate wins the race when punctuated by occasional sprints.

It's not enough to make daily, measured progress on your work if it's not deliberate progress. If you're not moving in a meaningful direction, then failure is a likely outcome. While most creative professionals know this, it often doesn't affect how we approach our work. Instead of defining our work effectively, we are carried along by its flow from day to day. Instead of clearly defining the problems we are trying to solve, we think in terms of big, conceptual challenges and thus set ourselves up for failure from the start.

Define what meaningful progress means today.

Don't be lulled into the idea that being busy and making progress are necessarily going to net you a win. You must be deliberate about your activity, and you have to be willing to sprint when the occasion calls for it.

Steady, measured progress (with occasional sprints) is the key to success.

> **QUESTION**
> Are you frantically approaching your work, filling days with busywork? How can you be more deliberate in your approach?

August
4

Don't Let Your Rituals Become Ruts

"A rut is just a grave with open ends." I remember hearing this phrase growing up, but I never fully understood what it meant until I entered the workplace. The mandatory meetings, problems to solve that felt more like irrelevant nuisances, and difficulty focusing on the work a manager removed from my day-to-day deemed most critical. That's when I learned that a ritual is a rail, *not* a magic formula.

Simply changing your circumstances or your productivity system might inject a measure of energy into your work and give you a boost for a short while, but that increase in output will be short-lived if you aren't committed to an outcome. Your systems and rituals exist only to serve the outcome you're trying to achieve. They are not an end but a set of guide rails to help you channel energy toward your goals. There is no magic bullet for creativity or productivity, only tendencies and rhythms. Ask yourself these questions:

- ► What outcome are you trying to achieve today?
- ► How can your routines/rituals be better channeled to help you achieve it?
- ► Which routines/rituals are undeniably in the way of it?

Rituals are more than just repetitive behavior. They carve out space to be filled by more substantial activity. They are open ends that facilitate the closing of creative loops. However, don't allow them to become mindless, distracting behavior, or they will drain the focus and energy out of your day. **Your rituals exist to serve you, not the other way around.**

> **QUESTION**
> How can you adapt your rituals and rhythms to better serve your goals?

August
5

Set Up for Another Year

A few years ago, I caught a short segment on the British Invasion on CNN (the musical one, not the military one), and I was snapped out of my half-attentive state by an interview with Mick Jagger of the Rolling Stones.

He was asked how long he thought the Stones could continue their run of success. His answer?

"I think we're pretty well set up for at least another year."

Did I mention that this was said by Mick Jagger in 1965?

In retrospect, statements like this seem ridiculous. Every big success appears inevitable after the fact. However, work that eventually becomes recognized as great rarely feels inevitable while you're engaged in the process of making it. Brilliant work is sometimes launched more with a shrug of the shoulders than a fist in the air. (Is this good? Not sure—I'm too deep into it.)

This is why expectation escalation can be so destructive to the creative process. When you compare your in-process work with the best of whatever is out there, it can squelch the very process that you need to deliver your best. You must allow yourself to live with the fragility and angst of whether the work will be successful. Ultimately, that's not your decision anyway.

And that is, I think, the genius of Jagger's response. He didn't seem too interested in the question. I really think he was giving it all he had to make the music great and to make the ride last as long as possible, whether a year or five or fifty.

Don't believe the lie that success feels inevitable to the successful. On the inside, where all the risk is being taken, it often feels like things could fall apart at any moment, and that's precisely how it should be.

Success only seems inevitable after the fact.

> **QUESTION**
> Are you allowing expectation escalation to cause you to feel your work isn't good enough?

August
6

What If It Were Easy?

When confronted with a difficult creative challenge, it's tempting to dive in and start building or making something without first stepping back to think strategically about the best way to approach it.

On his podcast, Tim Ferriss once shared a question that helped him find more clarity in his work. He said that when he feels overwhelmed by a project, he asks, "What would this look like if it were easy?" This is not a lazy question. He isn't implying that the work shouldn't require effort. Rather, he is asking how his approach to the work might be simpler so that he can pour his problem-solving efforts into the work itself instead of wasting mental cycles resolving the complexity of the process.

As you consider your work today, pause and ask, "What would this look like if it were easy?" Is there a way to simplify the process or the objectives so that you aren't wasting energy doing work that provides little return on your effort?

Simplicity of process yields complex, interesting ideas.

QUESTION
What would it look like if it were easy?

August

7

Be a Beginner

Sometimes experience is your worst enemy. While having a broad base of past work can help you form connections and make intuitive leaps, it can also cause you to make assumptions about what is and isn't possible and can limit the ideas you are willing to explore. Your own experiences can box you in and cause you to miss brilliant ideas that are right in front of you because you're looking past them.

This is especially true when you've experienced a degree of success in your life and work. Once you have something to protect, it can be difficult to take small risks that might put your reputation in jeopardy.

As you consider your work today, think about how you can become a beginner again. Ask: "What might I do if I didn't know what I know?" or "What assumption am I making that needs to be challenged?"

The beauty of being a beginner is that you don't know what you don't know. And that can mean new pathways to explore and unexpected dots to connect.

When we shed the assumptions and residue born from our experiences, we see our work in new and exciting ways.

QUESTION
How can you approach your work like a beginner today?

August
8

The Black Box Phenomenon

There's a dynamic in every organization that I like to call the "black box" phenomenon. All the decisions are made among a small group of leaders, then someone comes out of the black box and begins issuing orders: "Joe, do this. Jill, do that. Mark, you do the other thing." Then they go away, and everyone is left wondering, "Why are we doing this?"

It is difficult for talented people to do their best work when they don't understand why they are being asked to do it. To bring your full creative effort each day, you need to know not just what is expected of you but why it matters. I'm not talking about why in the grand existential sense ("Why am I here on this planet?") but in the very practical, tactical sense. If you understand the problem you're actually being asked to solve and why that problem matters, it allows you to think differently about it.

Today, be mindful of any work you're being asked to do for which the why isn't clear. It's your job to clarify that "why" so that you can approach that work more meaningfully.

It's difficult to fully engage your work if you don't understand why it matters.

> **QUESTION**
> Is there any work you're currently doing for which the why isn't clearly defined?

August

9

Defining the Edges

Imagine that you are about to run a race. As you step up to the starting line, you can't see the finish line, so you turn to the person next to you and ask, "How long is this race?"

"I don't know," they reply. "We just keep running until they tell us to stop."

That would be silly. There can be no race without defined terms of engagement. But we often do a similar thing in our work. We lack clear edges. We don't know how to tell when something is complete. Instead, we keep working until we run out of time or money or until someone else tells us to stop.

This is what often happens when we think about our work in terms of projects to do instead of problems to solve. Projects are open ended. They can always be made better or more complete, which is a challenge to creative pros, especially if they struggle with perfectionism. "Is this finished?" is a difficult question to answer. However, it's much easier to answer, "Did I solve the problem?" If so, then the work is complete.

As you consider today's work, have you clearly defined the problems that you're trying to solve? If not, how can you clearly define them so that you have clear edges for your work.

Your mind isn't wired to do projects. It's wired to solve problems.

QUESTION
How can you break up your important work today into problems to be solved instead of projects to accomplish?

August
10

On Mosquitoes

What are you actually paid for? More importantly, how much time do you spend doing that thing versus the hundred other things that often fill your day?

If you looked at where most creative pros' time goes, you'd think they were paid for answering emails or sitting in meetings. But in reality, you're being paid for the value you create each day. This is the bet that your company is making: that you'll provide more value for them than what they are paying you.

David Allen wrote, "Mosquitoes can ruin the hunt for big game." When you spend your day swatting away mosquitoes, you might miss the big game that's right in front of you. The big idea. The dots waiting to be connected. The intuitive leap that requires just a small amount of focused energy to get to.

Are you allowing those small, pesky tasks to prevent you from creating the value you're actually being paid for? If I looked at where you spend your time, what would I think your job is?

Yes, we all have to do things we'd rather not do. However, make sure that you are blocking significant segments of time for the work that you're actually accountable for.

Don't let the mosquitoes ruin your hunt for big game.

Small, pesky tasks can add up to big creative blocks.

QUESTION

How can you block time off today to spend uninterrupted on your most important work?

August
11

The Weight of What's Undone

Pause for a minute. Think about whatever is stressing you out the most at the moment. While I don't know exactly what you do for a living, I can almost guarantee that your answer has something to do with an uncertainty that has yet to be resolved.

It could be a project that you need a great idea for.

It could be a relationship that is strained and where you don't know the right path forward.

It could be a career move that you feel compelled to make but don't yet have a clear direction.

Whatever it is, I suspect that it has less to do with the stress of doing the work than it does with the weight of all that's left undone.

The problem is, you can't control that unresolved uncertainty. You don't know when the ideas are going to come, and you can't force them even if you wanted to. Thus the stress.

Make a list of all the things that are stressing you. Star the ones that you can actually do something about, then put time on your calendar to make progress. The best antidote to the weight of all that's undone is to plan for when it will get done.

And for those things you can't control, resolve not to stress about them but to instead be patient, look for dots to connect, and commit to act when an insight emerges. Don't stress about what you can't control.

When doing creative work, the greatest stress often comes not from the work itself but from the weight of all that's left to do.

QUESTION

Are you stressed about things you can do something about or things that are outside your control?

August
12

Looking Over Your Shoulder

One year, for my birthday, my wife found a complete set of posters from the Apple "Think Different" campaign. The posters featured artistic and cultural luminaries who shunned conventional approaches and carved their own paths. I thought these posters might make a nice addition to our offices, so I had them framed and placed them in strategic spots throughout the building as a way to keep the team inspired.

One day, a team member knocked on my office door. He asked me for a favor: Could I please remove the poster of Alfred Hitchcock that was hanging just outside his workspace?

I was puzzled because I knew that this person was deeply inspired by Hitchcock. That's why I placed the poster by his workspace. "That's the problem," he told me. "Every time I edit a video, I feel like Hitchcock is looking over my shoulder and judging me." Ah, OK, fair point. I took down the poster.

It's easy to allow comparison with the heroes of our craft to cause us to become paralyzed. Nothing ever feels good enough. It never feels like it will measure up to the work of others that we admire. What we forget is that all that deeply admired work was once a messy work in process just like ours. And our heroes probably felt the same way we do.

Don't compare your in-process work with someone else's masterpiece.

Don't become paralyzed through comparison with your heroes.

QUESTION

Are you frustrated that your current work doesn't meet the standards you expect? How can you make a little progress today?

August
13

Buffers

Who decided that meetings should be sixty minutes by default? Microsoft? Google?

For some reason, that seems to be the standard. If two people set up a meeting, it seems it's almost always sixty minutes. The problem is that means that you're likely running from that meeting to the next one, which also starts at the top of the hour. And then the next one.

There's no room to breathe. There's no buffer.

The same principle applies to the beginning and end of our days as well. We often rush straight into our work and race screaming out of it at the end of the day with no space to prepare or decompress. Again, we need buffers.

I encourage you to look at your schedule over the coming week and consider how you might carve out little pockets of time "in between." Give yourself space to prepare, think, ramp up and down, and not run from obligation to obligation.

We need space between to remain prolific, brilliant, and healthy.

QUESTION

How can you add a little space in between today? This week? This month?

August
14

Freewriting

What is on your mind right now?

Actually, you may not even *know*. That's often the case for professionals. In the flurry of activity and the myriad open loops you have yet to resolve, your mind is bouncing from thought to thought, and it can be easy to overlook the valuable creative patterns that are forming just beneath the surface of your conscious processing.

One very valuable tool that helps unlock those deeper thoughts is freewriting. This involves taking a dedicated amount of time—ten or fifteen minutes—to just write about whatever comes to mind. There is no editing, no forethought, and no intent of sharing your writing with others. The idea is to simply empty your mind on paper, then to see what's there.

You will be quite surprised at the nuggets of insight, concerns, and hidden feelings that show up during your freewriting sessions. They are also likely to yield breakthroughs from time to time, especially if you engage in the practice consistently.

Schedule some time today, or this week, to freewrite. Put on paper whatever comes to mind, and don't self-edit.

Taking a few minutes to let your mind wander through the written word can expose hidden creative insights.

QUESTION

Have you ever had an idea suddenly emerge in the midst of writing? How did it happen?

August
15

Don't Give Up Before It Gets Good

Some people say the hardest part of any creative project is the beginning. And some say it's the end. I disagree with both.

I believe the hardest part is squarely in the middle.

You have so much invested that it's difficult to turn back, but you aren't yet close enough to the end that you clearly see the payoff for your efforts. You are in a deep gray zone where the only path forward involves a tremendous amount of work and no promise of glory.

It's in these moments that many people give up on a project. You see, at the beginning of the work, we have the excitement, newness, and potential to keep us motivated. At the end, we are starting to clearly see the finished result. But in the middle, when everything is still forming, the work itself must sustain us. We must learn to fall in love with the process, not the outcome.

You may be tempted to quit a project you're working on right now because you're squarely in the middle and it's getting too difficult. You may even be tempted to justify quitting by switching to another project that provides that early-stage shot of excitement. But how many brilliant works of art or incredible products or world-class organizations will never be seen by human eyes because someone gave up before it got good?

Persist, friend. The hardest part of any work is squarely in the middle. And we're all right there with you right now.

Don't give up before it gets good.

QUESTION

Are you tempted to quit a project right now? What can you do to inject new energy into the work or to fall in love with the process?

August
16

Note Mining

Imagine what it would be like if every time a surgeon went in to perform an appendectomy, she started from scratch. She just forgot everything she knew about performing surgery and instead picked up a textbook and started reading about the process, how to use the surgical tools, how to make an incision, etc. It would be silly and impossible to do so, right?

Yet when you solve creative problems, you probably often do this exact thing. You have an entire library of experiences at your fingertips, yet how often do you leverage them?

There is something I call the "creative trash heap," and it's full of old insights, ideas, and solutions that might have been valuable but just weren't right for the situation. These discarded ideas fill your notebooks, your files, your hard drive. They are just looking for the right situation to be used. But you will never rediscover them if you don't routinely make it a practice to review your notes and mine them for gems.

I encourage you to spend some time today going back through some of your old notes and project notebooks to see what hidden gems are in them that you've long forgotten about.

You've probably already had the brilliant insight you're looking for. You just weren't ready for it.

QUESTION

How can you establish a practice of regularly reviewing your old notes and ideas?

August
17

The Value of Copying

What's the worst comment you can make about a piece of creative work?

Probably, "That looks just like..."

No one wants to be accused of copying others. And yet that's precisely how we begin the process of developing our own voice. We look to others who are already doing what we want to do, imitate them, learn from their style and experience, then over time begin to take small risks and find unique ways of expressing ourselves. This is true of everything from design to writing to management styles. Most early managers largely imitate their own managers prior to figuring out how to find their own leadership style. It's perfectly natural to do so.

If you feel stuck or want to develop a new skill, the best way to do it is to find someone who is already great at that skill and simply copy them. (A quick caveat: Don't do this in public work or work for hire! We're not talking about plagiarism but about skill development.)

Imitation is, indeed, the best form of flattery. It's also the first step toward growing as a professional and, eventually, being someone who is copied by others.

We develop our craft through strategic copying.

QUESTION

Who does work you admire, and what elements of their work can you copy and practice to help you develop your own voice?

August
18

Pep Talk vs. Prep Talk

In one of my all-time favorite *Saturday Night Live* sketches, Chris Farley plays the role of motivational speaker Matt Foley. Some well-meaning parents have brought him into their home to motivate their children to take school more seriously, and Farley spends his time with the children yelling at them, trying to amp them up, and warning them that if they don't get serious, they'll end up living in "a van down by the river" like him.

I've spent a lot of time speaking to organizations, and I have to confess that at times, I empathize with the Matt Foley character. Managers will often tell me that they are bringing me in to "motivate" their team members, but I always warn them ahead of time that that's not what I do.

Instead of a pep talk, most professionals actually need a prep talk. They need to be prepared to *bring* motivation to their work instead of waiting for the work to motivate them. Once they understand the subtle forces that drive their best, most engaged moments, they understand that it's not the tasks they do that motivate them or even some pithy slogan but how their unique motivation interacts with those tasks that is critical.

As you consider moments of peak engagement from your past, what is the common thread? Why were those moments so motivating and gratifying? And how can you craft more of those kinds of moments in your work today?

Stop waiting for your work to motivate you. Bring motivation to your work.

QUESTION

What are the common themes within your moments of deep engagement in life and work? Is it that you felt challenged? Worked with others? Taught something? How can you craft more of those moments today?

August
19

Serve Somebody

Who are the most *miserable* people you know?

OK, that might not be a fair question. And while it's unlikely that I know the person who immediately came to your mind, I want to predict that I know something about them: they are very self-centered.

The most miserable professionals I encounter are those who are only about one person: themselves. They feel like they're getting the short end of the stick. They never get what other people are getting. They blame the client anytime something goes wrong. And whenever credit is being doled out for work well done, they are always there to ensure that they get what they "deserve."

When you are self-centered, your world becomes a smaller and smaller set of concentric circles centered only on you. Your perspective. Your worldview. Your best interests. And eventually, you will get stuck. Stew on the perceived injustice for long enough, and it will take over your mind, leaving no space for creativity to flourish.

The antidote? As we've discussed before: generosity. Service. Doing things for others with no expectation of reciprocity.

Today, focus on doing something to serve another person. Offer to get them coffee. Give them credit for something they did. Write a note of encouragement. The funny thing is, when you commit to building into others, you will often find that you receive far more in return. Not just the feeling of having done something good but in real, tangible creative insight. It unlocks something in your mind.

Creativity thrives in the fertile field of generosity.

To get unstuck, get outside yourself.

QUESTION
How can you serve someone else today?

August
20

Develop a Root System

Imagine a tree in the middle of a rocky field. The soil is tough, and growing roots is a challenge. In the field next to it, there's an oak tree growing tall in the middle of a beautiful pasture with soft, rich soil and plenty of water.

Which tree will thrive?

The answer is both. Why? Because trees adapt and grow in the spot where they are planted. The tree in the rough soil will grow roots that circumvent the rocks and eventually reach the subterranean water and nutrients it needs to survive. The tree in the fertile field will grow roots as well, though it will not have to adapt in the same way.

It's tempting to wish that you were planted in a more fertile field. Maybe you don't like your manager, or you are surrounded by people who don't share your vision or ethics, or your organization isn't growing in the way it should.

There may come a time when it's necessary to replant yourself. However, don't do it until you've done all you can to grow in the spot you are planted. Every adversity is an opportunity for you to learn something, adapt, and develop new skills and a more resilient mindset.

Before you seek a new field, make sure you've grown all you can in the spot you're planted.

Grow in the spot you are planted.

QUESTION

How can you leverage your current situation for growth?

August
21

Opportunity Spotting

Despite "timing is everything" being a popular admonition, it's wrong. It's not timing alone that makes for creative or professional success. It's also intuition. And the biggest element of creative intuition is the ability to recognize an opportunity when it presents itself.

It's the ability to spot the aha moment. It's the capacity to recognize when dots connect and puzzle pieces snap into place. But many people miss it because they aren't even looking for it.

The unique challenge of doing complex, creative work is that focus must be both micro and macro. You must be able to zero in on a specific task and understand precisely what's required to accomplish it, but you must also be able to zoom out and understand that task in the grand scope of the bigger problem you're trying to solve.

When you become so fixated on the micro, you might miss the macro. You will overlook bigger patterns that begin to overlap or two converging problems that initially seemed like separate issues but now are one and the same.

As you consider your work today, take some time to zoom out and consider the problem you're actually trying to solve. Have you learned anything recently that might change your perspective on the work? Are there any new patterns that are beginning to emerge? Has there been any new communication that might present an opportunity for you?

Don't get so caught up in the micro that you miss big opportunities.

Most people miss opportunities because they haven't learned to spot them.

QUESTION

As you zoom out from the work you're doing, what opportunities do you see?

August
22

Commonplace Book

Brilliant creative pros are typically skilled collectors of inspiration. They clip things from magazines, have a repository of screenshots on their desktop, or keep a text file (or even boxes of index cards) full of quotes for future use. This repository is called a "commonplace book," and in some form, it's been practiced for centuries by some of the most recognized creatives, scientists, and leaders.

The benefits of a commonplace book are countless. It provides something to peruse when you are in need of inspiration. It reminds you of old ideas that weren't quite right at the moment but might be ready for primetime now. And it is a kind of record of your creative and intellectual curiosity over time.

Whether you choose to do it digitally (I do) or physically, start keeping a commonplace book. Add to it whenever you come across something that piques your interest or that inspires you. Keep your own fragments of ideas inside it, especially if they aren't quite ready to be seen by the world. Then make it a practice to review your commonplace book regularly to spark new insights.

We learn within the context of what we already know. We create within the context of what has already inspired us.

Keep inspirational items in a place where you can review them often.

QUESTION
What should you add to your commonplace book today?

August
23

Perceived Consequences

It's not true risk that inhibits creativity but perceived risk. We artificially escalate the perceived consequences of failure to the point where we don't act. We don't take little creative risks that are necessary to intuit larger possible creative leaps. Instead, we cower under the illusion of what will happen if we don't get it right.

"I'll lose my job."

"They'll laugh at me."

"I'll lose their respect."

"I'll never work again."

These kinds of narratives take root and justify our lack of creative risk, often causing us to live out a self-fulfilling prophecy. We don't want to fall, so we don't leap, so we do what's expected, so we fail. This is the paradox of how we often respond to fear: our timid response causes us to experience the very thing we were afraid of to begin with.

To loosen the grip of fear, we must change the narratives. We must notice the difference between perceived consequences of failure and likely consequences of failure. There are consequences to be sure, but they are often far less devastating than the ones that fear is whispering in your ear.

Fear thrives in the dark. Bringing your fears out into the light will often cause them to dissipate.

QUESTION

What fear or narrative is keeping you from taking a creative risk?

August
24

Your Pillars

What are you known for? Is there a kind of work, whether inside your organization or outside, for which you are the first call someone makes?

Everyone has unique "pillars" that stand in representation of their personal brand. They are the qualities of expression that stand out from everyone else and make them truly unique. It could be a particular way in which you think about a problem, a skill that you have that others don't, or a gift of wordsmithing that allows you to express something in a few words while others need a paragraph.

These pillars are your unique currency. Only you have it to spend, and you should leverage it whenever you can. Don't waste time trying to do things that anyone could do. Focus on the things that truly make you unique.

Take some time today to consider a few qualities that you possess that few others around you do. Then consider how you can leverage them in your work.

To succeed in life, you must identify the "pillars" that make you unique. Take time to consider why you stand out from the pack.

QUESTION

What are the unique pillars that make you different from others in your field?

August
25

Precision

Consider the most effective leader you know. Why are they so great at their work? I'm certain words like *competence, curiosity,* and *trustworthiness* come to mind, and those qualities are definitely important. But there is another quality of effective leaders that we often overlook: precision.

Good leaders, especially those who lead creative work, are precise about their expectations. They are precise in how they communicate with their team. They are precise in how they share feedback about the work. There is little ambiguity in their communication.

When their work is complex, many leaders become unclear in how they communicate. They want to hedge their bets in case they are wrong, so they lack precision.

Great leaders, on the other hand, are clear even when they are uncertain. This is also true of creative pros and the work they produce. They have a clear point of view even when they are uncertain that point of view is the right one.

To be effective as a creative pro, you must communicate and create with precision even when you are uncertain.

QUESTION

Where do you lack precision in your communication, your relationships, your work? How can you exhibit more precision today and be clear even when you are uncertain?

August
26

Crisis Phase

There are distinct phases of growth that we go through as we develop our skills and our craft. First, we typically imitate others as a way to build our basic platform for expression. This is how we master the basic elements of the craft. Then, we diverge as we begin to find our own voice and apply it in our work. This is when we may begin to experience success in our field, as we make a unique mark and deliver a unique contribution.

But then we hit what I call the "crisis" phase. This is when we suddenly realize that even though our work is fine, that it's delivering on expectations, and that everyone around us seems happy with our efforts, we feel stuck. We're doing the same things we've always done, and we're doing them well, but we no longer feel challenged. We're stuck.

To move beyond the crisis phase, you must go back to the beginning of the growth curve, choose a new skill to learn, and begin to imitate others again as you learn the skill. You must return to a beginner mindset.

Don't remain stuck in crisis phase. If you are not growing—developing new skills—your effectiveness will begin to wane.

The skill that you are known for today is unlikely to sustain you tomorrow. You must continue to grow.

QUESTION

What new skill would invigorate you and help you find new depths of engagement and effectiveness in your work?

August

27

Giving Feedback

No one likes delivering uncomfortable feedback to a peer or team member. It's difficult to look someone in the eyes and tell them that they've failed. However, candid feedback is necessary to build trust and ensure a healthy, well-functioning team.

When delivering feedback, ensure that you first turn the microscope on yourself. Were your expectations clear? Were they realistic? You cannot hold someone accountable for your own shortcomings.

Then distinguish between effort feedback and execution feedback. Was the failure the result of a good idea poorly executed or a bad idea well executed? If you are trying sufficiently difficult work, you will eventually fail in some way. However, failure of effort cannot be tolerated. This is the difference between a teaching moment (a bad idea well executed) and a corrective moment (a good idea poorly executed).

Finally, as discussed a few entries ago, always strive to be precise. "It's just not working for me" is not good feedback. You should aim to be clear, even when you are not perfectly certain of the right approach. Your collaborators need to know which target they are aiming for.

Clear, candid feedback makes the collaborative process more efficient. Make sure you deliver it with empathy but more importantly that you deliver it at all.

QUESTION

Is there any feedback you need to offer someone today but have been avoiding?

August
28

Discipline

Some people are just disciplined, and others aren't, right? Not exactly.

Most people you think of as disciplined aren't naturally that way. They—like everyone—would tend to default back to the most comfortable state if allowed to do so. The reason that they don't is that they have practices that prevent them from doing so.

Several years ago, I decided I was going to write every day. It's not always easy, and often the results are not up to my standard, but that matters little. What matters is that I engage in the discipline every day, because over time the quality of the work will take care of itself if I simply choose to practice my craft each day.

That's how discipline with creative work functions. If you establish a set of activities that you do every single day, it will begin to feel odd when you don't do them. Maybe it's a certain word count that you want to hit with your writing, a conversation that you have with your manager every day, or an expectation about how you close open loops with your teammates. Regardless of what the practice is, doing it consistently will become the expectation for you. And over time, others will begin to think you are one of those magically disciplined people.

Your practices provide the infrastructure for creative discipline.

QUESTION

What activity do you need to engage in every single day, no matter what?

August
29

Be Brave

What creative bravery is:

Bravery is doing the right thing, even when it's the uncomfortable thing. It's needed now more than ever in the marketplace, in the political realm, and in our schools and neighborhoods. *Most* bravery in the world is exhibited in small, everyday actions, not big efforts.

Bravery is a choice, not a trait. People who choose to do the right thing in the face of personal cost are choosing to sacrifice their life and comfort for a better future. Bravery is always empathetic. It's about the other, not about yourself. Bravery is action in spite of fear. People who act bravely feel fear and insecurity as much as everyone else. It's just that they choose cause over comfort. Bravery is willingness to fail in the pursuit of what matters.

What creative bravery is not:

Bravery is not stupid risk. A brave person counts the cost and decides to act because the cost of inaction is simply too vast to bear. Bravery is not bravado. Many people (especially some politicians) love to put bluster ahead of action. However, brave people do not feel the need to posture. Instead, they allow their actions to speak for themselves. They are fine being misunderstood, and even unliked if that's the cost of right action. Bravery is not for a select few. There are opportunities to be brave everywhere and every day. Bravery is not anonymous or remote action. Lobbing insults or politically correct attacks on someone from afar is not bravery. Stepping into their world, looking them in the eye, and learning to love what you don't understand is.

Be brave today, friends.

QUESTION

Where do you need to choose to be brave today in your life or work?

August
30

Assumptions

"What if this wasn't true?"

In the midst of a project, this can be one of the most powerful questions you ask. Often, we overlook key assumptions because we are so deep into the work that we can't see outside the grooves. That's when we begin to make key assumptions that limit how we think about ideas and possibilities. We miss obvious patterns that others, with less experience, might be more apt to see.

A way to avoid this trap is to routinely challenge assumptions, even if they're likely to prove true. It can seem inefficient in the moment to do so, which is why many won't do it, but when you stumble on a false assumption that's been blinding you, it's like discovering a diamond mine in your own backyard.

Consider a key problem you're working on at the moment but are still looking for a needed breakthrough. Now, as you think about the problem, consider any assumptions you are making about how to solve it. (There are many, for sure.) Are there certain methods that you keep going back to, wells of inspiration that are running a little dry, or rules that you are operating under that may no longer be relevant?

Once you've identified one or more, ask, "What if this wasn't true?" You will be surprised at the ideas that arise.

Don't allow assumptions to limit where you look for ideas. Challenge them.

QUESTION
What assumption will you challenge today?

August
31

Crafting Accidents

If you wish to be brilliant at a moment's notice, you must begin far upstream from the moment you need a brilliant idea. I call this process crafting "dangerous intersections" where "creative accidents" are likely to occur. (See my book *The Accidental Creative*.)

- ► Block regular, disciplined time to absorb a wide range of stimulus related to your field, Also, ensure that you are regularly absorbing stimulus that stokes your creative wonder.
- ► Don't just pay attention to the work in your industry but spend time asking why those particular decisions were made. What are the deeper themes within the work? How can you improve upon them?
- ► What assumptions are others making in their work? How can those be challenged?
- ► What assumptions might you be making in your work? How can those be challenged?

Consistently carve time in your schedule to think not just about the *work*, but about how you are *approaching* the work. Fill your mind with valuable stimulus. Do thought experiments. Challenge assumptions. You increase your chances of experiencing creative accidents.

To experience breakthroughs when they matter most, place yourself at "dangerous intersections" where ideas are likely to collide.

QUESTION

How can you be more intentional about your creative process today? This week?

September

*"I love inventing names, but I also collect unusual
names, so that I can look through my notebook
and choose one that suits a new character."*
—J. K. ROWLING

While they often seem to appear from nowhere, brilliant creative insights are the result of patterns suddenly becoming clear or dots suddenly connecting. Be mindful this month of collecting dots that could benefit a future project or shape a creative insight. Put them somewhere you'll see them often, and play with ideas as often as you can.

September

1

A Better Way to Brainstorm

Think back to any team brainstorm you've ever been a part of. What happened? Probably some version of this:

- Someone writes a problem (or project) on the board.
- They say, "OK, who has an idea?"

And sometimes that works really well, but often...well, it's not so effective. Why?

Because while some people thrive when put on the spot to generate ideas, others perform much better when given the time and the space to generate ideas on their own. One leader I met called these "fast twitch" and "slow twitch" people.

The next time you have a group idea session planned, try this:

- Assign the problem to your team a few days in advance, and tell everyone to come to the session with a few ideas.
- At the meeting, ask someone to share an idea that they were particularly excited about.
- Once everyone's had a chance to share, take the pulse of the group and see which ideas they're most excited about.

If you don't work on a team, this method works well in solo idea generation as well. Give yourself a few days' notice, and allow ideas to percolate rather than trying to summon them all at once.

A brainstorm is a seasonal process, not a one-time event.

> **QUESTION**
> What upcoming project do you need to give yourself space to think about?

September

2

We Make Time

"I didn't have time" is the most common excuse I hear for why important things don't get done. It's as if some magical unicorns roam this planet with an extra number of hours to spend while the rest of us have to make do with a mere 168 hours a week. But we all know that everyone we admire and respect has precisely the same amount of time in the day that we do.

If things are important, you *make* time for them.

What we are really saying when we say "I don't have time," is "It's not really that important to me," or sometimes "I don't want to deal with the uncertainty of it." But if an emergency arose, for example if you broke your leg, I guarantee that you'd find the time to deal with it. Everything else would become suddenly less urgent. Where did that time come from? Were you suddenly gifted the time to deal with your medical emergency? No, you prioritized it.

Today, I encourage you to shift your language from "I don't have time," to "It's not important right now." It's a small thing and very subtle, but it's a major mindset shift that is actually more honest and will keep you from making excuses that will eat away at your creative drive.

If something is truly important to us, we make time for it.

> **QUESTION**
> Are you really lacking the time to do what you need to do, or are those things just not as much of a priority right now?

September

3

Walk with the Wise

Despite what so many classic rock songs have told us about authority—
that it only exists to be resisted and challenged—it's actually a gift. Good,
trustworthy authority brings stability to our lives. Have you ever had a
really effective manager who made you feel like you were protected but
who also spoke directly and candidly to you when you needed it? That's
what really good authority looks like.

Not all of us are gifted with this kind of manager. Unfortunately,
some people use their authority to abuse others, get their own way, or
make themselves look good at the expense of the people they lead. Even
if that's the case for you, it's still possible to seek good authority in your
life to help you make better decisions, learn, and grow in your skill sets.

In my book *The Accidental Creative,* I wrote about the importance
of forming a "core team." This is a small group of people who have permission to speak truth to you and help you make better decisions. They
might be people who are a little further down the path than you and who
have visibility into your life and career. But most importantly, they care
about you. They want to see you thrive.

Do you have a core team? If not, who might be able to play that role
for you?

When we walk with the wise, we grow wise.

QUESTION
Who is, or should be, a part of your core team?

September

4

It's Not for You

The criticisms that others levy upon you can obsess your thinking, especially when negative feedback hits close to your insecurities. A particular critique targets an area that you're already unsure about, and before you know it, you are adapting your work to make it more palatable to people who probably don't care all that much anyway. At least they don't really care about you or about the work you do as much as they care about making their own opinions heard.

I was speaking at a conference a few years ago, and one of the other speakers, Seth Godin, said from the stage, "The moment you are willing to say 'it's not for you,' you are freed up to make art." What he meant is that not everything you make is for everyone who experiences it. You need to deeply understand who you are making things for and be unashamed about crafting your work with that person in mind. And if other people simply don't get it, it's fine. You can say "it's not for you."

To be clear, that means your work might not bring you commercial success. But most of the work that becomes culturally defining began with a specific point of view and an audience for whom it was crafted.

Not everything you make is for everyone. Become comfortable saying "it's not for you."

> **QUESTION**
> Are you shaping your work around the opinions of people who don't even care about what you're really doing?

September

5

As Goes the Leader

An old piece of wisdom says, "As goes the leader, so goes the team." This means that if you aren't taking care of yourself, you are in turn putting those who rely on you at risk. If you aren't taking care of yourself, you will have nothing to offer your team. Here are a few things to reflect on today:

- How is your margin? Are you protecting the space you need to think, connect dots, and do your deep work?
- How is your mind? Are you filling your well and seeking to find inspiration for your work? Have you dedicated time and space for study, reflection, journaling, and other unseen but essential and effective disciplines? These are often the very first things to disappear from your calendar when you're busy.
- How is the flame? Are you still connected with your productive passion? Are you effectively living out your principles?

Take some time at some point today to consider these three questions:

- How will I create space in my life to do the deep work that only I can do?
- How will I sharpen my mind and hone my intuition this week?
- How will I stay connected to my deeper why or productive passion this week?

If you want your team to be healthy, you must model health.

QUESTION
How can you better model health today to those you work with?

September
6

Clarity and Certainty

Creative work is—by nature—uncertain. You cannot know that any given strategy or decision is going to be the right one. Because of this, many creative pros and leaders become very unclear in how they communicate expectations and ideas. Because they are not certain of the right direction, they hedge their bets by refusing to commit to one.

As you can imagine, this becomes a problem when that lack of clarity begins to trickle down to their team, their peers, or their client. Where precision is lacking, misunderstanding and anxiety are almost certain to follow.

You don't have to be certain of your direction, but you must be clear about it. This is especially true if others are depending on you to make decisions for the work. The less clear you are, the more likely it is that others will misinterpret your expectations and get far off course—maybe even too far to correct in the time available.

As you consider your work today, look for any areas where you have become less clear simply because you are uncertain about the right direction.

To be effective, you must be clear about your strategy and direction even when you are uncertain it's the right one.

QUESTION

Is there any place in your work (or life) where you need to be clearer about your intentions or expectations?

September

7

How You Define Greatness

What does the word *greatness* mean to you? Think of someone you consider great. What qualities do they exhibit? What really makes them great in your mind?

Is it what they've accomplished? How others recognize them or what others say about them? The work they leave behind? Some ineffable quality of character or personality?

I believe that how you define greatness will determine a lot about the direction of your life and career. In fact, how you define greatness ultimately defines you, because it determines where you will choose to spend your time, energy, focus, and finite resources.

Have you ever considered what greatness really means? How will you know when you've achieved it?

If you don't take the time to define greatness for yourself, you might spend your entire life chasing vapor or someone else's idea of what it means.

How you define greatness defines you.

QUESTION

How do you define greatness for yourself and your work, and how will you know you've achieved it?

September
8

Ask What They Need

As much as the introverts among us (like me!) would prefer to avoid this fact, our primary role as leaders or peers is to understand, develop, and unleash the people on our team. It's all about people.

A great question to ask of others is "What do you need from me right now that you're not getting?"

This is an effective question for two reasons.

First, it gives permission to the team member to share needs with you that you may be completely unaware of. There may be resource constraints, relational conflicts, or other hidden dynamics that you simply don't see, and this question can open your eyes.

Second, it creates a patina of accountability within your relationship. If the team member doesn't share what they need with you, then they certainly forfeit the right to complain when they don't get it. By having this conversation on a routine basis, you are creating a rhythm of accountability for your team.

I encourage you to try this conversation at some point this week. The words *right now* are key, because they will prompt the team member to consider their current projects, conversations, etc., rather than thinking in big, broad terms.

When you commit to meeting the needs of your team, clients, or collaborators, you earn their trust. You also create a patina of accountability in the relationship.

QUESTION
Who can you have this conversation with today?

September

9

Ask What Others See

Some people don't ask challenging questions because they know the answers might make them uncomfortable. They'd rather live with the illusion that everything is great than open the possibility that things might not be as rosy as they seem on the surface. However, as you know, asking difficult questions is the *real* work of a creative pro.

One valuable question to ask a peer or collaborator (or someone on your team, if you lead one) is: "What's something you think I don't see but should know?"

Sometimes other team members see potential problems well before you do. They know that there's a conflict brewing between certain peers, that someone is struggling with a project (maybe even them!), or that there's an opportunity that you are not taking advantage of. By asking this question, you're giving others permission to tell you what they see, and you're also showing them that you value their ideas and opinions.

In asking this question, you're likely to receive responses that surprise you. You're also likely to learn who sees things clearly and who is simply phoning it in. If someone is consistently bringing you great insights about clients, the market, or the organization, then you might want to earmark them for development.

Again, this conversation is best had one-on-one but can also work in a group format. Do what's best for your situation.

Don't allow the fear of what you might hear keep you from asking questions. It's the only way to see reality for what it is.

QUESTION

Who in your life might give you some much-needed perspective on your work today?

September
10

What Gets Measured

You probably have a good sense of your organization's goals. Many of these were probably handed down to you by your own manager (or your manager's manager's manager), and you have little say over them.

Any expectation that you set for yourself or your team should also have an accompanying metric that you use to determine whether the team is meeting that expectation. If there is no metric in place, then you have no way of knowing whether the team is performing according to plan.

This means that any cultural expectations you set—such as timeliness of meetings, how conflict is handled, or how decisions are made—need to have some sort of metric associated with them so that you can clearly communicate to the team how they are doing. You don't need to communicate those metrics to your team members—they might just be for you—but they need to exist.

So is there any place where you've set an expectation that you're not prepared to measure? If so, spend a bit of time today considering how you'll know whether the team is living up to your expectations.

Every important effort you undergo should have a metric that helps you determine its success.

> **QUESTION**
> Is there any work you're doing that lacks a clear metric?

September

11

Negative Feedback

I read a bad review of my podcast today. I normally don't pay much attention to reviews, but I was doing some research that required me to be in a podcast app, and it was there right in front of me. Since I'd already done the unusual and read a review, I thought I would do a little experiment by copying the reviewer's username and pasting it along with the word "review" in the search bar of my web browser.

You know what I found? A bunch of negative reviews, all one star, all disparaging various podcasts. Not a single one was positive.

You will receive negative feedback for your work, and it's important to receive that feedback with grace and perspective. In this case, perspective means understanding that rather than building something of their own, some people just spend their energy tearing down the work of others. Maybe it's out of personal creative frustration, maybe it's a vendetta against those who are producing work, or maybe it's just a misplaced sense of when an opinion even matters.

When you receive negative feedback, pause and ask, "Is the intent here to help me get better or to tear me down?" If it's the former, learn from it, apply it, and move on with life. If it's the latter, sweep it into the dustbin and, again, move on with life.

Learn and apply what you can from feedback, then move on with your life. Don't dwell on it.

QUESTION

Is there negative feedback you've received that's bothering you more than it should?

September

12

Low Overhead

What does creative freedom look like to you? Is it being able to make whatever choices you want, whenever you want, about whatever work you choose to take on? Or is it something more like living where you want, working where you want, and having the space to never have to compromise your creative integrity?

We often think the key to creative freedom is more: more income, more career flexibility, bigger, better, and more expansive. But when we are thinking about freedom, we should also think about less: less expense, less responsibility, less dependence. Everything you add to your life requires some degree of maintenance, which is another word for overhead. More things equals more responsibility equals more time spent doing things other than creating. Lynda Barry once said, "The key to eternal happiness is low overhead and no debt."

By reducing your overhead, you give yourself more flexibility to make choices on your own terms without needing to consider how it will affect all those responsibilities. You gain creative freedom.

As creative pros, we must ensure that we don't take on so much overhead (literal or metaphorical) that it chokes our creative freedom.

QUESTION

How might you reduce your overhead so that you have more creative freedom?

September
13

Focus, Function, Fire

There are three key elements that work together to help you thrive in creative work:

1. *Focus:* What you allocate your finite attention to and spend your mental bandwidth on.
2. *Function:* The processes through which you solve those problems.
3. *Fire:* The underlying why behind what you do each day; the deeper drive or core motivation that propels you forward.

When someone drifts off course or when it feels like things just aren't working, it's usually because one of these three elements (or a combination of them) is misaligned. For example, they are focused on the wrong problems. Or their processes are so complex that they can't make meaningful progress. Or they've lost touch with their deeper sense of purpose.

As you consider your work today, how well aligned are these three elements with what you're actually trying to accomplish? Is your focus in the right place? Are you solving the right problems at the right time? Are your processes working well, and are they efficient? Do you understand why you are even doing the work?

When focus, function, and fire are integrated, you will experience deep engagement in your work.

To be effective, every creative pro must coordinate three elements: focus, function, and fire.

> **QUESTION**
> How well are focus, function, and fire aligned in your life?

September
14

Write It Down

It's my belief that the human race has likely cured cancer several times over, but some scientist forgot his pen and didn't write the solution down. Has that ever happened to you? You come up with an idea that is just amazing, and you think, "I could never forget that!" then ten minutes later, you're thinking, "What was the idea?"

It used to happen to me all the time, but then I found a solution: I write everything down. I take notes about the most mundane things that cross my mind. Sparks of intuition that have no bearing on what I'm working on are scattered throughout my notebooks. Little hunches I have or ideas that don't seem all that valuable are there as well. I've learned that by writing everything down, then routinely reviewing my notes, I often realize that ideas I had weeks ago are relevant to what I'm working on now.

Keep a notebook with your hunches, intuitions, ideas, and sparks. Then take just a few minutes each day to flip through it and see if any dots are connected.

Ideas that you think are irrelevant now might be perfect for next week's problem.

> **QUESTION**
> Where will you keep your ideas and sparks of insight, and when will you review them?

September

15

Cover Bands

As I wrote earlier, I spent a good portion of my early twenties as a performing musician. I got to know a lot of successful people who had made music their career and who had managed to carve out a bit of space for themselves in a highly competitive industry. However, not all of them had the same trajectory or staying power.

Those who began their careers by playing the music of others (cover bands) often gained large audiences right from the start. After all, the music was familiar, and they always played it pretty much like the original artist. However, when another band came along that played the song a little more like the original artist, they began to lose their spark and the audiences waned.

On the other hand, some people carved their own paths by playing original music. Their audiences started much smaller, and they had to convince people to give them a chance. However, as awareness grew along with the venues they played, their initial audience remained loyal because they loved the music, not just the performance.

Yes, the Beatles started as a cover band but transitioned to original music so that no one could copy them. I'm sure there were plenty of Liverpool cover bands that we have never heard of because they never made that leap. Being a cover band is pretty comfortable...until it's not.

Cover bands don't change the world. What is the thing that only you can do that people must come to you to get?

QUESTION
What is your unique offering to the world, that only you can offer?

September
16

A Change of Scenery

Your environment matters. Yes, it's true that a lot of brilliant creative work has been accomplished in miserable conditions, but that is often the exception. (Who knows how much more brilliant work may have been accomplished if the surroundings were more amenable?)

It's easy to get stuck in "place ruts" as much as we get stuck in creative ones. We sit down at the same desk, with the same tools, drinking out of the same mug, doing the same tasks day after day, and then we wonder why we feel like we're spinning our wheels. While it's the job of the pro to perform under any conditions, when you have some latitude to make your environment better or more varied, you should do so.

Today, try something different. Maybe it's taking your laptop to a park bench to work or even just sitting in the lobby of your building. Or maybe it's reorganizing your office space so that you are seeing something different when you sit down. By changing your environment, you shake your mind out of its comfortable ruts and can stimulate new kinds of insights.

Be careful not to get stuck in place ruts. Shake up your environment to stimulate new kinds of creativity.

> **QUESTION**
> How can you change up your environment today?

September
17

The Opinions of a Trusted Few

You are likely a terrible judge of your own work. It can be difficult to set aside your own expectations for the work for long enough to judge it for what it actually is. Even when the results are better than what you'd hoped for, your initial impression might be disappointment if your expectations were too high.

When you produce something you're not sure of, it helps to have a trusted few people you can share it with before it goes to your client, your manager, or the world. These should be people who will tell it to you straight and who won't tell you what you want to hear. They should know your work, what you're capable of, and how to speak to both your ambition and your insecurities. I have a trusted few people I send new work to (and have for well over a decade), and they have been invaluable in my own creative growth.

Trust the opinions of a few people close to you over the adulation or critiques of people who barely know you.

QUESTION

Who are your trusted advisers, or who should they be?

September
18

Who Are You Becoming?

Past successes can become a burden that you carry into all future work. They can cause you to do what's expected—because of your success—rather than what you think is best for a particular project.

Pixar didn't intend to make movies. They were a computing technology company. If they had remained stuck on their initial idea, the world would have missed out on *Toy Story* altogether.

How many potential Pixars are out there, both as companies and individuals, who are so stuck on who they have been in the past that they can't see who they are becoming? Life is about growth, which is about change, which is about releasing what has *been* so you can embrace what is *yet to be*.

It's only when you are willing to finish one chapter that you can start the next. Otherwise, you're simply stuck in the same story loop over and over.

So definitely leverage your experiences and successes to make you better, but don't allow them to define you. "Who are you becoming?" is a much more interesting question.

To continue to grow, you must let go of who you have been and embrace who you are becoming.

QUESTION

Who are you becoming through your work? Do you need to let go of something so you can embrace the next thing?

September
19

Pulled in Two Different Directions

There are a few inevitable tensions that we live in as creative pros. One big one is the time vs. value tension, meaning that although we are expected to work for a certain number of hours each week, we are actually paid for the *value* we create during that time. This creates an inherently contradictory set of expectations—be here always, but be great when needed because that's why we're paying you.

However, some creative pros work most effectively when they work in such a way that can't really be measured by how much time they spend in a particular place. Some need a lot of time to think, while others need to iterate quickly and often to get to a good result. Some will spend hours to get to a great idea, and others will spend ten minutes and generate something remarkable.

Understand that regardless of which approach works best for you, you are paid for the value you create, *not* for the time you spend creating it, no matter what your company is measuring. Negotiate for whatever you need to produce that value.

Creative pros are paid for the value they create, not for the time they spend creating it. Do whatever you must do to negotiate for the space to produce your best work.

> **QUESTION**
> When and how do you produce your best work? How can you negotiate for more space to do what works best for your creative process?

September
20

Seasons for Everything

To everything there is a season. (Did that Byrds song just play in your head?) More specifically, there is a season for planting, for cultivating, for harvesting, and for resting.

Planting is about faith. You put seeds in the ground with no guarantee of a return, just the hope that if they are given the right conditions, some of them will grow up and produce an eventual harvest.

When you are cultivating, you care for the vulnerable seedlings, assessing their needs and adapting to ensure that they don't get squashed by the elements. You must protect and defend them and make sure they are nourished.

Harvest is what we all hope for. It's when we get to experience the fruits of our labor and finally see what it's all been for.

Finally, resting is about allowing the ground to recover and become refreshed. Good farmers know that crop rotation is important so that the land doesn't become depleted. There needs to be a rhythm of rest to ensure a good future harvest.

Many people try to live in perpetual harvest, but that is a recipe for disaster. You must honor all the seasons to be effective.

Where are you planting seeds right now?

Which seedlings are you cultivating?

Where are you experiencing a harvest?

How will you rest so that you aren't depleted?

Effective creative pros honor the seasonal nature of their work. To everything there is a season.

QUESTION

Which season are you in right now? How should you adapt your rhythms to reflect it?

September
21

Bamboo

I once read a fascinating article about bamboo. Bamboo takes about three years to get established. During that time, there is little discernible growth that takes place. Then, shoots appear and the bamboo tree can grow as quickly as three feet per day!

Often, the daily practices that we implement, such as study, idea time, strategic leadership conversations, and others, seem like they aren't giving us the payoff we desire. It seems like it's all for nothing. However, just like with the bamboo, much of the growth is happening "underground." It's very likely that one day, we will begin to experience incredible results "out of the blue," when they are really the result of long and steady effort.

Success comes in layers, not all at once. It's often the result of a lot of small and seemingly insignificant moments, not big and obviously important ones. The growth is happening underground, where no one can see. But that growth ultimately culminates in results that surprise us.

If you're not seeing the immediate results of your efforts, don't give up. Keep developing your roots so that you will be able to bear the weight of the successes when they come.

Much of your growth happens underground before anyone else can see the visible results of your efforts.

> **QUESTION**
> Where are you tempted to give up because you aren't yet seeing the results you want?

September
22

The Three Gaps

Few creative projects truly match the original aha moment that inspired them. Ideas always appear much more perfect in our minds than they do once they are brought into the world, where compromise and tension are inevitable.

Author Scott Berkun described this dynamic in a recent interview as a series of gaps that must be navigated to do creative work from inception to completion.

- *The effort gap:* Some people become paralyzed at the thought of taking action on their idea. It feels perfect in their minds, and they fear that any execution will never live up to their standards.
- *The skill gap:* According to Berkun, it's easy to become paralyzed when you compare your in-process work with the work of the best performers in your field.
- *The quality gap:* Even the most brilliant contributors still experience insecurity about their work. Your work is unlikely to ever live up to your expectations, no matter how hard you work on it. That's simply a fact of life for creative people with high standards.

This isn't necessarily a bad thing though. As Berkun shared, "To be perfectly satisfied with something you made likely means you didn't learn anything along the way, and I'd rather be a little disappointed with projects now and then than experience the alternative of never learning anything at all."

Creative work is an assault on uncertainty, and it requires persistence, focus, and bravery. Don't allow the three gaps to lock ideas up inside your head.

QUESTION
Are any of the three gaps preventing you from taking action today?

September
23

Build Your Networks (Before You Need Them)

In June 2011, I was preparing for a trip to New York to launch my first book, *The Accidental Creative*. This event was for two hundred people in Manhattan, including several important publishing figures. I had a connecting flight through Philadelphia, and as we prepared to board the plane, I learned that a storm had grounded flights into La Guardia, effectively stranding me and making it impossible to make my book launch speech. To make matters worse, because of the storm's impact on other flights, all the trains were filled to capacity, and all the rental cars were gone. It seemed like my book launch, which I'd planned many months for, was destined to be a massive failure.

Distraught, I took to Twitter to share my frustration. I couldn't have predicted what happened next. A woman named Mindy, who lived in Philadelphia, happened to be on Twitter at that moment. She had been following my work and said that if I could navigate to the central Philly train station, she would be happy to drive me to Manhattan for my event. I followed her directions, and she lived up to her word, delivering me to the doorstep of the venue with only twenty minutes to spare.

I share this story because it is often a reminder to me that when you are generous over long periods of time in giving yourself to others, you will often find that your networks are there for you when you need them most. You need to build your network through unexpected generosity well before you need it. Then you will be delighted to find it there for you when you need it most.

Be generous with others, and build your network well before you need it.

> **QUESTION**
> How can you be generous toward others today?

September
24

Escape Routes

What does it mean to have faith in your idea? In the early days of a project, everything seems clear and the spark of insight so profound that you fight vigorously for what you believe to be the right direction. Then, as you work your way through the project, things become muddled and uncertain. You begin to have your doubts. You might even publicly waver in your commitment to the idea so that you have an "escape route" in the event the idea doesn't pan out.

Two things happen next:

On a personal level, you begin to find ways of covering yourself in case things end poorly. This means that you are half-heartedly committed to making the idea work, because the other half is trying to mitigate the downside.

On a leadership or collaboration level, your communication with those around you might become obfuscated by your lack of commitment to the idea, and others begin to waver in their commitment as well. "I'll jump if you jump first" is a real thing, and no one wants to feel foolish for being the only one in the pool.

Don't build escape routes. Speak clearly about your ideas, and either be committed to them or not. It's fine to be uncertain—we all are—but you must be clear.

Don't build premature escape routes when you fear an idea may fail. Be fully committed until the moment you choose another direction.

QUESTION
Is there any area where you are building escape routes?

September
25

Creative Bravery

Creative bravery exists when you believe in a better possible future and you believe you have the ability to bring it about. It is at the intersection of optimism and agency that your best work emerges. Without optimism, it's easy to slip into futility or nihilism and fail to see how even your most brilliant ideas would matter. Without a sense of agency, you will never put the effort into the work necessary to put it into the world, because you don't believe you're capable.

When you operate at the intersection of optimism and agency, you are a powerful creative force. Your narrative is one of hope and possibility rather than frustration and pointlessness.

Cynicism, which is often an indicator of a lack of optimism, is corrosive to the creative process. You must guard your heart against it.

As you consider your mindset today, where do you lack either optimism or agency? Is there any place where you struggle to see a better possible future or where you don't believe you have the ability to help bring it about?

When you operate squarely at the intersection of these two powerful forces, your best and bravest work will result.

Creative bravery is forged at the intersection of optimism and a sense of personal agency.

QUESTION

Where do you lack either optimism or a sense of agency at the moment? How can you remedy it?

September
26

What Will You Regret?

If you ask people who are near death what they regret the most, they rarely talk about the aggressive mistakes they made. Rather, they will tell you about the opportunities they didn't seize, the risks they deferred, or the relationships they chose not to reconcile until it was too late.

It's inaction that leads to the larger regrets, not action.

Many creative pros take their best work to the grave with them because they didn't make every effort to put it into the world where it can be of service to others. Instead, they allowed comfort or cowardice to convince them that the risk was too great, the effort too much, the gap too wide to cross. So they lulled themselves into complacency and passed through days until they reached the ends of their lives and all those ideas, that brilliant work, those missed opportunities were buried with them dead in the ground never to be seen by human eyes.

You will never get the chance to accomplish everything you want in this life. I hope that on the day I die, I have more ideas and ambitions than I had the day before. But because we can't accomplish everything, we convince ourselves that it's all right to settle in, to ride it out. As a result, the entire world misses out on our contribution.

Refuse to allow the lull of comfort and complacency to rob you of your best work.

QUESTION
What risk have you been avoiding that you need to take today?

September
27

The Idea Factory

I once came across a copy of the Walt Disney Company's business strategy, circa 1958. It had a lot of arrows pointing in different directions—licensing, theme parks, books, comics, music, etc.—but all those arrows ultimately centered around and pointed back to one thing: the creative talent of the film studio.

Disney understood that no matter how good the company might be at squeezing value out of its properties, everything ultimately hinged on its ideas. At the very center of the Disney business model was the "idea factory."

This guiding principle that allowed a multinational, multibillion-dollar company to dominate the entertainment industry is the very same one that will allow you to produce the best work of your life. As a creative pro, everything hinges on ideas. The creative talent of the idea factory is what generates value.

Are you caring for your factory? Do you dedicate time and space for generating ideas? Do you put creativity and idea generation on your calendar each week, or are you still trying to squeeze value out of yesterday's ideas?

To produce brilliant work consistently, you must care for your idea factory. Make time each week to generate ideas and produce unique kinds of value.

QUESTION

What would it mean for you to put the idea factory at the center of your work life?

September
28

Ritual Voyeurs

A few years ago, a number of books were published about the daily rituals of famous achievers. Readers scrambled to discover what Richard Branson ate for breakfast or which brand of notebook Adele uses to capture ideas. There is an understandable desire to know how the people we admire structure their lives, but we often mistake correlation for causation. It's not the specific rituals they implement that made them successful; it's that they actually have some. They have implemented a bounding structure that channels their focus and energy in meaningful ways.

We make our rituals, then our rituals make us. They are the bounding arcs that keep us moving in the right direction, day by day. As I write this, we are just emerging from the COVID-19 epidemic, and many of our lives have been upturned by something we never saw coming in ways we couldn't imagine. Except those of us with bounding rituals of study, reflection, writing, and connection maintained a constancy and stability that only ritualized disciplines can provide.

Don't worry about the rituals of others, but make certain that you have some of your own. They are what keep you grounded even when the world and your work devolve into chaos.

Rituals that work for one person may not work for another. Adopt daily rituals that channel your creative energy toward your own personal goals.

QUESTION

Which rituals are indispensable for you? Are you practicing them consistently?

September
29

On Creative Anxiety

I often meet what I call "nervous" creative pros. They are on edge, constantly worried about perception, risk, or organizational standing, and perpetually scanning the horizon for danger.

The phrase *productive paranoia* was introduced by Jim Collins and Morten T. Hansen in their book *Great by Choice*. They discovered that a healthy amount of the right kind of paranoia can lead to better results. They argued that for leaders, paranoia led to preparation, which led to ultimate success. "By preparing ahead of time, building reserves, preserving a margin of safety, bounding risk, and honing their disciplines in good times and bad, they handle disruptions from a position of strength and flexibility." I agree with this assessment. However, there is a big difference between productive paranoia and paralyzing paranoia.

Paralyzing paranoia is the kind that prevents you from taking any form of risk whatsoever because you are always more focused on the potential problems with an idea than with its possible upside. When this happens, even the smallest risk—introducing an idea, having a difficult conversation, investing a few hours on a hunch that might not pan out—can feel overwhelming. However, not doing those things comes with its own burden, which adds to your send of anxiety and paranoia. It's a never-ending cycle.

It's good to be "on edge" enough that you recognize the consequences of your behavior. It's bad to be so on edge that you invent consequences that don't even exist.

Paralyzing paranoia can prevent you from acting on your hunches, which only adds more weight to your anxiety.

> **QUESTION**
> Where are you experiencing paralyzing paranoia right now?

September
30

Free Association

It's easy to get stuck in your own head and fail to see potential ideas that are just outside your field of vision. This often happens when you become so fixated on solving a problem in a specific way or using a certain set of tools that you keep going back to the same wells of inspiration over and over, failing to leverage your own creativity.

Creativity is the process of connecting dots in a new and unique way. However, sometimes those connections only emerge when you intentionally force them to occur. One way to do this is by the process of free association.

Think of a problem that you're trying to solve. Now, take out a sheet of paper and write the one word that comes to mind when you think of that problem. Then, write the first noun that comes to mind when you think of that word. Then, repeat the process with the new word. Then, again.

So for example: *Website (makes me think of...) --> Links (makes me think of...) --> Golf (makes me think of...) --> Funny pants (makes me think of...) --> Clowns (makes me think of...) --> Small cars (makes me think of...) --> Etc.*

Once you have two or three dozen words on the page, start forcing them together and applying them to the problem you're solving. (For example, how might combining *links* and *small cars* help you better reach customers with your new marketing campaign?)

This process can take time, but it will force you to generate ideas you never would have thought of otherwise.

Using free association can help you forge ideas you never would have imagined otherwise.

QUESTION

What project can you use free association on today?

October

"There must be courage; there must be no awe. There must be criticism, for humor, to my mind, is encapsulated in criticism. There must be a disciplined eye and a wild mind."

—DOROTHY PARKER, ON WRITING HUMOR

We often confuse wild, imaginative thinking with risk. The truth is, there is zero risk in allowing your mind to wander, explore crazy and fringe ideas, and push the bounds of what you think possible. Then, accompany that wild thinking with a disciplined eye that recognizes the difference between impossible and difficult. It's at that intersection that you'll deliver your best work. This month, push yourself to think of ideas that make you a little uncomfortable, then seek to implement them with a disciplined eye.

October

1

Play

When my children were little, one of my favorite activities was to sit in the next room, just out of view, and listen to them play. The conversations they had were simply unbelievable. They would concoct elaborate storylines, invent new worlds, and defy the laws of physics as a matter of course. There were no limits on their creativity, because they were simply playing. There were no stakes.

When was the last time you truly just played with your work? I mean with no pressure on yourself to get it right, no one judging you, and no stakes. The strange irony is that much of our best work results from moments of serendipity sourced in playful creativity, then at some point, we turn it all into very serious business, we pile pressure onto ourselves expecting to get it right from the very start, and we leave no room for inefficiency and error. And in so doing, we shut down access to the parts of our minds that could truly provide the breakthroughs we crave.

Take a bit of time today—even just fifteen minutes—to play with an idea, a concept, or a project. Just sketch something. Play around with words. Make it fun, and lower the inhibitions.

Your breakthrough idea will often come when you lower inhibitions and simply play with your work.

> **QUESTION**
> How can you engage in some work-related play today?

October

2

Do the Work

A few years ago, I received a lunch pail in the mail from Steven Pressfield. If you're not familiar with his work, he is the author of *The War of Art* and *Do the Work* among many other bestsellers. Steven believes that the job of a creative pro is to show up every morning, check in at the work site, put on the hard hat, and get to work. That's why he sent the lunch pail—it was a reminder that our mindsets should be the same as someone who shows up each day to a job site.

There is probably something that you need to do today that you're putting off. Maybe you don't feel like doing it because it seems difficult, or you haven't yet figured out the best way to attack it, or you just don't have the energy to wrestle the uncertainty of it to the ground. No matter. Your job today is to show up and do the work, to attack it. You don't have the luxury of waiting until you're inspired. If you dive into the work, you will find inspiration in the midst of it.

Make progress right now on the thing that seems daunting or uncertain, and you will find inspiration in the midst of your action.

> **QUESTION**
> What is "the work" for you today?

October
3

Bird by Bird

In *Bird by Bird*, her phenomenal book on writing, Anne Lamott shared the story of a time when her younger brother was overwhelmed by a school project. He was supposed to categorize a large number of birds but had put off the project until the last minute. Distraught, he sat at the kitchen table ready to break down in tears. Lamott's father sat beside him, put his arm around him, and said, "Bird by bird, buddy. Just take it bird by bird."

It's easy to feel overwhelmed with the amount of work required to complete a project. Sometimes that feeling is due to a lack of definition of the work, and sometimes it's the result of an overall sense that we're never going to get it done.

In both cases, charting a clear, measurable course for completion is the best approach.

Break the work down into manageable chunks. Make a list of those chunks. Block time for each chunk. Then take it chunk by chunk. It's amazing how simply making a small amount of progress can lighten your spirits and cultivate a sense of momentum.

What is the "bird" you need to complete next to make progress on an important project?

All creative work is accomplished task by task. Don't allow the weight of the undone tasks to cause you to despair. Take them one at a time.

QUESTION

What is the next task that you need to complete?

October

4

Wild Ideas, Practical Implementation

If you aim from the start for only practical ideas, you are likely to end up with very predictable and possibly very stale projects. It's rare that an idea goes from boringly safe to edgy and cool during the course of a project. Typically, ideas that feel like a bit of a stretch are toned down in order to make them more practical.

Because of this, at the start of a project you should aim for the sky. Be wild, imaginative, and thoroughly impractical. Come up with ideas that could never work in practice. However, what you discover in those initial impractical ideas is often a spark that leads to much more practical, yet still novel concept.

When you aim for practical, you typically wind up with predictable and stale projects.

When you aim for the impossible, you often wind up with simultaneously practical and interesting ideas.

Remember: ideas are easy and cheap. It's not dangerous to have one. Don't shy away from letting your mind run wild just because you fear you won't be able to implement it.

Aim for the sky with your ideas and sometimes you'll surprise yourself with what's possible.

QUESTION

Are you ever too safe with your ideas? What wild idea can you think of for a current project?

October

5

Clean and Dirty Fuels

People sometimes offer well-meaning advice like, "Remember the people who didn't believe in you, then use it as fuel to prove them wrong!" Yes, positioning doubters as the enemy can give you a boost of quick motivation to help you succeed. However, that motivation is very temporary. Once you've proven them wrong, what will drive your next effort? Or will you need to keep living in the past, perpetually stewing on all those people who didn't think you could do it?

There are clean fuels, and there are dirty fuels. Anger and resentment are dirty fuels because they leave a residue on you that can affect your optimism and creative drive. If you are motivated to prove others wrong, you are not focused on possibility; you are looking for the way to show others that you are right. You have tunnel vision. There is residue blocking your field of view.

However, when you are driven by a desire to succeed for the sake of others, like making their lives better through your work or achieving an outcome that improves the standing of others along with you, you are driven by clean fuel. There is no residue, only clear sight.

Is there any part of your work right now that's being driven by dirty fuel?

Anger and resentment are dirty fuels, and they leave residue that obstructs the creative process. Strive to be driven by clean fuels.

> **QUESTION**
> What drives your desire to succeed in your work? Why?

October

6

Automate

Unnecessary complexity isn't just a function of making a problem too complex or creating pointlessly difficult processes that have to be followed to do the work. Yes, bureaucratic red tape can inhibit creative effectiveness, but sometimes it's the smaller things that stand in the way of focus and clarity. Scheduling meetings, back-and-forth email volleys, and other activities that require you to spend energy that's not directly tied to the value you are tasked with creating can zap the drive you need to deliver great work at the right moment.

I am a big believer in automating as much work as possible. With the array of tools at your disposal, there is really no excuse for wasting precious creative time on anything that can be fully automated. Given the amount of uncertainty that must be resolved in the course of the work you do, strive to eliminate as much pointless uncertainty as possible by automating tasks that don't really require your decision-making prowess. What in your life should be automated so as to free up creative mental cycles?

Automate as much of your process as possible so that you can spend your valuable creative cycles on work that truly matters.

QUESTION

Which elements of your work could be automated to free mental bandwidth?

October

7

Resignation Letters

If you're doing work that matters to you, conflict is inevitable. It may even become a part of your everyday work experience. The natural response when conflict becomes the norm is to entertain the thought of moving on. Before entertaining leaving your job, here's something you can do to clarify what's really at the heart of your frustration: write a letter of resignation, but don't deliver it.

Convey all the reasons you need to move on, all the frustrations you experience daily, and all the ways in which you feel underutilized. Be as personal as you'd like, since no one will ever read it.

Once you've written your letter, ask yourself a few questions:

- ► How much of what's in this letter could I change if I really wanted to?
- ► Am I looking to my job to provide something a job cannot ultimately give me (identity, self-worth, etc.)?
- ► How much of what's in this letter is recent frustration vs. old wounds that haven't healed?
- ► How much of what's in this letter have I experienced in other workplaces as well?
- ► Are there any unexpected patterns I see within this letter?

Before considering leaving your job, first write a resignation letter but don't send it. You might discover ways in which you are contributing to your own frustration.

> **QUESTION**
> Do you need to write a letter to express your frustration, whether for work or something else causing strife?

October

8

Working against Something

One of the keys to unlocking your creative voice is asking yourself: "What angers me?" I'm not talking about road rage or a disappointing season of your favorite TV show. I mean what fills you with compassionate anger.

Compassionate anger is anger on behalf of someone else. It's anger that you feel because there is a wrong that needs to be righted or there is an injustice happening around you. It's anger that you feel when someone isn't delivering on their promises or you see a customer or client being taken advantage of. It's anger that you feel when an inferior product is causing problems for your customers.

For example, I am profoundly moved by the stories of underdogs. If I see someone being taken advantage of or who is working against incredible odds, I immediately spring into action and take their side. Some of my best work is done with underdogs.

What fills you with compassionate anger? And, more importantly, how can you channel that into work that matters to you and the world around you?

Sometimes, your best creative work will arise when you are working against something or when you are fighting something.

QUESTION
What fills you with compassionate anger?

October
9

Twenty-Mile March

Steady, deliberate progress is the key to making meaningful progress on big, complex projects. In their (already referenced!) book *Great by Choice*, Jim Collins and Morten T. Hansen share the hypothetical story of two people walking across the United States. One sets out on the first day, which was beautiful, walks twenty miles, then stops. The other, because it's beautiful, decides to walk forty miles. The following day, the temperature is unbearably hot, but the first person again walks twenty miles. The other person, already worn out from the big first day effort, decides to wait for more optimal conditions to trek again. This goes on for day after day, in good and bad conditions. Who will arrive at their destination first?

Collins argues that successful companies (and I would add people as well) are those who commit to the twenty-mile march even when they don't feel like it or when conditions aren't optimal.

For you, that might mean doing a specific number of hours of work on a project each day, writing a certain number of words no matter your circumstances, or having your check-in meeting even when it's inconvenient. By committing to steady, deliberate progress, you are more likely to arrive at your destination than if you only do work when you feel inspired to.

Commit to steady, deliberate, measured progress on your big projects. And do it every day, even when you don't feel like it.

QUESTION
What is your twenty-mile march right now?

October
10

Influence vs. Control

Early in your career, you are rewarded based on how effectively you control your work. You are primarily tasked with executing decisions being made by others, and if you deliver on expectations consistently, you will eventually be rewarded with more responsibility. You might even be promoted into a role where you are managing others.

This is the critical moment when many people slip up. Once you are in a position of leadership, your job is no longer to control the work; it's to influence it. If you attempt to control the work of the talented creative pros on your team, they will eventually disengage until you tell them exactly what to do. This means that you won't get the best work out of them, because they will stop spending energy thinking of ideas that you're likely to change anyway.

To lead by influence, whether you're leading a team, a client, or your peers, means to spend less time telling them how to do the work and more time teaching them how to *think* about the work. Establish guiding principles that help them understand what successful work looks like (instead of them guessing what you want), how to know when an idea is good (instead of them waiting for you to tell them), how to deal with conflict (instead of always stepping in and resolving it), and other elements of your leadership philosophy that will help them deliver great results.

To help your team deliver brilliant, unique results, focus on leading with influence instead of leading by control.

QUESTION

Where are you trying to control the work right now instead of influencing it?

October
11

Disappointment

You invest tremendous time, energy, and emotional engagement into work that you don't know for certain will succeed. You may do your best to create something that others will find valuable, but in the end, no matter what you do, there will be times when it simply doesn't work. You will fall short of your expectations.

In those moments, disappointment can begin to whisper in your ear. "I told you so," or "It was destined to fail," or "You were never good enough," can begin to play like a soundtrack in your mind. You can begin to lose hope and confidence in your abilities.

Friends, don't allow disappointment to devolve into despair. There is a difference between "I have failed," and "I am a failure," but it's easy to allow the latter to obsess your mind when you fall short.

Though you may not want to recognize it, when you choose to do creative work, you are choosing to engage in work that is uncertain, challenging, and likely often to result in failure. Don't allow the narratives in your head to cause you to play it safe just to avoid the disappointment of falling short. If you never take the shot, you never hit the game winner.

In creative work, disappointment is inevitable. Don't allow "I failed" to become "I'm a failure."

QUESTION

Where are you experiencing disappointment right now? Are there any unhealthy narratives playing in your head?

October

12

Stability and Challenge

As referenced a few months ago, there are two key things that creative pros need to thrive: stability and challenge.

Stability means that you need clarity of process, clarity of expectations, protection of your time and focus, and protection of the runway needed to do your work.

Challenge means that—whether you know it or not—you need and want to be pushed, to take risks, to try new things, and to be operating on the edge of your abilities from time to time.

The problem is that stability and challenge exist in tension with one another. As you are challenged, the environment in which you work often becomes less stable because there is more uncertainty and less clarity about the process that will get the results you need. When you increase stability, you feel less challenged because things are more predictable.

Much of the success in creative organizations lies in getting the balance of stability and challenge right. If teams are overly challenged without the corresponding stability needed to support the effort, they grow frustrated and angry. If there is high stability but little challenge, talented people grow bored and begin seeking better horizons.

Whether you lead a team or not, it's important to be mindful of these two dynamics—stability and challenge—and which of them you might need more of at the moment.

So much of the success of creative teams lies in striking the right balance of stability and challenge.

QUESTION

Of these two forces—stability and challenge—which do you lack the most right now? What can you do about it?

October
13

Brachiation

A technique called *brachiation* is an important phase of physical development for children. For example, when a child is swinging from one side to the other on a set of monkey bars, there is a moment when they must let go with one hand before the other hand is fully secured on the next bar. If they fail to let go at the right moment, as often happens when they get scared, they will likely fall (or be stuck between the two bars with no momentum).

A key reason why they don't let go at the right moment is a fear of falling. Ironically, that fear is self-fulfilling. It's precisely because they don't let go that they fall. You must learn to let go at just the right time—not too early but still at some point before you know for certain that everything is going to work out fine.

Creative work is very similar. You have to know how to let go of an idea and move on to the next one. If you don't and try to grasp onto it long after it has served its purpose, you are likely to end up with something mediocre.

We all mastered this skill as children, but emotional brachiation can be much more difficult. There is so much of our self-identity wrapped up in our ideas or projects. However, we need to train ourselves to let go and move forward.

If you don't know when to let go of an old idea and move on to the next one, you are destined to struggle creatively.

QUESTION

Are there any old ideas—or anything at all in your life—that you simply need to let go of so you can grasp ahold of the next one?

October

14

Simplicity by Principle

As a principle, nothing goes from complex to simple on its own. It requires outside energy to bring simplicity to a complex process or to a complex organization. In fact, on their own, things devolve into ever-greater chaos.

How do you bring simplicity to a complex situation? One way is by establishing principles that guide your decisions and behaviors. If you have to approach every single project or creative problem in a fresh way, your world is going to be remarkably complex. However, if you have a set of guiding principles to help you make decisions and frameworks to shape your decisions, you already have a head start. Premake as many decisions as you can by thinking through the governing principles that guide your work and your leadership. For example, what are the specific qualities you look for in a good idea? How do you handle conflict when people disagree about direction? What are the values you refuse to compromise, no matter what?

By establishing some core principles ahead of time, you carve out a space for simplicity in the midst of complexity. You bring order to your world.

Nothing goes from complex to simple on its own. Establish principles to guide your work so that you begin from a point of simplicity.

QUESTION

What are the core three to four principles that govern your work?

October
15

Right Now

What is the most powerful question you can ask your team or collaborators? I'm a big believer in, "Is there anything can I do for you right now?"

A lot of managers toss out, "Let me know if I can do anything for you," or "Let me know how I can be of help," but team members often don't take them seriously because those phrases are too generic and vague. They don't mean anything, because they are a promise of something to be done at an undetermined time in the future about a yet to be experienced problem.

However, adding the qualifier "right now" implies urgency. It means, "I will drop everything at this moment and take care of your issue." It's a promise of immediate action. Simply adding that qualifier to the end of the question completely reframes it. It shows the person you're communicating with that you are serious.

As you interact with others today, strive to avoid vagaries and empty offers of help. Instead, add a sense of precision and seriousness to your offer by indicating that you will act right now.

Asking, "What can I do for you right now?" is a powerful way of showing that you are committed to helping your team or collaborators success.

QUESTION
Who can you ask this question of today?

October
16

Intelligent Adjacency

If you go into a grocery store, you'll see that items are typically placed together that are frequently purchased together. For example, you won't find the toothpaste with the asparagus (although that actually might not be a bad idea!). You'll find it next to the toothbrushes, because people who are looking for one item are more likely to also be looking for the other. This is a concept in store planning called "intelligent adjacency," and it's designed to make things more convenient for the shopper but also to increase likely impulse purchases.

There is another kind of intelligent adjacency that applies to your time and focus. It's often the case that you spend ten minutes answering an email, then a half hour in a meeting, then fifteen minutes actually doing deep creative work, then another ten answering an email, etc. When you bounce between different kinds of tasks like these, you pay a task-switching penalty, and your overall effectiveness is likely to suffer. Instead, consider how you might be able to group certain kinds of similar tasks together so that you are not shifting your mindset as often between highly conceptual creative work and highly tactical administrative work. Try to block space for each kind of work today, and you will see an uptick in your engagement.

By protecting blocks of time to do similar kinds of work, you minimize the task-switching penalty that stifles creative thinking.

QUESTION

How can you carve out intelligent adjacency in your work today?

October
17

Make It Convenient

I love playing the guitar. When I was in a band and played almost every night, I definitely got my fill of music. It seemed like the guitar was in my hands all the time, and I was writing songs in every spare moment. As I got older, changed career paths, and moved into leadership, those moments of creative expression through music took a back seat. In fact, there were long stretches of time when I didn't pick up the guitar at all.

About a year and a half ago, I decided that I wanted to reincorporate music into my life. I had the desire to write songs, but whenever the mood struck me, it seemed like too much of a hassle to go all the way to our basement, take the guitar out of its case, and bring it back up to my home office where I could write. So I decided to hang the guitar on my office wall so that it was always within reach. (I did the same thing with the mandolin my family bought me for Father's Day.) Now, I often find myself picking up the guitar to noodle while thinking through an especially difficult problem. And in the year since I hung it in my office, I've probably written twenty-five or thirty songs.

The lesson is that if you want something to happen more often, make it more convenient. Surround yourself with easy access to things that inspire you, that help you express yourself, or that stoke the fires of your imagination.

Eliminate unnecessary barriers to creative expression. Put the tools you need in convenient places.

> **QUESTION**
> How can you adapt your environment to make creativity more convenient?

October
18

Don't Be a Romantic

When I was younger and imagined what it would be like to write a book, I pictured myself sitting in a busy coffee shop on a cool, breezy day sipping on a latte while thinking deep thoughts about…something profound. Now, having written and published six books, I've learned something very important: the creative process is rarely romantic. More often than not, I carve out time in between meetings to ensure that my daily allotment of words gets written and that I make steady progress on whatever project I'm into at the moment. It's less "spontaneous Parisian café bliss" and more "purposeful, functional progress."

Now, please know that these moments of pragmatic creating are peppered with unexpected insights, excitements, and breakthrough celebrations. Those moments are very special indeed. However, if you rely on moments like those to fuel your progress, you will inevitably stall.

To be a pro, you must commit to the steady, methodical, progressive attack of your work, day by day, and release the notion of romantic creativity. However, just like any good marriage has its fill of everyday moments and relatively humdrum mechanics to accompany the deeply romantic moments, your work will also surprise and delight you with occasional romance.

Drop the notion that creative work is romantic. Engage in steady progress on your creative work, and the romance will sneak up on you.

QUESTION

What does steady progress on your work look like today?

October
19

Burnout

As I write this, the world is beginning to emerge from a global pandemic. While technology allowed many to work remotely in a way that was never before possible, that gift was accompanied by certain struggles, such as creative burnout. In the face of uncertainty and especially when the entire world has been turned upside down, many pros did everything they could to hold things together. However, the emotional toll of creating under pressure every day inevitably led to a sense of overload.

Here are six quick tips for dealing with these moments of burnout:

1. *Pause and organize:* Sometimes the burnout is due to the weight of all that's left undone. When you don't have a clear sense of what's left to do, the emotional pressure can be palpable.
2. *Clear the decks:* Prune any unnecessary commitments from your life.
3. *Reprioritize:* Line up your existing commitments in order of priority, starting with the most urgent and important open loops that need to be closed.
4. *Time block:* Allocate time on your calendar to tackle those priorities.
5. *Care physically:* In busy times, make certain to get plenty of rest and exercise.
6. *Root in your productive passion:* Reconnect with your core "why."

For creative pros, burnout is at some point inevitable. You need to have a plan for dealing with it when it happens.

> **QUESTION**
> Is there any place in your life or work where you are feeling a little burned out?

October
20

Declaring Undeclarables

Trust is the foundation of all great creative work. Without it, it can be nearly impossible to take risks, venture into uncharted water, or mention an idea that might not be received well by others. You must trust that on the other side of that effort is the possibility of a brilliant result and that others are on your side and will help you deliver on your objectives.

However, we often breach trust in silly, avoidable ways. For example, we make promises to others that we aren't certain we can deliver on. I call this "declaring undeclarables." We declare things like, "We are absolutely going with your idea for this project," or "I will definitely meet with you on Tuesday at 1:00 p.m.," with every intention of delivering, but circumstances change and we're unable to do so. While it might seem minor in the moment, these small breaches of trust add up over time, and they can compromise our ability to garner team trust in important moments when we need to rely on one another to take a creative risk.

Don't declare undeclarables. Make certain that you can deliver on your promises before you make them.

> **QUESTION**
> Have you breached trust by declaring an undeclarable? How can you mend the damage caused?

October
21

Rejection of Work and Worth

Creative work is subjective. You can labor for weeks on a project and deliver something that you fully believe in only to have it rejected by the stakeholders for some nebulous, maybe even undefined, reason. In those moments, it's easy to take the rejection personally and feel it deeply. After all, it was your idea, your execution, your risk. It stings, and rightly so.

While it's perfectly fine to feel the pain of rejection when it occurs, it's important to be mindful of what happens next. Sometimes that moment of rejection can morph into a season of feeling like a reject. The temporary moment of rejection turns into a nametag bearing the name "Reject," and you begin to wonder if you've lost a step and if you'll ever be as good as you once were.

A rejection of your work is not a rejection of your worth. Yes, it's natural to feel the sting when your work isn't chosen, but that is not a statement about the value that you inherently carry as a human being, nor is it a statement about your capabilities as a creative pro. It's a statement about one moment in time, with one project, in one specific situation, with one set of stakeholders.

The rejection of your work is not a rejection of your worth. The best path beyond rejection is to throw yourself into the next project.

> **QUESTION**
> Are you allowing the rejection of your work to define you?

October
22

The Big Three

You probably have more priorities on your plate than you can reasonably handle. Where will you find the ideas you need?

One method that works very well is a technique that I call the "big three." Write the three most pressing open creative loops in your world (problems to be solved) on a Post-it, an index card, a whiteboard, or someplace where you are likely to see it often. Keep these three problems in front of you as you go through your day.

Why would you want to keep these three open loops in front of you? Because you are priming your mind to look for potentially useful ideas and information as you go through your day. By keeping these problems at the front of your mind, you might notice ideas or connections that you would otherwise have simply glossed over. Sometimes, the best ideas are right under our noses, but we simply can't see them because we're not paying attention.

Always keep your most important creative problems in front of you so that you are primed for potential breakthroughs.

QUESTION

What are your three most important, unsolved creative problems right now? Write them down and keep them in front of you today.

October
23

Your Circle

The legendary myth of the lone creator is powerful. We envision the solitary genius sitting in her studio, tinkering with a project, until one day she emerges and unleashes her brilliance on the world. However, this is simply not reflective of how most brilliant work is accomplished. Most of the effective professionals I've met have a strong network of peers, friends, and mentors who help them stay aligned and inspired.

One practice that I recommend building into your life is to create a circle. This is a group of people that meets about once a month to ask each other three questions:

1. What are you working on right now?
2. What do you need help problem-solving right now?
3. What's inspiring you right now?

These three questions yield brilliant conversation and will likely spark new inroads of creative thought. Relationships are a powerful source of creative inspiration and—when approached intentionally—will help you see new opportunities for growth and creative expression that were previously in your blind spot.

Relationships are an important contributor to creative growth. Make certain to carve out time to connect with others who inspire and challenge you.

QUESTION
Who should be in your circle?

October
24

Break the Glass

If you walk into any public building, you'll see a glass panel on the wall containing a fire extinguisher etched with the words "break glass in case of fire." Although fires are incredibly rare, having a fire extinguisher handy when one breaks out can make all the difference between a minor blaze and a roaring, five-alarm event. Planning for that contingency, even though it might never happen, is important and maybe even critical.

In a similar way, there are many "fires" that break out in our lives and work. Maybe it's a client emergency that's going to require you to work late hours or all weekend. Maybe it's someone on your team getting sick or suddenly quitting, leaving everyone else to pick up the slack. It's inevitable that at some point, there is going to be a fire that needs to be extinguished. Do you have a "break the glass" strategy?

We often react in these moments rather than responding, and the reason is that we haven't developed a plan for what to do when they arise. (They inevitably will.) So what are the fires that are most likely to arise over the coming weeks? Do you have a plan for how to resource putting them out, how to fund your effort if necessary, and how to communicate with others about the situation? Don't react. Make a plan to respond.

Develop a "break the glass" strategy so that you are able to respond in moments of crisis rather than reacting.

> **QUESTION**
> What contingency should you be planning for, just in case?

October
25

No-Fly Zone

Having predictable time on your calendar for important priorities is critical to making progress on creative work. Without knowing that you'll have the time you need to do the work, you are prone to stress and anxiety, which can consume your world and choke your creative energy.

One strategy that was implemented by a client of mine was called "no-fly zone" time. The policy stated that between the hours of 11:00 a.m. and 1:00 p.m. Monday through Friday, there were to be no meetings, no phone calls, and no expectations of returned emails. Everyone in the organization had that predictable two hours every single day to do their deep creative work. What this did for the organization was provide steady, predictable windows for people to do their work, regardless of how many meetings they had to sit through outside it. They knew that at least ten hours a week would go to the work they were accountable for.

How can you implement the same strategy in your life? Is there a window you can block off as "no-fly zone" time? Maybe it's 7:00 to 9:00 each morning, as you ease into your day. Maybe it's 3:00 to 5:00 each afternoon so that you can leave on a high note, having tackled important priorities.

Block some time each week, preferably each day, for doing your most important creative work.

> **QUESTION**
> When will you schedule "no-fly zone" time?

October
26

The Likability Trap

Everyone wants to be liked. And there's nothing wrong with being liked. However, there's a dynamic that I call "the likability trap." Some creative pros, especially leaders, begin to believe that the key to earning their team's respect is to be liked. So they do everything they can to ensure that others like them. However, sometimes—as you well know—the right thing to do may not be the popular thing to do.

That's why I believe that you cannot chase being liked and being effective at the same time. You can be both liked and effective, but you can't chase both. At some point, you will be forced to choose between the two.

Again, there's nothing wrong with being liked. Just make certain that your desire to be liked isn't interfering with your ability to make wise, even if unpopular, decisions.

To be effective, you will occasionally have to do things that aren't liked by your team. However, making the wise choice, according to principle, will earn respect. (And you may be liked as well.)

You cannot pursue being liked and being effective simultaneously.

QUESTION

Is there any place where you are compromising your effectiveness to be liked?

October
27

The Stimulus Queue

There are few things that affect your creative process more than the quality of the stimuli that you allow to enter your mind. The better and more diverse "dots" you have to connect, the higher quality ideas you are likely to generate. But some people leave their raw creative inputs to chance. They read whatever comes across their field of view or spend time mindlessly surfing the web, Instagram, or Twitter for something that sparks their interest.

As a pro, you can't afford to leave your stimulus to chance. I recommend that you have what I call a "stimulus queue." It's a list of items that you plan to read, experience, and watch next. You might use a tool (there are any number of apps that allow you to aggregate articles from the web) or the back page of your notebook or simply keep a stack of books next to your desk. (That's what I do, and mine is growing tall!) But the key is that you file away interesting stimuli and work through them in a processed way.

Don't leave your stimulus to chance. Keep a stimulus queue or list of things you want to experience, read, or watch, and work through it over time.

> **QUESTION**
> Where will you keep your stimulus queue?

October
28

Step, Sprint, Stretch

In my book *Die Empty*, I wrote about three kinds of goals that can help you accomplish your creative ambitions. The biggest and most challenging are what I call "stretch goals." These are goals that take a long time to accomplish, will push the boundaries of what you think to be possible, and bring a sense of hope and possibility to your work.

Once you've set a stretch goal, you can break it into a series of "sprint goals." These are shorter-term (usually a few weeks at a time) goals that help you measure your progress on the larger stretch goal. For example, if your stretch goal is to write a book in a year, your sprint goal might be to write a chapter every two weeks. You stack enough two-week sprints together, and soon you have a book.

However, it's the "step goals" that really make progress happen. These are the daily, regular activities that you engage in that propel you forward. For example, my stretch goal for this book is to write the entire manuscript by the end of September. This means that I need to write three months of content each month, which means that I need to write approximately ninety entries per month. I write five days per week, which means I need to write about five entries per day to stay on course (and have some days left over). That's my step goal for this project. If I hit it, I'm on course.

To accomplish something big, set a stretch goal, then break it down into sprint and step goals.

QUESTION

What stretch goal are you pursuing? What are the corresponding sprint and step goals?

October

29

Checkpoints and Road Signs

For our honeymoon, my wife and I were able to take a two-week driving trip across France. While it was an incredible experience, one of the things that you learn quickly when driving in the French countryside is that there aren't a lot of road signs. Instead, you infrequently come to a roundabout with several signs marked for cities pointing in different directions leading to different roads. If you happen to miss just one of those signs because you aren't paying attention, you might end up many, many kilometers away from where you intended to go.

Your creative process is very similar. Maybe you think you know the direction you need to go, so you keep your head down, do your work, and settle into a rhythm. However, it's possible that the environment around you is changing and you're missing the signals. The result could be that you end up very far from where you intended to be.

It's important to have frequent checkpoints—weekly, monthly, quarterly—to make sure that you're still on course. Are you still solving the right problems? Do you need to build new kinds of stimulus into your life? Do you need to shift how you are using your time? Building checkpoints prevents you from getting too far off course before you're able to make a correction.

To ensure that you stay on course for your objectives, it helps to have frequent checkpoints built into your life.

QUESTION

When could you do a weekly checkpoint? A monthly one? A quarterly one?

October

30

Use More of the Hoop

My father has been a basketball coach for over forty years. People from all over Ohio ask him to help them with their shooting, which is his specialty. One of the things he taught me at an early age is that—within obvious limits—when you put more arc on your shot, you increase the chances of making it. A shot with more arc approaches the rim from a higher angle, thus increasing the size of the opening the ball can fall into. When your shot is flat, with little arc, you are essentially shooting into an oval, and your technique has to be nearly perfect to succeed. By increasing the arc, you add some degree of tolerance for imperfection.

I've found that the same principle applies to the creative process. When you try to squeeze everything into a very tight deadline, with little room to maneuver, it's the same as shooting a flat shot. Everything has to go perfectly for you to succeed. However, when you schedule just a bit of room—flexibility of schedule, space to think and process and adapt—you give yourself some tolerance for variability. You are "using more of the hoop."

To increase your chances of eventual success, build into your process a bit of extra space for thinking, processing, and experimenting.

QUESTION

How can you use more of the hoop with the work you are planning?

October
31

Fear

In his book *The Now Habit*, author Neil Fiore describes an experiment in which someone is shown a wood plank on the floor and asked, "Do you think you could walk the length of that plank?" Of course, they answer yes.

"Now, imagine that I suspend the plank one hundred feet in the air between two buildings. Do you think you could walk the plank?"

"No way!" is the response.

Here's what's interesting to me about this scenario: nothing has changed about the technical skill required to walk the plank. If you can do it on the ground, you can do it in the air. What's changed are the perceived consequences of failure. (Which, in this case, is plummeting to the ground, so I kind of understand!)

However, I would submit to you that as creative pros, we do the same kind of thing all the time. We artificially escalate the perceived consequences of failure to the point that we don't act. We don't take even small risks. They seem too scary to us. This is what fear does—it paralyzes us.

There are real consequences for failure, for sure. But please make sure that you are not artificially escalating the perceived consequences of failure to the point that it inhibits your creating.

Don't allow fear to paralyze you. Refuse to artificially escalate the perceived consequences of failure.

QUESTION

Are you escalating planks in any area of your life, your work, or your leadership?

November

Some people believe that constraints of any kind are harmful to their creative process. This is untrue. Our habits, self-imposed limitations, and healthy boundaries help us channel our creative energy where it can be most effective. This month, focus on establishing healthy habits and boundaries that help you spend your finite time and energy wisely and will generate momentum heading into the end of the year.

November
1

Bounded Autonomy

Orson Welles, the great filmmaker, once quipped, "The enemy of art is the absence of limitations." Without some form of limitation, it's difficult to make priority decisions about focus, energy, and time.

As creative pros, what we should strive for is bounded autonomy. This is freedom within limits. Effective limits help us make critical decisions about our finite resources. Sometimes, the reason we are stuck is that we either have too much autonomy (not enough boundaries) or we are too bounded (too many limits), and the net result is that we can't see a meaningful path forward. By considering these two factors, we can sometimes find just the right solution to our stuck-ness. Do you need better limits to define where you look for ideas? Better definition of the problem? Or are you overly constricted by tight boundaries and need more freedom to explore?

Complete freedom is not helpful. The creative process thrives within the context of bounded autonomy.

QUESTION

Think about a problem you're stuck on. Do you need more autonomy or better boundaries?

November
2

The Creative Habit

In her book *The Creative Habit*, choreographer Twyla Tharp shares a fascinating insight into the formation of habits. She wakes very early each morning and goes to her studio for a workout. On many mornings, she doesn't really feel like going, but she does anyway. However, going to the studio isn't the habit. The habit is hailing the cab that will take her to the studio. She says that once she hails the cab, she knows that the rest of the process will be on autopilot, but the hardest part is getting down to the curb to hail the cab. So that's the habit she focuses on.

It's far too easy to overcomplicate habits and rituals, but if you try, you can probably simplify many of your most valuable ones down to that very first trigger action. It's the thing that gets you moving. For me, every time I write, I light a candle. Not just any candle: an Archipelago Havana Cigar scented candle. I go through several each year. It's an important part of my writing habit because it sends a signal to my brain that it's time to begin to write. Once I light it, I'm already on the way. And I only light that candle when I'm writing.

Trigger habits can you help you get moving on difficult creative work.

QUESTION
What trigger habits can you begin to instill in your life today?

November

3

Normalization of Deviance

A phrase was coined in the wake of the space shuttle *Columbia* disaster to describe the very dynamic that allowed it to occur: normalization of deviance. It seems that for years prior to the *Columbia* exploding on reentry, it was routine for foam to shed off the external fuel tank during launch. This was so common that they used the term *foam shedding* to describe it, and even though it was concerning at first, eventually it was determined to be harmless. Until one fateful launch when the foam happened to damage a heat shield that subsequently failed on reentry, leading to the disaster.

This is why the term *normalization of deviance* was used to describe this event. Abnormal, deviant events were normalized over time, even though they were unacceptable. This happens in many organizations as well. Undesired behavior like missing deadlines, being late to meetings, snapping back with sarcastic comments, and the like become normalized parts of the culture to the point that no one even questions them. However, the long-term consequences of normalizing these behaviors can be significant, or even disastrous.

You can't allow unacceptable behavior to become normalized, whether in yourself, your team, or the people you lead.

Normalization of deviance can quickly erode a culture and the collective creative process.

QUESTION

Do you see normalization of deviance playing out in your work? In your team's culture? What can you do about it?

November

4

At the Intersections

Great contributions are often made by those who, rather than just focusing on one discipline or craft, work at the intersection of two or three disciplines. Leonardo da Vinci was a brilliant artist not only because of his raw ability to paint or draw but because of his insatiable curiosity about anatomy, botany, and science. It was the confluence of these disciplines that makes his work so resonant. The same can be said of Steve Jobs, who combined technology and art to help create computing devices that were intuitive and useful for businesses, musicians, artists, and students alike. It was at the intersection of these multiple disciplines that real creative value was generated.

At which intersection(s) are you operating? Which disciplines do you uniquely combine to create work that uniquely defines you? Maybe it's your ability to teach and your attention to detail. Maybe it's your consumer intuition and your design sense. The greatest and most unique value you will offer your organization, your clients, and the world at large will be at the intersection of multiple aptitudes.

Discover where your unique talents overlap and complement one another, and you will discover a sure path to creative value.

QUESTION

Which two or three aptitudes intersect to allow you to produce your unique work? How can you leverage them more?

November
5

Nouns and Verbs

Author and artist Austin Kleon wrote, "Lots of people want to be the noun without doing the verb." This means they want to be thought of as a certain kind of person—a writer, a painter, a musician, an editor—without doing the hard work necessary to actually do the work. To them, it's more about being a certain *kind* of person than doing the actual work that person would do.

Of course, to be any of those things, you have to do the things those people do. If you want to be a writer, you must write consistently. If you want to be a musician, you must make music. If you want to be a leader, well...lead. If more people focused on the verbs instead of the nouns, the world would certainly be filled with compelling work. And if you focus more on the verbs, you will make steady progress on your goals.

If you're not yet the thing you *want* to be, begin doing the thing that person does. Write every day. Make music. Build the business, one day at a time.

If you want to be the noun, focus on doing the verb.

> **QUESTION**
> What verb should you do more consistently to help you become the noun?

November

6

Timing

How do you know which of your ideas is ready to put into the world? Phil Libin, founder and former CEO of Evernote, believes that the best ideas are ones that technology has just made possible for the first time in history but that are still difficult to achieve. Difficulty means that many won't try them, but the fact that it's possible for the first time means that you can step into a space that others haven't yet considered. The convergence of *just became possible* and *still kind of difficult* is the place where tremendous, unexpected value can be created.

Are you working on anything that meets that description? Maybe there's an idea that you've been exploring, but it doesn't quite seem like it's ready for prime time. How can you alter the idea so that you're doing something that's only recently possible and still really difficult to do? By concentrating your efforts on these sorts of ideas, you are likely to uncover value that others haven't. And you may even surprise yourself with what you accomplish.

The biggest value in your work lies at the intersection of things that just became possible and things that are still difficult to accomplish.

QUESTION

As you consider your work, which ideas lie at the intersection of these two dynamics?

November
7

Your Branch

I once asked world-famous DJ Z-Trip how he discovered his voice as an artist, and he used the analogy of a tree. He said that when he began his career, he—like everyone else—was climbing the trunk of the tree because it is the safest and most stable part. However, as he began to progress in his career, he began to step out onto branches that took him farther away from the trunk, or what was expected. His DJ peers wondered what he was doing, because he was taking risks with his work that separated him from the pack and could result in failure or rejection by the industry. However, Z-Trip said that as he began to venture out onto new branches, he became so unique from other DJs that he began to carve his own space in the market, defined by his own voice. People were coming to him for the unique thing that only he could do.

So much of the process of discovering the unique value you offer is in choosing to step out onto one branch at a time, separating yourself a little bit from the predictability and stability of the trunk. Over time, you define your own space until soon you are sitting all alone out at the end of a winding branch.

To develop a unique voice, you must venture away from security and what's expected. However, it's best to do it one small decision at a time.

QUESTION

What "branch" can you step out onto to separate you from the pack?

November

8

The Aspiration Gap

NPR radio host Ira Glass once shared insight into the struggle of making great art: "What nobody tells people who are beginners—and I really wish someone had told this to me—is that all of us who do creative work, we get into it because we have good taste... But it's like there's a gap. That for the first couple years that you're making stuff, what you're making isn't so good... It's trying to be good, it has ambition to be good, but it's not quite that good."

However, Glass said that the key to producing work you're proud of is to follow your creative instincts as you develop your skills. "A lot of people never get past that phase. A lot of people at that point, they quit... Most everybody I know who does interesting creative work, they went through a phase of years... It is only by actually going through a volume of work that you are actually going to catch up and close that gap. And the work you're making will be as good as your ambitions... It's going to take you a while. It's normal to take a while. And you just have to fight your way through."

It's natural to feel disappointed with the work you make. However, you must push through that discomfort and continue to create until your work catches up to your aspirations.

QUESTION

Where are you currently disappointed that your work doesn't live up to your aspirations? Don't quit. Keep developing.

November

9

Be a Laser, Not a Lighthouse

Many people—especially leaders—focus on all the things that could go wrong rather than on a compelling vision of what's possible. They operate like a lighthouse—"Don't go here. Don't go there."—pointing out all the potential problems or danger areas but not really indicating what others should do.

Instead, you must be a laser. A laser is pointed in a clear direction and cuts through the fog. There is no mistaking its direction, and it's easy to follow. When you communicate about your work, focus on being clear and precise about expectations, direction, strategy, and priorities. When you do this, it provides just the right kind of clarity that will trickle down to the rest of the team.

Consider your current priorities. Is there any place where you are being less than clear in order to avoid potential dangers? Could that be affecting the kinds of risks others take or the ideas they will share?

Focus on being a laser, not a lighthouse. Be clear, precise, and direct in how you communicate with others.

QUESTION
Where are you acting as a lighthouse instead of a laser?

November
10

Your Manifesto

Do you remember the movie *Jerry Maguire*? Sports agent Maguire spent all night writing a manifesto about how dysfunctional his industry had become and how to fix it. He delivered copies to his entire company, hoping it would set the stage for a massive change. Instead, he was fired.

Did Jerry do the right thing? Well, sort of. Just going along with the way things are as a way of keeping the peace is no way to produce a body of work that you'll be proud of later. However, making copies for everyone may have been a lapse in judgment.

Still, getting clear on your values and principles is important to doing work you can stand behind. I challenge you to write your own manifesto. It doesn't have to be dozens of pages. It can simply be a list of five or ten principles that define how you will engage your life and work each day. They can be simple, and they only have to matter to you. However, they should frame up how you will make decisions each day and the principles by which you will live, work, and produce. (Just learn from Jerry Maguire and keep this manifesto to yourself.)

Writing your own personal manifesto is a great way to clarify what really matters to you and to build a framework for making personal and career decisions.

> **QUESTION**
> What are the principles of your manifesto? Don't have one?
> Write it!

November
11

Reaction vs. Response

Our instincts keep us safe, help us navigate relationships, and help us discern between good and bad ideas.

However, our instincts can also mislead us. It's possible to react in the moment instead of responding meaningfully and with reasoned wisdom. When we react instead of responding, we make very bad decisions that we may have to live with for months or longer afterward.

To react is to operate purely on instinct. To respond is to listen to your instincts but pause and allow wisdom and experience to guide your actions. When we respond rather than reacting, we are far more likely to make wise choices and far less likely to cause ourselves trouble down the line.

Does this ring true to you? Can you think of moments in your life, your work, or your relationships where reaction got you into trouble and a more measured response would have served you better?

When you react, you are operating purely on instinct. Brilliant creative work is forged when instinct is in submission to wisdom and experience.

QUESTION

Where might you be tempted to react rather than respond this week? How can you prevent it?

November

12

WIGs

You probably have a number of objectives you are trying to deliver on at the moment. However, there are likely only a few very critical goals that will build momentum for everything else you are doing. In his book *The 4 Disciplines of Execution*, Chris McChesney calls these wildly important goals, or WIGs. They are the critical areas of focus into which all your other activity should channel during a season.

I'll give you an example from my own work. For the past year, my WIGs have been quality, awareness, and revenue diversity. *Quality* means that I am working to improve the overall quality of the work I produce, the content I generate, and the talks and trainings I offer to organizations. *Awareness* means that I am working to increase awareness for my work and to play on a larger scale. *Revenue diversity* means that I am seeking to find new and more diverse sources of revenue for my business so that I'm not overly dependent on just a few.

By establishing these three WIGs, I've been able to set smaller goals that channel up into them and thus focus my work on what will truly move the needle rather than working on many disparate projects with loose connections to my overall objectives.

As you consider your work during this season, what should your WIGs be?

Wildly important goals help you focus your projects and your everyday goals on activity that will actually move the needle.

QUESTION

What are your wildly important goals?

November
13

Sorry, Not Sorry

"Don't apologize for your existence."

This is a phrase I coined to help people on my team stop apologizing for sharing a bold point of view. I noticed that a lot of creative pros—myself included—struggle with "sorry under my breath" syndrome, or the need to apologize any time they express an opinion. I think it connects to the deep insecurity that many creatives feel about whether their work is truly good and the subsequent fear that they will never measure up to expectations. So "sorry" becomes shorthand for "I really shouldn't be speaking right now."

But...you should.

We need a diverse set of perspectives in order to get to the right idea. We need one another in order to see things clearly. We need our peers to be willing to say what they see. And they need you to do the same.

Apologies are for when you've genuinely wronged someone. And when you do, please apologize loudly. But don't follow the compulsion to apologize for sharing your perspective. It's part of your job as a pro to do so, and apologizing for it means that you are devaluing yourself, the person listening to you, the person who hired you, and the very space that you're occupying.

Don't apologize for your existence.

QUESTION

Are you overly apologetic in certain situations? Why do you think that's the case?

November
14

Reality behind Reality

You know that feeling when things suddenly make sense in a way they didn't just a few moments before? When you see things more clearly and all the dots connect? It's like there's a sudden clarity that's always been there, but you never noticed. You've seen through the looking glass. You've peered through to the heart of the issue.

Pay special attention to those moments, because they are sacred. I don't mean sacred in a spiritual sense but in a "set apart" sense, which is what the source word of *sacred* means. Pay attention to the circumstances that led to those breakthroughs, what you did just before, what you were reading or listening to, the conversation that was happening. It's not that you can fabricate more of these moments, but you can learn to create environments in which they are more likely to occur.

Think about the breakthrough moments you've experienced. What did they have in common? What were you doing just before? What were the circumstances that led to the breakthrough? What question did you ask?

Breakthrough moments are a glimpse of reality behind reality. Pay attention to them, and learn from them.

QUESTION

What do your breakthrough moments have in common? Are there any through lines that you notice?

November
15

It's Going to Be OK

Inevitably, every creative pro reaches a moment when they begin to think that maybe they've lost their touch. What came so easily just a few years before feels more challenging, and what once would have felt intuitive now takes a while to understand.

It's going to be OK.

One of the blessings of inexperience is naivete. You don't know what you don't know. Everything feels so intuitive and clear and black-and-white. As you gain experience, things begin to appear grayer. The curse of experience is that you know all the things that could go wrong because you've seen it all before. By the time the newcomer shouts "I love it!" you've already subconsciously concocted ten ways the idea could go off the rails.

You haven't "lost it"; you're just more nuanced in your thinking. You see things as they are—shades of gray. You realize that life is a probability set, not a clear-cut math equation. That is valuable. It doesn't feel as good in the moment, but it's far more valuable than wide-eyed optimism.

Experience brings wisdom, which brings the curse of knowing that life is a probability set, not a clear-cut math equation.

QUESTION

Have you ever felt like you're "losing it"? Where have you seen your experience pan out when less-experienced pros thought a different direction to be best?

November
16

The Spark and the Scorpion

In my book *Herding Tigers*, I wrote about two common kinds of people you might find on your team. The first is what I call "the spark." This is a person who has never met an idea they don't like. They are in perpetual idea-generation mode and can toss out a hundred of them in a half-hour meeting. They see possibilities everywhere, which may not be useful when you need to choose an idea and move on.

The second profile is "the scorpion." They dislike every idea and immediately dismiss new thinking. Their very presence brings down the vibe of the room, because everyone knows they will be the first to offer critique. In fact, people may even look right at them when sharing an idea in anticipation of their response.

Both of these qualities can be useful. It's important to be able to spot possibility and to play with ideas. It's also important to be able to critique ideas to improve them. However, maintaining a balance of each quality is necessary to be effective.

Both the spark and the scorpion can disrupt the flow of your team. Strive to maintain a balance between possibility seeking and critique.

QUESTION

Do you skew toward one profile or the other, the spark or the scorpion?

November
17

Optimal Creative Time

When do you do your most effective thinking? Some people jump out of bed and are halfway into their work before they even hit their desk, while others seem to do their best creative work late in the evening or even after hours. Unfortunately, most of us do not have an option to work whenever we want to. However, that doesn't mean that you can't take advantage of those extra productive times, even if they fall outside your normal work hours.

Some creative pros set aside time very early in the morning to do their creative thinking, before they go into the office. Yes, I understand that it's important to have a separation between work space and home life, but for some people, those precious few hours in the morning or the evening after everyone else is in bed might actually save us many hours of trying to think while juggling all our daytime priorities. An hour in the morning or evening might actually save us five later.

When do you do your best creative thinking? Strive to block off just a bit of time this week during that optimum time for idea work.

Dedicate your best creative thinking time for generating ideas, even if that's in the morning or evening.

QUESTION

When do your best ideas generally happen? How can you structure more thought time during those windows?

November
18

The Power of Yes

A commitment is a powerful force of nature. Something magical happens when we say yes. It seems that the moment we commit to something, we begin to orient our lives around bringing that commitment into existence, even if subconsciously. Our minds begin to connect dots that we couldn't see before. Other people come into our lives at just the right moment to provide an opportunity. (In reality, they were already there. It's just that we weren't looking for them.) A commitment channels our focus and energy toward an end.

Many people fail to make commitments because they are afraid of failing. Instead, they like to "keep their options open," but in so doing, they are unwittingly working against their own best interests. They fail to channel their energy effectively because it is spread across too many possibilities.

When you make a commitment, you channel your focus, time, and energy toward making it happen. When you keep your options open, you will often subvert your goals because you try to do too many things at once.

> **QUESTION**
> Where are you trying to keep your options open instead of committing? What do you need to say yes to today?

November
19

The Power of No

Entrepreneur and author Derek Sivers says that if something isn't a clear yes, it's a no. Life is too short to half commit to things that you really have no interest in spending your time on. We do this out of guilt or shame or obligation, but if we aren't really putting ourselves fully into it, we're not really doing it anyway. This applies to discretionary work, relationships, personal obligations, and more.

In many ways, creative work is about choosing what you'll say no to. Others may never see what was left on the cutting room floor, but that material is just as crucial to the finished product as what made it into the project. It's the negative space gives substance to the work. A brilliant musician knows which notes *not* to play.

Is there something in your life that you need to say a clear no to right now? Doing so will help you channel your energy into what really matters.

Closing a door by saying no allows you to channel your finite energy into the places where it can really matter. Do not commit out of guilt, shame, or obligation unless you plan to give it your full effort.

QUESTION
What do you need to say no to today?

November

20

Work Is Not a Family

Some workplaces like to parade the notion that their work culture is a family. No! The workplace is not a family. Family membership is unconditional and is not contingent on performance. On the other hand, a job is contingent on delivering on expectations and maintaining appropriate behavior, and at any point, your employment can be revoked if you don't measure up.

When companies talk about work culture as a family, they give people a false sense of security that really shouldn't be there. Yes, it's important to feel psychologically safe, but at no point should the signal be sent that work peers are similar to their bloodline.

Why is this important? Because whether you lead a team or are on one, it's easy to slip into this family mindset out of insecurity. It's important to have a clear understanding of where you stand in relation to your manager, your peers, and the people you lead and to not allow insecurity to cause you to make promises you can't keep or expect treatment that is unrealistic.

Don't confuse your work team for your family. Teams are not family.

QUESTION

Do you consider your work team a family? How might you adapt those perceptions to be more accurate?

November
21

EPIC Ideas

How do you know when an idea is the right one?

One framework that I've taught creative pros uses three aspects of the idea, rated on a scale of one to ten, then discussed with the team. (This also works for solo projects, by the way.)

1. *Effective:* How effectively does the idea solve the problem you set out to solve?
2. *Practical:* How practical would it be to execute the idea, given present resources (time, budget, etc.)?
3. *Interesting and Cool:* How much energy do you or the team have about executing the idea? Is it something you could get excited about, or does it feel underwhelming?

Once you've rated the idea for these qualities on a scale of one to ten, you can begin to have a more productive chat about ways in which you might make the idea more palatable.

- ► How could we make it more effective?
- ► Could we scale it down to make it more practical?
- ► How could we make it more interesting to us?

Using a framework to evaluate an idea makes a very subjective process (choosing an idea) into a more objective exercise.

QUESTION

Is there an idea you're evaluating right now that could benefit from the EPIC framework?

November
22

One for Me

In his books about the creative process, author Steven Pressfield shares an ethic that is common among screenwriters in Hollywood: "One for the studio, one for me."

"One for the studio" means that to do your job, you need to do work—in this case, write screenplays—that matches the expectations of the people paying the bills and not worry so much about whether it satisfies you creatively. This might mean cranking out a summer action sci-fi script that hits all the expected notes for such a movie.

However, "one for me" means that you also need to have some creative work in process that satisfies you creatively and may be on the less practical side commercially. This might be a side project or something on the back burner that you're working on as a way to grow your skills and take creative risks or to express yourself in ways that your on-demand work won't allow.

When you slip toward a "six for the studio, one for me" approach, it's easy to begin to lose your heart. It feels like you are cranking out widgets to match everyone else's specs but aren't able to scratch your own creative itch.

Adopt the "one for the studio, one for me" approach to ensure that you are keeping your creative fires stoked.

> **QUESTION**
> Are you too lopsided in how you are leveraging your creativity at the moment? Do you need to develop a personal project to help you keep the embers burning?

November
23

Listen to Your Life

Just before I left for my honeymoon, a colleague handed me a little book by Parker J. Palmer called *Let Your Life Speak*. The book explores the nature of vocation and how we often miss the clues to what we are truly wired to do and be because we aren't listening for the patterns all around us. Palmer argues that to uncover your vocation, or what is being uniquely called out of you, you must listen to your life and hear what it's saying to you. We think that vocation is "out there" somewhere, but it's often actually right under our own noses.

- ► Where do you seem to add distinct value to the lives of others in a way no one else does?
- ► What kinds of activities seem to bring you alive more than others?
- ► What do other people consistently come to you for?
- ► What perspective do you have that others think is a little crazy?

Any of these questions can help you begin to identify your vocation, which can help you develop the unique voice that marks your creative work.

To uncover your vocation, you must listen to your life. Look for the patterns that are all around you.

QUESTION

As you consider the patterns in your life, how would you describe your vocation? What do you uniquely offer the world through how you engage each day?

November
24

Thankfulness

I've always preferred the term *thankfulness* over *gratitude*. When I express that I am thankful, it means that I'm full of thanks. I'm filled up.

It's easy to turn your eyes to the next thing—the next project, the next meeting—without pausing to express thankfulness for the good thing that just happened.

Did an idea appear out of nowhere that solved an important problem?

Was a conflict resolved?

Did you read something that helped you understand a topic in a new way?

It's important to pause in those moments when something good happens and allow yourself to be full of thanks. Reflect on your good fortune, not in a pandering way but in a way that recognizes how very different things could actually be. Mark the moment.

What are you thankful for?

Why?

What does it mean to you?

Making the practice of thankfulness a part of your rhythm will open your mind to new opportunities, new creative possibilities, and new relationships. (People want to be around those who are full of thanks!)

Make the practice of thankfulness a part of your rhythm. Pause to be full of thanks when something good happens in your life or work.

QUESTION

Take a few minutes today to pause and be full of thanks. What do you have to be thankful for?

November
25

Discipline

The word *discipline* is polarizing. To some, it implies the grind. It means sweat, grit, blood, and sacrifice. To others, it sounds like obligation. It's something I ought to do but probably don't want to. It's guilt inducing.

I'd like to simplify the word for all of us. Discipline simply means to make an agreement with yourself, a promise to yourself, and then keep it.

If you agree that you're going to run for two minutes and you do it, you are disciplined. You did what you said you would. You don't have to run a 5K; you just do what you say.

If you say you're going to write fifty words a day, or two hundred, or a thousand and you do it, you are disciplined.

We get into problems when we make promises that we can't or don't intend to keep. We say, "I'm going to write twenty-five hundred words on Tuesday," then something comes up and we only write a few hundred, and we feel terrible and undisciplined. The reality is that we set unrealistic expectations.

To be disciplined, set realistic expectations of yourself, then deliver on them. Always do what you say.

Discipline simply means to make an agreement with yourself, then keep it. Don't make agreements you don't intend to do everything you can to keep.

QUESTION

What agreements do you have with yourself right now? What does discipline look like in your life?

November
26

Peaks and Troughs

At times, it seems like you are on fire, have plenty of energy, and could go on at your current pace forever. Then you inexplicably hit a wall, and your output suddenly changes. You are in a trough with no clear explanation why.

When you have high expectations, it's tempting to believe that the solution to consistently impressive productivity is to remove the troughs so that you have no "off" moments. However, by removing the troughs, you also inadvertently limit the peaks. You force yourself into a very narrow bandwidth of productivity that is predictable but also stale.

To be effective, you must embrace the rhythmic nature of the creative process. The peaks are inexplicably linked to the troughs. There must be downtime to accompany your frenetic uptime. Every hill you climb means an eventual valley to endure.

The key is to not resent the troughs but to instead recognize them as seasons when your creative process has gone underground for a while. Use those trough moments to learn, to look for new opportunities, and to rest.

The creative process has peaks and troughs. Instead of resenting the troughs, learn from them and leverage them to look for new opportunities.

> **QUESTION**
> Are you in a creative peak or trough right now? What does that mean for you?

November
27

Busy Boredom

There's a dynamic that I like to call "busy boredom." A lot of pros I meet suffer from this malady. They are very, very busy. Much to do. Work to create. Meetings to attend. Yes, their schedules and their task lists are full, but they are bored out of their minds. They are no longer curious. They are not asking questions. They are not filling their minds with valuable stimuli that spark new ideas, new insights, new connections.

Here are a few questions to ask that will help diagnose busy boredom:

- ► Have you learned anything exciting this week?
- ► Are you working on a project that energizes you and maybe even scares you a little?
- ► Are you doing any work right now that runs the risk of failure?
- ► Have you asked *why* in a meeting recently?
- ► Do you find yourself scrolling on your phone in every available down moment?

The cure for busy boredom is curiosity. Ask questions. Come alive. Try something new. Read or experience something that challenges your point of view. Immerse yourself in a new perspective. Do something that rekindles the pilot light of your creative imagination.

You can be busy and bored at the same time. Strive to avoid falling into the trap of busy boredom.

QUESTION
Have you experienced busy boredom? How will you handle it the next time you recognize it?

November
28

Others' Expectations

I once had a wonderful conversation with Richard Hytner, who was the former global deputy chairman of advertising great Saatchi and Saatchi. He told me that he spent many years of his professional life striving to climb the ladder and become the person in the organizational spotlight. He wanted to be the CEO of a publicly traded company, because it had become engrained in him that to aspire to any less was unacceptable.

The problem, as Richard conveyed, was that he simply wasn't wired to be CEO. He thrived as the "number two" in an organization, driving alignment, developing strategy, helping bring the CEO's vision into being, but he simply wasn't the right person to be in the spotlight. He learned that it was better to thrive at what you're wired to do than to aspire to something that others tell you that you should want.

There are many narratives in the marketplace that shape the aspirations of creative pros. In the "up or out" ethic of many organizations, you're deemed unmotivated and unambitious if you don't aspire to be on top. However, I encourage you to consider that your life and career might be far more productive and enjoyable if you make decisions according to who you are, not according to who others want you to be.

Know yourself. Don't make career decisions according to what other people would do in your situation.

QUESTION

Are you making any decisions right now because of what is expected of someone in your situation rather than because of who you actually are?

November
29

Victimhood

When you hear the word *ego*, it conjures up images of bombastic managers charging into the room, barking orders, and expecting everyone to bend to their every whim. This is certainly one form of ego. But there is a more subtle form of ego that often plays out in organizational life, and it can be equally destructive. It sounds something like this:

"Oh, you don't like my idea? OK. That's fine. I'm just going to sit over here in the corner, silent, until you recognize how incredible I am."

Playing the victim is a form of ego, because it means you are putting your ego ahead of your productive passion. You feel slighted in some way, so you decide that you are going to disengage until you feel that you are being recognized in the way that you deserve.

When you play the victim, you essentially abdicate your contribution. You withdraw from the conversation and forfeit your body of work. The price is high.

Don't allow your bruised ego to cause you to forfeit your body of work. Refuse to play the victim.

QUESTION

Is there any area of your life or creating where you are playing the victim? Are you in any way withholding your contribution because you feel unappreciated?

November

30

Pomodoro

The creative process flows best when you alternate between deep engagement and deep rest. It's in the fluctuation that you often experience breakthroughs, because you are forcing your mind to shift gears, which can forge new and unexpected insights in the most unlikely ways.

One method that I've found effective is the Pomodoro technique. It involves engaging in a series of twenty-five-minute deep work sessions punctuated by five-minute breaks. So you set a timer, work uninterrupted for twenty-five minutes, then when the alarm goes off, take a five-minute break. Get up. Walk around. Grab some coffee. Stretch. Do something that shifts your mode for a few minutes. Then reset the timer and dive in once more.

Many pros who have implemented this technique will set a goal for their session. For example, "I'm going to do three Pomodoros this morning," or "I will do five Pomodoros throughout the day." Simply planning these short, deep work sessions in advance can drastically improve your daily productivity and your overall sense of energy.

Creative productivity happens best in short, frequent bursts of work. Schedule them in advance to ensure that they don't get squeezed out by your busy life.

QUESTION

How can you plan a few short bursts of creative productivity today? Can you work in two Pomodoros at some point to do your deep, creative work?

December

*"For last year's words belong to last year's language.
And next year's words await another voice... And
to make an end is to make a beginning."*
—T. S. ELIOT

Every year's end offers the opportunity to reflect on the past and adjust for the future. This month, spend some time reflecting on how things have been for the past year and on small things you might want to prune, eliminate, adjust, or continue doing over the coming year. End strong, and build momentum going into the new year.

December

1

Rubber and Glass Balls

In 1991, Brian G. Dyson, the former CEO of Coca-Cola, gave what has become known as one of the most memorable commencement speeches ever recorded. He said, "Imagine life as a game in which you are juggling some five balls in the air. You name them—work, family, health, friends, and spirit—and you're keeping all of these in the air. You will soon understand that work is a rubber ball. If you drop it, it will bounce back. But the other four balls—family, health, friends, and spirit—are made of glass. If you drop one of these, they will be irrevocably scuffed, marked, nicked, damaged, or even shattered. They will never be the same. You must understand that and strive for balance in your life."

There are some things in life that are incredibly pliable. If you make a mistake and lose a client, you can likely find another one. If you produce work that is subpar, you'll likely get another chance at it tomorrow. However, there are some things that are not quite so resilient. Relationships, your health, your friendships, your spiritual life: these are all much more fragile and must be handled with care. If you neglect them for too long—drop them—they may shatter.

You must know which things in your life are pliable and which are irreparably fragile.

Handle the fragile elements of your life with care. To be prolific, brilliant, and healthy, ensure that you are not neglecting them for the sake of your work.

QUESTION

What are the fragile elements of your life? What do you do to ensure they are protected?

December
2

The Breakout Principle

In their book *The Breakout Principle*, Herbert Benson and William Proctor taught that brilliant insights often occur when you are deeply immersed in a problem, then break away and engage in some sort of mindless activity like knitting, walking, or humming. Upon returning to your work, you will often see things more clearly because your mind has continued to process the problem while your executive brain was otherwise occupied. Benson and Proctor argue that we can strategically implement this method in our daily lives to help achieve creative breakthroughs when under pressure.

Consider an important problem you are working on. Block some time today or this week to delve deeply into it, attacking it from all angles. Then structure time to break away and engage in some sort of mindless activity, and after a time, reengage the problem. It's likely that you'll have a fresh perspective when you return, and maybe even a breakthrough awaiting you.

To achieve breakthroughs, we sometimes need to break away from the problem and engage in mindless activity.

QUESTION

How can you implement the breakout principle in your work today?

December

3

The Long Hallway

British philosopher Alain de Botton is reported to have said, "The more people you have to ask for permission the more dangerous a project gets." One huge mistake that many creative pros make is perpetually revisiting their previous decisions. They grow uncertain about their direction, so they waffle and turn alternative ideas over in their head long after a decision has been made. This behavior is *especially* damaging when your work depends on others or when they depend on you. Your collaborators will eventually learn to just wait until you've made up your mind before acting. This means that the entire project will stall until they know for *certain* that you've made up your mind.

Imagine that a project is like a long hallway. Once a decision is made, a thick steel door closes behind you, and you have no choice but to move forward. Yes, you can go backward, but it's going to require a lot of time and resources to make it happen, so you must be decisive and move forward at each phase. I find that this is a helpful way to think about a long-arc creative project. As we all move forward through the stages of the project together, we make decisions and agree to live with them unless we learn something new that impacts the work.

Don't constantly question or revisit your old decisions. Doing so will train others around you to wait until you've made up your mind.

QUESTION

Do you frequently second-guess and revisit decisions on projects? Is there a decision that you're questioning now that you simply need to commit to?

December
4

Just One Song

Jeff Tweedy, songwriter and founding member of the band Wilco, recently released a book called *How to Write One Song*. I immediately resonated with the title, because that's precisely what the creative process is.

Make *this* thing, that's here in front of you, right now.

It doesn't matter how many of them you've done before, the only one that matters is *this* one. Now. And typically, for professionals, it must be delivered under a deadline.

In the book, Tweedy writes "I happen to love deadlines. Not everyone does. I do, because they fit with my belief that art isn't ever really complete. As the saying goes, 'No work of art is ever finished; it can only be abandoned in an interesting place.'"

Whatever you are working on today, how can you approach it as if it's your first time? How can you refresh your perspective, ask new kinds of questions, and reclaim the joy of solving problems with your skills? How would you approach it if you were a beginner?

And, when the deadline arrives, how will ensure you abandon it in an interesting place?

Approach each project like a beginner, and treat it like it's the only one you've ever worked on.

QUESTION

What would it mean to approach your work like a beginner today?

December
5

The Culture of Blame

Some creative teams devolve over time into a culture of blame. A few signs that this may have already infiltrated your team include the following:

- *A general lack of accountability:* If it's difficult to identify the single point of accountability for delivering a project or if there seems to be ambiguity about responsibilities on the team, it's possible that some of this is the result of a culture of blame.
- *Hesitancy to admit mistakes or frequent attempts to cover them up rather than fix them:* Everyone makes mistakes. If your team is really stretching itself to do great work, it will probably make many of them. But mistakes need to be dealt with, not disguised.
- *An overall lack of commitment to the excellence of the work or the needs of the client/organization:* Some of the most toxic blame shifting is the kind that involves blaming the client or customer for the problems the team is facing. When this happens, it can cause a downshift in the team's drive to go the extra mile.
- *Frequent whispers in the hallway or gossip:* These little side conversations are like cracks in a dam. Every one of them erodes the integrity of the team slightly and puts the entire team at risk.

Don't play along with a blame culture. Refuse to point fingers, always take accountability for your actions, and refuse to throw others under the bus.

The blame game erodes trust and squelches the creative process.

QUESTION

Is there any place where you are pointing fingers rather than assuming responsibility?

December

6

The Edge Pieces

My family *loves* to do jigsaw puzzles. There is typically an unfinished one sitting on our dining room table for weeks at a time, and every so often, someone will sit down and work on it.

If you've ever attempted to complete a jigsaw puzzle, how did you begin? Did you just pick up random pieces and try them together to see if they fit? Or did you stare at all the pieces on the table, trying to mentally place them all together? No, of course not. You probably started with the edge pieces, because you know at least one thing about them: they belong on the outside of the puzzle. Once you've identified all the edge pieces, you can begin to fit them together to form a frame around the rest of the puzzle. In this way, you work your way from what's known to what's unknown.

You can follow a similar process in your creative work. Start with the knowns, and work your way to the unknowns:

- ► What do I know for certain about this problem?
- ► What has definitely worked well in the past?
- ► What do I know is off-limits?
- ► What resources do I have to spend, whether time, money, or energy?

Once you've identified the edge pieces, you can begin filling in the puzzle.

In your creative work, start from what's known, and work toward what's unknown. Begin with the edge pieces.

> **QUESTION**
> Is there a problem you're stuck on right now? How can you step back and identify the edge pieces so that you have more clarity about how to proceed?

December
7

Difficult Managers

Everyone—even the CEO of a company—reports to someone. This means that you not only have to learn how to manage those on your team, you must also develop the ability to manage up to get what you and the team need to succeed.

Sooner or later, you are likely to have a difficult manager. How do you handle a conversation with someone who seems to want nothing more than to make your life more challenging?

First, approach each conversation with respect, and assume the best. Go into each interaction with the mindset that everyone is on the same side.

Second, have your supporting facts in order, and make your case clearly. Make certain that you can back up your hunches and intuitions with data. Strive to make your argument airtight.

Finally, aim for small wins, and build from there. You're unlikely to get everything you want, so aim for small progress, and use it to build relational momentum.

Be strategic in how you manage up. Aim for small wins with your manager and build on them.

QUESTION

Is there a difficult conversation you need to have with your manager? How can you approach it strategically?

December
8

When You're Working

What do you do when you're working? I mean actually working?

Thomas Edison once said, "Being busy does not always mean real work. The object of all work is production or accomplishment and to either of these ends there must be forethought, system, planning, intelligence, and honest purpose, as well as perspiration. Seeming to do is not doing."

There are a number of activities we engage in every day that are grouped together under the heading of work, but not all of them are truly what we're paid to do. We are very, very busy, but not all that busyness results in actual value.

There is a select set of activities that you do each day that truly constitute work. For me, that would be writing, thinking, solving a client problem, or producing teaching that helps someone else do better work. There are a number of activities that I have to do to keep things moving forward, but those activities are my actual work or the value I'm paid to produce.

So what do you do when you're working? What set of activities produce 80 percent of the value that you're accountable for delivering? How can you set up more of your time and energy around your actual work?

Not all activity is work. Know the critical value that you're actually paid to deliver, and set your days up around delivering it.

QUESTION

What do you do when you're actually working?

December

9

Make It Simple

One of the worst insults you can hurl at someone is to call them naive. When you do, you are essentially saying that they aren't mature enough or wise enough or worldly enough to understand the depth of the complexity of the situation. If only they were as mature as you, they would actually see things for what they are!

In an effort to not appear naive, we love to make things more complicated than they actually are. We mock simple answers because they insult our pride. We love thinking the truth is complex, because that makes us seem sophisticated and experienced. But the reality is that simple answers are often the right ones. I'm pretty certain that Einstein wasn't disappointed when he arrived at $E=mc^2$.

When you're stuck, seek simplicity. How can you make what you're working on as simple as possible? Can you restate the problem in a new way that eliminates needless complexity of language and thought? Are there assumptions clouding your view of the problem?

It's not naive to seek simplicity in your work. It's a mark of maturity to do so.

Seek to state your creative problem as simply as possible.

QUESTION

Is there any place where you are overcomplicating your work?

December
10

Who Do You Listen To?

Who do you listen to? We listen to all sorts of people, some of whom may not even be in our lives any longer. We listen to teachers or coaches who once said something cruel to us or who marked us with self-doubt. We listen to parents who expressed their disappointment in a career choice. We listen to managers who used us for their own gain but never really built into us in a way that would help us achieve our own goals.

These people are no longer speaking to us, but we are still listening to them because their words echo in our minds. As Ralph Waldo Emerson wrote, "Whatever course you decide upon, there is always someone to tell you that you are wrong. There are always difficulties arising that tempt you to believe that your critics are right. To map out a course of action and follow it to an end requires courage."

There will always be people in your life to tell you what you do. You must choose who you will listen to. Receive the words of people who actually have skin in the game. Listen to people who want what's best for you, not just for themselves.

Don't listen to the voices of those who would only seek to squelch your ambition. Choose to listen to people who actually want what's best for you.

QUESTION

Are there any voices from the past (or present) that are limiting your view of what's possible?

December
11

Avoiding the Circus

Have you ever had a client, another team, or even another person in your organization that you dreaded having to work with? You just knew that the entire project was going to be chaotic and that you would end up having to deal with not only the complexity of the project itself but also the complexity of the other person or team. This is not uncommon in highly collaborative work. Different people and teams have varying standards for how they organize and what they expect from one another.

Here's the thing: you cannot allow yourself to be drawn into the chaos of your client or collaborator. You must maintain your standards of engagement and refuse to allow yourself to get swept away by the other person's lack of organizational skills or by their lack of health.

I've always loved the Polish saying, "Not my circus, not my monkeys." It means that you refuse to take responsibility for the chaos that everyone around you creates. All you can do is own your own work, stay focused, and avoid getting drawn into the circus.

Don't get drawn into the chaos of your client or collaborators. Stay organized, maintain clear expectations, and own your process.

QUESTION

Is there any place where you're getting drawn into someone else's circus? What can you do about it?

December
12

Legacy vs. Tombstone

"What do you want your tombstone to say?" I remember going through this exercise a number of years ago as a participant in a team-building exercise. Everyone struggled to come up with a few words that would describe how they wanted to be remembered after they die. What words could be carved into a hunk of stone to summarize an entire life?

In retrospect, I really don't like this exercise at all. Mostly, I dislike it because it simply isn't a practical way to consider the impact you want your life to have. A tombstone is a cold piece of granite that will sit in the middle of a field, rarely seen, as a testament to the fact that you were once here. However, memories are living things. Your impact on others is a force multiplier.

Rather than worry about the handful of words that will go on your tombstone, I think it's far more effective to focus on the investments you are making in the lives of others. Focus on developing a living legacy that will continue to echo for generations to come.

Don't worry about how you'll be remembered. Make investments in other people that will echo for generations to come.

QUESTION

What investment will you make in the life of another person today? Who can you spend time with, encourage, build up?

December
13

Fighting for Your Work

It's wonderful when you find an advocate, someone who is willing to step up and argue for your work. When these people arrive in your life, it often feels like a breath of fresh air and a gift from above.

But here's a hard truth: no one cares about your work like you do. *No one.*

If you're waiting for someone else to kick down a door for you, prepare for disappointment. If you're hoping for someone to vouch for you and get your foot in a door, then you may be waiting for a long time.

That's not to say that these things don't happen. Of course they do. However, recognize that no one thinks about your work as much as you do, and if you aren't willing to fight for it, no one else will either. When people see you fighting for your own work, they are inspired to join you.

No one else will fight for your work like you will. Period.

No matter how great the trainer, every boxer has to step into the ring alone. You must be prepared to go twelve rounds if necessary.

You can't afford to put the fate of your work into someone else's hands. Fight for it and be tenacious.

QUESTION
How do you need to fight for your work today? Don't abdicate that responsibility!

December
14

Take More Shots

In basketball, you cannot make a shot that you don't take. Thus, the more shots you take, the greater your chances of making some of them.

How many shots are you taking in your life? How often are you putting work into the world? How many different kinds of activities are in your portfolio of risk? The more shots you take, the more likely some of them will actually land in the metaphorical basket.

- ► Have a few projects in your life that you're working on purely out of passion or curiosity.
- ► As a team leader, encourage people to explore ideas that could be a "moon shot" but could also provide unimaginable value to the organization long term.
- ► Refuse to settle for the first idea, even if it's acceptable. Keep pushing until you are a little scared of where you landed.
- ► Refuse to allow fear of failure to limit your perspective. If you want to do good work, you will fail. If you're not failing occasionally, you're probably not stretching yourself.

The more shots you take, the more you are likely to make.

Winning is often a game of percentages. Practice and hone your skills through unnecessary creating, follow your instincts for opportunity, and don't be afraid to take shots and miss.

QUESTION

How can you increase the number of shots you are taking with your work?

December

15

Nervous

I used to think being nervous about launching something new was a sign of weakness or a lack of confidence in one's ability. Now, I realize that it's actually a big part of doing things you deem worthwhile.

Nerves are a sign that you care about your work. If you never get nervous about what you're putting out into the world, it could mean that you don't think your work is important enough to fret over. If you value the work you do, you should on occasion feel a little nervous about whether it will hit the mark and create the value you intended.

Nerves are a sign that you know you can still improve. If you never get nervous, it means that you believe yourself to be at the very top of your game and there is no room for improvement. One of the reasons I get nervous when I launch something is that I know there is always something more I could have done to tweak it and make it better, but perfect is the enemy of great.

Nerves are a sign that you respect your audience. If you respect the people you serve, you will feel a little nervous about whether your work will truly hit the mark for them. I greatly respect the people I have the honor of creating for and working with, and I want to ensure that I deliver something that's worthy of them.

Don't mistake nervousness for weakness. It means you care deeply about your work.

QUESTION

Are you nervous about any of your work? Why? What does it mean?

December
16

Uncertain

I have had conversations with people at the top of their industry or craft. In fact, some of them are household names. You know the one overriding thing that I kept thinking after I met them? They are—just like me, just like you—figuring it out as they go along.

There is a myth that many people carry around that convinces them that some people just have things all figured out, and if they could simply figure out the secret that they know, everything would lock into place. Only the secret doesn't exist. They are—mostly—just figuring it out as they go along like the rest of us.

Yes, experience yields wisdom. Yes, as they get better at their craft, they discover some shortcuts or leverage some economies of scale that the rest of us don't have access to. But for the most part, they are just figuring it out as they go along.

There is no secret out there for you to discover. The path forward is to make things, learn, grow, and figure it out as you go along.

Even the people at the top of their craft or industry are mostly figuring it out as they go along.

QUESTION

Have you ever been discouraged because you couldn't seem to figure out the secret?

December
17

Excellence, Not Perfection

A leader once shared with me a tenet that he teaches his team:

"We value excellence, not perfection."

He said that this leadership tenet has been important to his team, because many who are drawn into his field tend to skew toward the perfectionist side of the spectrum. They want everything to be exactly right and might work for hours extra to make it so. The problem is that all those extra hours might yield just a small amount more quality but create a lot more pain and frustration for the team. So he will tell them, "It's fine. It's already excellent."

This is an important point for all of us who make things. Is there any place where you are striving for perfection instead of chasing after excellence? All those extra hours spent trying to squeeze just a little more value out of the project could be better allocated against something new.

Here are a few signs you're succumbing to perfectionism:

- ► If a project keeps you awake at night, even once it's finished.
- ► If you keep others waiting even after your work has been approved by your manager.
- ► If you start over again and again and again until you get something exactly right.

Chase excellence with your work, not perfection.

> **QUESTION**
> Is there any place where you are trying to be perfect?

December
18

Rapid Task Switching

Congratulations! You're quite the multitasker, no? You can write, check your email, watch a show on Netflix, and monitor your notifications all at the same time. Amazing.

Actually, it's not. And you're not really multitasking. You're doing what psychologists call "rapid task switching." You are quickly moving your attention and executive function back and forth between multiple tasks, which means that you are abandoning what you're actually working on—writing something important—each time you check your email.

The problem—and this really is one—is that each time you break your attention, you don't go back to exactly where you left off. Instead, your mind needs time to reengage with your work and get back to the level of creative thinking you were previously experiencing. It might not seem like anything has changed, but your creative flow has been broken inside your mind.

You will always do your best work when you are doing a single task at a time. Just one thing. This is most certainly true of any kind of work that requires creative problem-solving.

When you have important creative work to do, eliminate as many distractions as you can, and commit to focusing solely on that work. You will find insights that are lurking just beneath the surface of your conscious mind that are ready to break through.

Don't rapid task switch. Do one creative task at a time.

QUESTION

Do you try to multitask? How can you structure your work so that you are doing one thing at a time?

December
19

Risk Is Relative

A question I often encourage managers to ask of their team is: "What was the last risk you took, and how did you feel about it?" This question reveals an important understanding about collaboration: everyone has a different tolerance for risk.

What feels risky to you may feel completely safe and predictable to someone else and vice versa. What's normal for the spider is chaos for the fly.

It's important to note this because we often ascribe our own sense of risk tolerance to others and believe that risk is objective. It's not. Not by a long shot.

If you are early in your career, something might not feel risky because you don't understand the potential consequences of getting it wrong. This might yield confidence, but it's a false confidence based on immaturity.

If you are later in your career, something might not feel risky because you've seen it before and know how to tread the waters. This is mature confidence.

In the middle, where most of us reside, things are a little murkier. So it helps to have conversations about perceived risk. Don't assume everyone sees things the same.

Risk is relative. Have a conversation about perceived consequences of failure with your collaborators.

QUESTION

Is there any place in your current work where your perception of risk might be at odds with your collaborators'?

December
20

Your Defining Question

Often, there is one "defining question" that hovers over everything you do, begging to be answered.

How do I grow awareness for my new product?

How can I improve my rapport with my manager?

How do I deal with that difficult coworker?

Where is this job headed? Am I stuck?

In the day-to-day you probably ignore this defining question because you have much to do and little space to think about anything not directly relevant to your work responsibilities. Yet, this defining question clouds your thinking and creates a sense of misalignment and dissonance when not addressed. You know that something isn't right, but you can't put your finger on what it might be. The defining question is the one question that, if answered, could provide massive clarity in many areas of your life and work.

Your defining question could be related to your work, your relationships, your ambitions, your calling, or something else entirely, but if it's not addressed you *will* struggle to feel like you're making meaningful progress, even as you check tasks off your lists.

Your defining question defines your sense of everyday engagement. Identify it, then seek to find answers to it.

QUESTION
What do you think your "defining question" is right now?

December
21

Be Someone Worth Listening To

Why should people listen to or follow you?

Sorry to be blunt, but I think it's a question that everyone should ask themselves every so often. If you expect others to follow your lead, you need to be a leader worth following.

Have you ever known someone who became so subsumed by the organization that they basically became a tool of the company? There was no longer any distinction between them and the organization's priorities. All the best, most unique parts of their personality and perspective had been rounded off so that they could fit whatever role they were playing.

It's sad, and it's all too common.

The problem is, this not only affects their ability to do the work they're capable of doing, it also eliminates their team's ability to trust them. People don't trust automatons. They need to know that there's something driving your decision-making process other than climbing the ladder.

They need to know what you value.

Do you have a decision-making framework that is visible to your collaborators?

Do they know what you value?

Have they ever seen you make a decision that's counter to your best interests for the sake of the team?

Your team needs you to be someone worth following, and that means that they need to know that you're in it for them, not just for yourself.

QUESTION

How can you make your values more apparent to those you work with?

December
22

Comfort and Creativity

This is a pervasive and sinister belief that has—at times—caused me to compromise more than I should. When I aspire to comfort as the greatest goal of life, I refuse anything that might cause me pain or hardship, even if that means I have to abandon my pursuit of true north.

It is struggle that gives life its meaning and the pauses and blessings that punctuate its landscape. Sometimes that struggle is against self and the laziness that craves only comfort. The creative process is a personal assault on the beachhead of apathy, and to succumb to the path of comfort is to turn our backs on the greatness that is on the other side of sacrifice. I refuse to allow comfort to be my ambition. Comfort is often the enemy of greatness.

When you succumb to comfort as your ethic, you will compromise whatever you have to in order to preserve it, and this means not taking creative risks or even sacrificing meaning and purpose in your life.

Here's my challenge: Where in your life are you falling prey to "comfort worship"?

The love of comfort is often the enemy of greatness.

QUESTION

Is there any place in your life or work where you value comfort over creativity or comfort over effectiveness?

December
23

Scarcity Mindset

I've never lived in poverty, though when I was a full-time musician in my early twenties, I would celebrate having fifteen dollars in my account after monthly bills were paid. (It's steak dinner time! Well, cheap steak dinner anyway.) Still, I realized recently that for much of my life, I've held the belief that I was only a few mistakes away from losing everything and that it was more important to protect what I have than to focus on what is possible.

A scarcity mindset invades every area of life, and when I'm more concerned with protecting, I might lose my ability to recognize opportunities, or I may refuse to act on them because of what could be lost.

For creative pros, this lie is always on the prowl. It can cause you to shrink back from investing in yourself or to skimp and cut corners, which affects the long-term viability of your work. When you succumb to a scarcity mindset, you cannot be generous in a way that fuel creativity and passion.

Embrace possibility. Don't believe the lie of scarcity. There is abundant opportunity for you.

> **QUESTION**
> Where in your life do you have a mindset of scarcity rather than possibility?

December
24

You Are (Not) Your Work

As a creative professional, so much of what you make is defined by your intuitions, preferences, and influences. As a result, your work is highly personal, as it should be. At the same time, there is a subtle switch that can be thrown that causes you to begin to believe that your work defines your worth. You are only as good as your latest project.

You are not your work, and you are especially not defined by how your work is received. That is not an excuse for laziness; it's permission to engage fully and freely without worrying so much about how others try to define you. This is hard medicine to swallow in a culture that celebrates title and fame even above valuable contribution.

Here's the challenge: Where in your life might you be over-identifying with your work?

You are not your work, and you are especially not defined by how your work is received.

QUESTION

Where in your life are you over-identifying with your work? Where are you allowing how you appear in others' eyes to drive your decisions?

December
25

The Gift

Your creativity is a gift, but it's not for you. It's a gift that's given through you to others. Your job is to be a good steward of the gift, develop it, and use it to be a blessing to those who experience it. It doesn't matter if you are developing commercials, writing marketing strategy, making music or paintings, or building a business. Your creativity is a gift to be enjoyed by those who experience it. Do you see it that way?

What are the qualities of a good gift?

It's thoughtful. The person who gives the gift had you in mind when they made it. Are you thinking about the people for whom you are making your work? Are you considering how the work will be a gift to them?

It's timely. There's no use giving a gift after it's no longer useful. Are you considering how your creativity can be given to others in a way that meets them where they are?

It's simple. Sometimes, complex gifts don't feel like a gift at all. They feel like a burden. How can you simplify your work for others?

Your creativity is a gift, but it's not for you. It's for others who will be blessed by your work.

QUESTION

How can you use your creativity to be a gift to others today?

December

26

Three Questions to Ask Someone You Trust

You need other people in your life to help you see yourself fully. You only see a certain perspective, but people around you can help you see opportunities for growth and advancement that are invisible to you.

But by default, community doesn't naturally come to you. You have to go to community. You have to seek it out.

If you have people in your life you trust to help you grow, there are three questions that you should be asking them often. Also, if you are a manager, these three questions can help you unlock areas of growth for yourself and your team and can illuminate places where you're slipping into ruts or overcontrolling the team.

The three questions are as follows:

1. What am I doing right now that I should stop doing?
2. What is something obvious that you think I don't see?
3. How can I be of help right now?

If you ask these three questions consistently of people you trust, you are likely to get answers that surprise you. And you are likely to find that the answers you receive lead to breakthroughs both personally and professionally.

We need community around us to help us see ourselves, our gifts, and our growth opportunities more fully.

QUESTION

Who can you ask these three questions of this week?

December
27

Year in Review

Humans are wired to think in terms of rites of passage. Birthdays, especially important ones like your eighteenth, twenty-first, or fiftieth, mark critical seasons of life. In a similar way, each new year offers the promise of possibility and change. But many people move forward without a clear sense of what's behind. What's behind is what makes us who we are, and if we ignore it, we are flying blind into the future.

There are a few questions that I ask each year to help me assess any changes I might want to make in the coming one. This week, being the last of the year, is a great time to begin asking them.

- ► What went well this year? What success did I achieve, whether expected or unintended?
- ► What didn't go well this year? Where did I fall short of my objectives? Why did I fall short? What were the controllable contributing factors?
- ► How did I grow this year? How am I different now than I was at the beginning of the year?
- ► What did I learn this year? What new concepts shaped my worldview?

Doing an honest assessment of your past year can help you set new rhythms for the coming one.

> **QUESTION**
> Answer the four questions. Do you see anything that surprises you?

December
28

Year in Preview

Every great achievement begins as a quiet aspiration in someone's mind. You will change over the coming year—that's for certain. The question is, will you change in a way you desire? What do you aspire to?

Here are a few questions I encourage you to ask over the coming week. Spend some time writing and reflecting on them. Don't just settle for the first answer. Probe deeply.

- How do I want to be different this time next year? What changes do I want to see in myself both professionally and personally?
- What do I want to experience this year? What places will I go, what environments will I experience, what will I do, and who will I do it with?
- What will I do to stretch my mind this year? What will I read, study, watch, absorb? What topics will I pursue?
- How will I serve others this year? How will I get outside myself and help others pursue their dreams?

Spend some time with these questions this week. They will help you fix a vision of the person you want to become.

Taking time to prepare for the upcoming year will help you get off to a more productive, structured start.

QUESTION
Answer the four questions. What stands out the most to you?

December
29

Bury the Butterfly

A few years ago, I was on a walk, and as I glanced down at the side of the road, I noticed a beautiful butterfly sitting perfectly still on a leaf. I don't know why it caught my attention, but as I studied it, I realized that it wasn't resting or disguising itself. It was dead.

In that moment, I was moved, and I decided to bury the butterfly. It didn't seem right to just leave something so beautiful to rot in the sun.

After I buried it, I continued on with my walk and began to think about my past dreams and ambitions. They were beautiful pursuits and mattered to me deeply. But they were not to be. However, instead of burying them, I let them rot in the open because I wasn't willing to let them go. As a result, it took years to get over some of them.

Your dead dreams deserve the dignity of a decent burial. It's important to mark the moment and choose to move on from them. If you don't, you leave them out in the open, and you may never fully get over them.

Even good, beautiful things must come to an end. Give your dead dreams the dignity of a good burial.

> **QUESTION**
> Are you still holding on to a past dream that didn't pan out? Maybe it's time to bury the butterfly.

December
30

Accelerate into the Turn

When my son was learning to drive, he was often overly cautious when going into a curve in the road. He would slow down to the point that it became dangerous to us and to anyone behind us who wasn't expecting the sudden change in speed. I explained to him why it can be helpful to accelerate into a curve rather than slow, but to a new driver, it seemed counterintuitive. It took some serious convincing to help him see that accelerating through the curve is how you maintain better control of the car.

In a similar way, many people slow way down when they encounter uncertainty. Almost to a crawl. This is not only counterproductive in many instances, it's actually dangerous. When you slip into creative panic mode, you don't think clearly. You take a defensive approach rather than an offensive one, which means that you aren't seeking answers but are instead trying to avoid mistakes. You aren't aggressively pursuing your goals; you are trying to avoid messing things up.

As you consider the coming year and any changes you know are coming, how can you accelerate into the curve instead of becoming paralyzed with inaction?

Good drivers understand the importance of accelerating into a curve.

QUESTION

Is there any place where you are currently behaving in a manner that is too cautious? How can you accelerate?

December
31

Good Endings Lead to Good Beginnings

You made it through another year. That's something to celebrate.

I mean it.

You should celebrate. Marking moments is an important aspect of mental health. We need to mark the passage of time, celebrate wins, and look back at the mountain we've just climbed.

What in your life needs to be celebrated today?

What good things in your life are you grateful for?

What adversity did you overcome this year?

How have you proven to yourself that you are able to persist?

What risk did you take that you look back on with deep satisfaction?

In what ways did you grow this year, whether in perception, skill, or emotion?

What new relationships have entered your life that you should celebrate?

What old relationships remain that should be marked?

What have you moved on from this year that you need to celebrate and leave behind?

Take some time today to end the year well by marking the moment, celebrating your wins, remembering why you're grateful, marking the moment, and preparing to move ahead.

Good endings lead to good beginnings.

Take the good with you, and leave the bad behind.

QUESTION

How will you mark the moment today? Take some time to celebrate all that the last year brought your way.

Read This Once You've Completed Your First Pass through the Book

First, let's mark this moment. You've just completed your first pass through *Daily Creative*. What a huge accomplishment! I trust that the daily practice you've instilled over this past year has had a profound effect on your life and work.

And notice I said *first* pass. With most books, once you've read them, they just occupy a space on your bookshelf or get recycled through a used bookstore. *Daily Creative* is designed to be a lifelong companion. I recommend that you continue to dedicate five minutes each day to its daily practice over the coming months and years. Even though the entries won't magically change from year to year, you most certainly will. As Heraclitus wrote, "You cannot step in the same river twice." The river is always flowing and changing, as are you. Your next pass through *Daily Creative* will yield fresh insights and new passages to growth that you didn't notice the first time. It's a new river, and you are a new you.

If you'd like to take a deeper dive into the concepts in *Daily Creative* or would like to connect with others who are also working through the book, please join our community at DailyCreative.net. There you will find daily audio versions of each entry as well as worksheets, meetups, and more designed to help you get the most out of your daily practice. I'd also love to hear how the book has

impacted your creative journey. You can contact me at DailyCreative
.net.

It's such a joy to be on this journey with you.

And as always, may you be prolific, brilliant, and healthy!

Acknowledgments

It's fair to say that we are living through interesting times. *Daily Creative* was written squarely in the midst of a global pandemic, while most of us were working remotely and much of the world was on pause, and it took incredible flexibility from a team of pros to bring it into the world.

Many thanks to Meg Gibbons and the entire Sourcebooks team for believing in the project. Your diligence and vision helped this book embody its potential.

Thank you to my long-time literary agent Melissa White and the team at Folio for finding the perfect home for this project.

I'm full of gratitude for our early readers and *Daily Creative* community members. Your feedback shaped and refined the daily entries until they felt practical and helpful. Your effort will continue to help creative pros everywhere, every day for many years to come, so thank you!

Writing a book that's nearly twice as long as any I've written in about a third of the time it normally takes certainly added a little stress to the system. I'm thankful for the support of my wife, Rachel, and my entire family for understanding when I needed to sneak away for an hour to get some writing done. I love you all.

To the reader, the creative pro, the dreamer, the visionary, the one who suspects there's a better possible future and is working diligently to bring it about, thank you for sharing your work with the world. This book is for you. May you be prolific, brilliant, and healthy

About the Author

Positioning himself as an "arms dealer for the creative revolution," Todd Henry teaches leaders and organizations how to establish practices that lead to everyday brilliance. He is the author of six books (*The Accidental Creative, Die Empty, Louder Than Words, Herding Tigers, The Motivation Code, Daily Creative*). which have been translated into more than a dozen languages, and he speaks and consults across dozens of industries on creativity, leadership, and passion for work.

With more than twelve million downloads, his podcast *The Accidental Creative* offers weekly tips for how to stay prolific, brilliant, and healthy.

Learn more at AccidentalCreative.com.